COLONEL STEPHENS

INSIGHTS INTO THE MAN AND HIS EMPIRE

Compiled by

Philip Shaw

and

Vic Mitchell

MP Middleton Press

EVOLVING THE ULTIMATE RAIL ENCYCLOPEDIA

Front cover:
(Upper) Holman Fred Stephens in about 1904 is from a tinted photograph, which hung in the offices at 23, Salford Terrace, Tonbridge.
(Lower): Rolvenden in 1932, from a watercolour by George Heiron. Newly-arrived "Saddleback" locomotive No 4 (ex LSWR No 335) pauses at Rolvenden station. In the shed are No 1 **Tenterden** (Hawthorn Leslie 2420/1899) and Ford Railcar set No 2, constructed for Colonel Stephens in 1924. (© P.Shaw)
Back cover: The original desk and chair used by Colonel Stephens is in the re-creation of his office within the Colonel Stephens Railway Museum at Tenterden. Its historian, Philip Shaw, is in the great man's seat, in March 2005. (Brian Stephenson)

Published July 2005

ISBN 1 904474 62 4

© Middleton Press, 2005

Design Norman Langridge

Published by
     Middleton Press
     Easebourne Lane
     Midhurst, West Sussex
     GU29 9AZ
Tel: 01730 813169
Fax: 01730 812601
Email: info@middletonpress.co.uk
www.middletonpress.co.uk

Printed & bound by Biddles Ltd, Kings Lynn

CONTENTS

INTRODUCTION

Lt Colonel Holman Fred Stephens (1868-1931) did not in his lifetime receive the public recognition for his services to transport that he so evidently craved. Yet, since the revival of the Kent & East Sussex Railway as a heritage line in 1972, interest in Colonel Stephens and his railways has grown.

This book, which charts the life and career of Stephens, draws on articles, many no longer available, first published in the *Tenterden Terrier,* the house journal of the Kent & East Sussex Railway. Although they do not represent a complete biography, these articles do provide a good introduction to both Stephens, the man and the railways with which he was associated. The authors have drawn on unpublished material from the Colonel Stephens Museum archive at Tenterden, notably the papers of William Henry Austen and James Arthur Iggulden, both key employees of Colonel Stephens, who salvaged material which would otherwise have been destroyed when the offices at Tonbridge were closed in 1948.

Colonel Stephens was, by all accounts, an unusual employer. Eccentric in manner, autocratic, impatient, even bombastic in his management style, he was, nevertheless, immensely popular with his staff. In private life, a bachelor, he had few interests outside his railway and territorial army activities. Stephens was essentially a man of little railways who abhorred large organisations and the bureaucracy that goes with them. His philosophy as a consulting engineer and manager was simple: "I don't make a lot of money out of my railways, but I do have a lot of fun".

Stephens' legacy was largely ephemeral and most of the railways that he constructed or managed are long gone, as are his methods of operating them. Publishing the articles in a single format, will bring the history of the man and his railways to a new and wider audience. Many of the original photographs have been reproduced, whilst new ones have been included to illustrate the themes which have been developed since the articles were first published. They are from the Colonel Stephens Historical Archive, unless otherwise stated.

Finally, I would like to thank Vic Mitchell for the idea to publish in the first place, without which this book would not have come about. He has also compiled the captions. Appreciation also to Mr A Carder and Mr D & Dr S Salter for their help.

Philip Shaw
Editor, *Tenterden Terrier* (1974 to date)

Chapter 1

H F Stephens MICE - Education, List of Works and Qualifications.
A Curriculum Vitae published by himself in about 1918.

EDUCATION

University College School London	1877-1883
With Private Tutor	1883-1884
Vitre (Ille et Villaine)	1884-1886	French, &c.
Carlesruhe (Baden)	1886-1887	German, Mathematics, &c
Matriculation, London University	1887	
University College, London	1887-1888	Pupil, Sir A W B Kennedy, Civil Engineering.
Workshops and Loco Dept., Neasden Works	1889-1890	Pupil, J J Hanbury, Mechanical Engineering.

LIST OF WORKS

Name of Works.	Period.	Mileage			Remarks
		M.	F.	C.	
Paddock Wood & Cranbrook Railway	1890-94	11	3	5	Resident Engineer during construction. (Now worked and maintained by SE&CR)
*Rye & Camber Tramway (Steam)	1895	2	0	0	Engineer and Locomotive Superintendent. Designed and equipped line organised traffic matters and worked line.
*Chichester & Selsey Tram Road (Steam.)	1897	8	0	0	Engineer and Locomotive Superintendent. Designed and equipped line organised traffic matters and worked line.
*Rother Valley Railway (Now Kent & East Sussex Railway)	1898	12	0	4	Engineer, Locomotive Superintendent, and Managing Director. Designed and equipped line, organised traffic matters and worked line.
Sheppey Railway	1900-02	8	5	0	Engineer (Now worked and maintained by SE&CR)
*Rolvenden & Tenterden Railway (Kent & East Sussex Railway)	1902	1	4	6	Engineer, Locomotive Superintendent, and Managing Director. Designed and equipped line, organised traffic matters, and worked line.
*Kent & East Sussex Railway, Tenterden to Headcorn extension	1903-04	7	6	9	Engineer, Locomotive Superintendent, and Managing Director. Designed and equipped line, organised traffic matters, and worked line.
Bere Alston & Calstock Railway	1904	4	1	8	Engineer in conjunction with Messrs. Galbraith & Church, Locomotive Superintendent and General Manager. Designed and equipped line, organised traffic matters, and worked line.

Name of Line		Period	Mileage			Remarks
			M.	F.	C.	
East Cornwall Mineral Railway (Reconstruction and conversion of gauge)		1904	6	0	0	Engineer in conjunction with Messrs. Galbraith & Church, Locomotive Superintendent and General Manager. Designed and equipped line, organised traffic matters, and worked line.
Burry Port & Gwendraeth Valley Railway		1909	12	2	3	Engineer, reconstructed and converted line from mineral to passenger.
*Shropshire & Montgomeryshire Railway		1910-11	24	0	24	Railway reconstructed. Engineer, Locomotive Superintendent, and Managing Director. Designed and equipped line, organised traffic matters, and worked line.

WORKS LOCATED AND DESIGNED.

Name of Line.	Period.	Mileage.			Remarks
		M.	F.	C.	
*East Kent Railway	1911-16	18	0	0	Engineer, Locomotive Superintendent, and General Manager. Designed and equipped line, organised traffic matters, and worked line.
*Weston Clevedon &, Portishead Railway	1911	14	0	0	Engineer, Locomotive Superintendent, and General Manager.
Medway Upper Navigation (Maintenance & Renewal)	1896-1901	16	0	0	Engineer. (Number of Locks on River, 13)
Tenterden Railway (Parliamentary Line)	1894	31	5	9	Passed. Charge of Survey and Sections.
Rother Valley Railway (Parliamentary Line)	1895	12	1	3	Passed. Sole Engineer.
Railways under Act of 1896 &c					
Rye & Camber Tramway (Steam)	1895	2	0	0	Sole Engineer.
Gower Railway	1896	13	6	6	Passed. Sole Engineer.
Hadlow Railway	1896	11	5	5	Passed. Sole Engineer.
Central Essex Railway	1897	27	5	1	Passed. Sole Engineer.
Sheppey Railway	1897	7	6	1	First 5 miles rejected subject to diversion, remainder passed. Sole Engineer.
Chichester & Selsey Line (Steam)	1897	8	0	0	Sole Engineer.
Sheppey Railway (Diversion)	1898	8	5	1	Passed. Sole Engineer.
Cranbrook, Tenterden & Ashford Railway	1898	21	0	2	First 9m 7f 1¾ch passed. Remainder rejected. Sole Engineer.
Kelvedon, Coggeshall & Halstead Railway	1898	9	4	1	First 2¼ miles passed, remainder rejected. Sole Engineer.

St. Just, Land's End & Great Western Junction Railway	1898	17	1	0	Rejected. Sole Engineer.
Land's End, St. Just & Great Western Junction Railway	1898	23	3	1	Rejected. Sole Engineer.
Hedingham & Long Melford Railway	1898	15	2	7	Rejected- Sole Engineer.
Orpington Cudham & Tatsfield Railway	1898	7	6	8	Passed. Sole Engineer.
Long Melford & Hadleigh Railway	1899	15	0	9	Passed. Sole Engineer.
Maidstone & Faversham Junction Railway	1899	12	1	3	Passed. Sole Engineer.
East Sussex Railway	1899	7	2	8	Passed. Sole Engineer.
Rother Valley Railway Extension to Headcorn	1901	7	7	1	Passed. Sole Engineer.
Surrey & Sussex Railway	1901	25	5	6	Rejected. Sole Engineer.
Maidstone & Sittingbourne Railway	1904	11	1	6	Pending. Sole Engineer.
Headcorn & Maidstone Junction Railway	1906	10	0	8	Passed. Sole Engineer.
North Shropshire Railway	1907	24	0	0	Passed. Sole Engineer
Bere Alston & Calstock Railway, North Hill Extension	1909	6	7	0	Passed. Sole Engineer.
Burry Port & Gwendraeth Valley Railway	1909	12	2	3	Passed. Sole Engineer.
North Devon & Cornwall Junction Rly	1910	19	6	0	Passed. Sole Engineer.
East Kent Railways	1911	19	7	6	Passed. Sole Engineer.
East Kent Railways Extensions	1911	10	3	2	Passed. Sole Engineer.
East Kent Railways Extensions	1912	5	2	1	Passed. Sole Engineer.
Cadbury Railway	1912	1	6	4	Pending. Sole Engineer.
East Kent Railways Extensions	1913	21	6	8	Pending. Sole Engineer.
Gower Railway	1913	13	6	6	Pending. Joint Engineer.
East Kent Railways Extensions	1914	7	4	9	Pending. Sole Engineer.

West Sussex Railway	1915	8	1	0	Passed. Sole Engineer.
Edge Hill Railway	1917	11	2	8	Passed as regards 5 miles 5 furlongs 8 chains. Sole Engineer.
Ashover Railway	1918	6	0	8	Pending. Sole Engineer.
Shropshire Railways (Shrewsbury & Market Drayton Extension)	1918	22	1	2	Pending. Sole Engineer.
Siding from L&NWR to Castner Kellner Alkali Co's Works, Weston Point, Cheshire	1918	0	7	6	Pending. Sole Engineer

*Lines worked and maintained.
Mileage of Railways constructed, 130 miles at a cost of £842,225

Considerable experience re Parliamentary work, also organisation of traffic matters and the complete equipment of Railways with rolling stock and stores.

At present responsible for a considerable number of standard and narrow gauge engines, coaches, and trucks of various types; also other rolling stock, with workshops, etc.

Total mileage of lines over 450; total estimates, £2,900,000.

Considerable experience in locating, designing and working railways of economical construction.

Acted as Inspector to the Railway Department of the Board of Trade, under notice of Accidents Act, 1894, for several years.

Admitted Student of Middle Temple, 1906.

General consulting work and reporting on various schemes, cases, &c., from 1890 to present date.

Has had special opportunities for acquiring knowledge of Government requirements for the working of both heavy and Light Railways.

Member of the Institution of Civil Engineers.

Raised 600 men (Royal Engineers) for South African War.

Raised and commanded 2,400 men and 220 officers (Royal Engineers), in 1914, for European War; mentioned in despatches 1916; returned to Railway Work 1916 with rank of Lieut.-Colonel Royal Engineers (TA)

1.1   Stephens studied the principles of mechanical engineering in the workshops of the Metropolitan Railway at Neasden. He can be seen in the bowler hat on the footplate of a 4-4-0 Beyer Peacock locomotive, built in 1866.

1.2   Stephens was caught on camera while inspecting progress on his Shropshire & Montgomeryshire Railway, in 1911.

1.3   In stand-easy posture, Stephens posed near the WC&PR at Clapton Road, about one mile south of Portishead. There was no platform - only a nameboard and timetable.

1.4   In the official photograph of the opening of the Ashover Light Railway on 6th April 1925, Stephens is in the back row, second from the right.

Chapter 2
Childhood - My Dear Dah and Mam
by Kay Smailes (1990/91)

In the early summer of 1989 a chance encounter, leading to a surprising discovery, gave me a unique opportunity to embark on a strangely rewarding assignment. At the request of the KESR Archivist I was entrusted with the responsibility of transcribing a miscellaneous collection of letters, post-cards, telegrams and hastily scribbled memos, most of them written by or to the young Holman Fred Stephens (familiarly known as Holly) to or by his parents (Dah and Mam) between the years 1876 and 1911 - first during his early childhood and as a schoolboy, then as a student and later as an ambitious and enterprising engineer of many early Kent railways.

Like those of most children, Holly's first letters, carefully preserved and dated by Mam, were in the form of drawings: water-colours or pen-and-ink sketches, - of a steam-engine, a train travelling over a long, high viaduct, a coastal scene with sailing-ships. In this collection his first real letter, with a poem as introduction, was written at the age of eight for his father's birthday -

"I awake in the morning the robins are thair
Flying abougt in the sweet sentedair". H F S

"dear Dah, i wish yu menny happy returns of the day". Holly.

Holly's parents, Frederic George Stephens, a leading artist and critic, editor of the "Athenaeum" for many years, a member of the Pre-Raphaelite Brotherhood, and Rebecca Clara, lived at 10 Hammersmith Terrace, W from 1877 until 1883. Holly, a godchild and namesake of the artist Holman Hunt, attended University College School in London. After leaving he was sent to learn French with the family of Monsieur and Madame Rossignol at Vitré in Brittany, initially for two months. It is from that time on that we have the most vivid and lively descriptions of his activities and interests - swimming, fishing, driving a trap, riding a bicycle (very easy), later to be given up in favour of learning to play billiards in the evenings, as an honorary member of M Rossignol's club.

Holly was greatly struck by the kindness of everyone he met in France. The French, he thought, were very nice people. M Rossignol and his family were considered gentlemen (gentry?) and used to dine with the best families in the department (= county). Water-colour sketches of the medieval, turreted castle and of the Hotel Rossignol, by far the largest in the town and next to the Railway Station, accompanied his first letter from Vitré, and what most impressed him about his "dear little room" was the English furniture and an electric bell!

His detailed accounts of visits and conversations with people he met reveal his early interests - amongst others, the Commandant of the 70th Regiment of Infantry, with whom he went to hear Military Music in the Public Gardens, and who expressed a keen desire to see portraits of English soldiers. On a visit to the barracks the critical eye of the 15-year-old described the portion allotted to "reservists" as not fit for a cow to live in, let alone a man. "The soldiers are all very little men with very big red trousers, (in which I believe they must carry their tents), a blue tunic and a ridiculous hat." Holly's letters and cards, some written with a "dredful nib", are outpourings of infectious enthusiasm, with intermittent punctuation, erratic and varied spelling, and little thought of paragraphs, but the reader cannot fail to share in the sense of enjoyment he so obviously felt in visits to local fairs, military manoeuvres, and all the details of everyday life.

He much preferred to progress conversationally rather than by attending lessons, and had no fear of talking to the Mayor of Vitré or dining with the President of the Tribunal. He enjoyed his 6-course meals with wine and coffee, "when we all talked french like steam-engines," but his great moment came at the Dépôt of Locomotives, when he rode one kilometre back to the station on an engine ("very jolly") with the Government Inspector, "who has taken a fancy to me, and very often I go to his cosey little office and talk with him and his colleague about English railways which interest him very much." In a letter to her husband after Holly's return from Brittany Mrs Stephens wrote - "I think that you will be pleased with Holly. It is fun to hear him take off Frenchmen he has met. He says the utmost enjoyment he has ever had was at Cromer and at Vitré."

In later letters (1886-7) from Karlsruhe (Baden) in Germany, where Holly at 18/19 went to learn German, are plans and diagrams as well as detailed descriptions of scenery and excursions into the Black Forest, visits to historic houses and castles, his bathing in the Rhine and his encounters with many different types of people all of which show that he was a good mixer, friendly, sociable, observant and talkative, always keenly concerned about his progress and eager to become fluent in both French and German. He enjoyed frequent friendly spars with his host, Professor Kienitz, on colonial questions, such as the Cameroons, and gave his own curious view of the Prince of Wales' (later Edward VII) visit on his way from Cologne to Baden in August 1886 - "he was warmly received, people cheering him repeatedly. They don't cheer in a Christian manner but give vent to long Ho-o-o-ohs which sound as if the whole assemblage had suddenly been afflicted with violant toothache".

Karlsruhe he found a dull town, on the dead flat, 3 miles from the hills and 8 from the Rhine, rather large with rows and rows of well-built old-fashioned stone houses. He made frequent visits to the floating swimming baths, carefully calculating the cost of every journey, and soon knew the details of his local line and all other railways and Channel crossings that might be useful to him. It was here that he first saw the Simplon-Orient Express, where the up and down engines change at 7.33 am...... "all the passengers were at breakfast in the hotel car and looked very comfortable." Although Holly's letters are packed with information and descriptions, and show a mature knowledge of historical events, he begs Dah to excuse his scrawle, having only a quill, and very often he is rushing to catch the post. Overlooking the blots, smudges and crossings-out, the reader has, nevertheless, a sense of being in the company of a lively young man on his first trips abroad. He would dearly have loved to stay longer in both France and Germany, just as he was beginning to take part in conversations. Eight weeks is not enough to get a "speaking power" over the language, he wrote, but he knew it was impossible with the "exam bogey" (London Matric) hanging over him.

Holly's devotion to and concern for his parents (love and 10,000 kisses to you both, Your affectionate son) shows through all his letters. They were undoubtedly his closest friends and supporters. His anxiety about their health, their need for short holiday breaks, to brace themselves up -in Cornwall (Port Isaac), Norfolk (Cromer), the South Coast (Lymington), N & S Wales, is often expressed. His offer of free passes ("such a pity not to use them, it would not look well to send them back"), often to cross the Channel to Calais, and then on to Paris (for 19/- in 1903), or via Boulogne (for 15/6 in 1893), were balanced by requests for tickets to the Royal

Academy Private View, a privilege not easy to obtain, and introductions to influential friends, so important for his future railway undertakings.

Throughout the 1890s, his early railway building years, Holly, now a qualified Civil and Mechanical Engineer, based in Cranbrook (Hartley) or Tonbridge, continued to keep in close touch with his parents, joining them at home or on brief holidays whenever possible. With the helpful influence of his father, he was elected to membership of the Reform Club in 1898. Already a Board of Trade Inspector at 26, "getting a little known", and travelling all over the country to advise and to learn, as well as to Belgium, the chief centre of light railways at that period, he was much occupied with Parliamentary business which kept him to the grindstone, particularly with the Rother Valley scheme, a project dear to his heart. In April 1900 he was at last able to write to Mam - "I have got this line open for traffic at last and hope that it will be a success. The prospects are good so far. . . ."

Earlier that year he had proudly sent his parents a photo of one of his Rother Valley engines built to his designs - "they are wonderfully powerful and very successful taking 40 trucks of goods at 20 miles an hour!" A year later he wrote with a mixture of pride and modesty that he would be delighted to take them over the Chichester, Rye, Rother and Sheppey lines "but you will be disappointed as they are not great works at all!"

The rest is history, already recorded and well-known, but what emerges most clearly from the handling and reading of this very personal family correspondence, a refreshing experience in itself, is a sense of being part of living history, its failures and successes, but still in the process of being made, 90 years on.

* * * * * * *

Further study on a selection of letters and postcards concerning. the young Holman Fred Stephens (Holly) and his parents, Frederic George and Rebecca Clara (Dah and Mam), exchanged during some 35 years of the late Victorian period and the first decade of this century confirms earlier impressions that H F S was a man of indomitable spirit and extraordinary vision, whose experiences and interests during his early years seemed to be closely linked with the ideals and achievements of his later life. Although many of his plans for railways proved to be too ambitious, too costly and too impracticable to succeed for long, we have in this historic correspondence many colourful and often amusing glimpses not only of how H F S saw himself, but also of how others saw him in his formative pre-military years.

Holly's artistic heritage and loving devotion to his parents, his interests in money and in getting full value for it from early youth onwards, his instinct for detailed calculations, and his dedication to the fulfilment of his aims, are all evident. So also is his desire to do the right thing, to meet the right people and to behave correctly. All these aspects of his character are revealed in a medley of extracts together with reports from others in this miscellany, which are left to speak for him as they were written. Undoubtedly Holly's most joyous letters and cards came from Brittany. At no time later could one imagine him saying "I am as happy as the day is long", words he wrote to Mam from Vitré (1883, at the age of 15), and we soon learn the symbol of true happiness at that period was for him an oil-colour paint-box. Many parents will be familiar with pleas from their children away from home to send more money, but the imperious manner of some of Holly's demands seemed to expect miracles too . . . "Please let the Post Office order reach me before Monday next." During his stay in Karlsruhe to learn German, he carefully calculated that instead of paying for private lessons, it would have been cheaper to attend the Polytechnic in term-time, corresponding exactly to University College School. There he could have attended German classes of one hour every day for 6 months for 30/-, and additional classes in any other subject for the same moderate sum. He wrote "The next time I come to Germany I will go to N Prussia. It is much cheaper because one goes by sea in 24 hours to Hamburg, and I could live there for just one half of what it costs in a family in S Germany."

In spite of professional discouragement being given at that time to young fellows wishing to become Civil Engineers (the prospects were not very bright), Holly, with strong support from his father, took the vital steps to acquire qualifications and experience. A letter dated July 26, 1890, from F G Stephens to J Bell Esq. of the Metropolitan Railway at Neasden forms the link between Holly's school days and his first ambitious steps into the future. F G S wrote "Thank you very warmly for your great kindness in allowing my son to enter the Company's workshops at Neasden and work there for a considerable time. I hope that those under whom you gave him opportunities of learning his profession found him energetic, practical and teachable. I am sure he has been very anxious to learn. I should therefore in view of his future regard it as an additional favour if a certificate of his having worked at Neasden could be granted to him. I am, dear Sir, Yours very faithfully, F G Stephens".

Dated October 9, 1891, the first letter from Holly to Dah headed "Cranbrook & Paddock Wood Railway, Engineer's Office", although written from Horsmonden, illustrates two commonly recurring themes - "Thank you for the money duly received", and "Will you please ask my Mother if she has arranged some clean collars for me." Father, we learn later, made him a monthly allowance of £8 and paid his subscriptions until the launch of the Rother Valley Railway in 1900. Mother received and returned his washing ("underthings"), usually via the cloakroom at Charing Cross station, a convenient clearing-house, much used by members of the Stephens family for all manner of goods lent, borrowed, given or exchanged, as well as serving as a laundry collection point. A brass fender and picture frames for Holly's bare walls were dispatched and collected in this way.

His first years with Cranbrook & Paddock Wood Railway were not easy for H F S, but his life offered him the challenges he seemed to need and kept him increasingly busy with travel, planning advice, Board of Trade inspection demands and contacts with a variety of lines and enterprises.

His letters over the next 15 years from 1891 are a strange mixture of the important and the trivial, the formal and the familiar, revealing his character and philosophy of life, expressing gratitude for presents received and for introduction to well-known people. In June 1892 - "It is absolutely essential to have a policy and to stick to it. If it fails try some other way. I'm sure this is the only way to get on." In 1895 he wrote "Can you get me an introduction to the Hon. F D Smith (son of the late W H Smith) or the Marquess of Bristol? I want to interview them." A few years later, in July 1901 - "Many thanks for your letter and enclosed card of introduction to Mr. Kipling. Please thank Sir P Burne-Jones for me". As we shall see in Chapter 9, earlier, in November 1896, he wrote "I have a letter of introduction from Lord Medway to Lord Harris 're' a proposed line in Isle of Sheppey. You know so much better than I do how to manage these sort of things. How shall I address Lord Harris? I write 'My dear Lord Medway' because I know him, but I don't know Lord Harris. Shall I say 'Sir' or 'My Lord'?"

From a letter of November 1898 we learn - "Mr. McLaren said if I was judiciously pushed I might yet do well. He said he would help in any way, but I was to bear in mind that most things went through influence nowadays, and if we were not willing to use what we had it would be wasted."

In November 1903 he wrote "Many thanks for the delightful (tie) pin you sent me. It is rather gorgeous for a simple person like myself but I will try and live up to it. Personal adornment is rather out of my line." From a letter dated March 1897 we read "I want very much to come to the Boat Race. Will you let me have a post-card 're' time. May I bring my man (W H Austen) with me? He has never seen the race and would appreciate it I think . . ." At Christmas 1898 Stephens wrote to his parents thanking them for " . . . the beautiful pipe, a handsome present which will be very useful to me. My man nearly swallowed the sixpence Mam put in his pudding and when he has got over the shock he is going to write to Mam and thank her."

By the end of 1895 H F S was living at Ashby House, Tonbridge, soon to acquire an office at Salford Terrace, from where he could travel more easily. From the twenty letters dated 1896 in this collection it would seem the busiest years were now upon him. There was mention of his involvement with the Cranbrook & District Water Company, and with the Rye & Camber Tramway. He was hoping to obtain flood prevention work in Tonbridge which would be "a bit of experience in another direction", and in a letter from Swansea Vale his advice was sought on making a Light Railway to some coal villages up the Clyddach valley if the scheme were practicable and possible to carry out at reasonable cost. There were letters from Ambleside and Westmorland C C asking advice on projects for tram roads and Light Railways.

Stephens was also busy with the Chichester to Selsey line, and with possibly extending the North Cornwall line to Truro; he was involved in travelling from Essex to Penzance, with attending public meetings all over the Gower Peninsular, and with the Swansea and Mumbles to Worms Head line. He returned home dead tired but was hard at it again the next day. There is mention of an order to extend the Rye line 1½ miles, and of a similar line from Sandwich to the coast.

Perhaps the most vivid impression of H F S at work, as others saw him, comes not from a letter but an article in the East Kent Advertiser of 12 October 1895, which was headed "A Steam Tram for Sandwich!", and continued - "Who would have thought it? To picture a snorting, whistling vehicle wizzing into the sleepy old place is certainly peculiar, but it is by no means improbable that the scheme for a steam tram to run between Sandwich, the Golf Links and the shore will be carried out by local enterprise. A meeting which was held at the Bell Hotel was well attended. All the principal big-wigs were there. More than this, the proceedings were quite enthusiastic. Mr. Stephens, the engineer, was a host in himself. He depicted the future career of the Sandwich Steam Tram Company in glowing colours, and his sanguine, buoyant remarks infected his hearers with his own enthusiasm and carried them in imagination over any difficulties or hindrances which suggested themselves to the cautious mind."

In February 1896 H F S wrote "I am glad to say that the schemes I have in hand are going on as well as I can hope." and in October of that year, "So far as I am concerned I am very busy and as you know I can't afford to keep a proper assistant. You can guess that to keep my own practice going finds me full employment. It is rather an uphill game but I think that in the course of a short time the benefit of the work I have in hand will become apparent." After the turn of the century, in July 1901 we hear that - "I am very busy indeed with the negotiations 're' my Headcorn line which is giving me a great deal of trouble and anxiety" and in July of 1908 that - "We have had some very bad weather here during the last week. Tonbridge station was flooded and my man Austen was washed out of the lower part of his house ... We are making the borings for the piers of the Calstock viaduct and hope to start work soon." A year later, in October 1904, he confides to his parents – "As for my money matters, I hope I have made enough to keep me from the workhouse and also those dear to me if the need comes."

Not until April 1904 was there any misunderstanding apparent between father and son. Holly had not been told of his mother's accident (a fall) and her period of ill-health since the previous December; he queried the choice of medical advisers, and the slowness of her recovery. "It is perfectly clear that some means must be discovered to put her on her legs again and be the dear one she has always been to all of us." A long and detailed reply from Dah (his last letter in this collection) asks Holly - "Can it be that you have got it into your head that I am withholding help from your Mother on any account whatsoever, least of all because of its cost? I share your anxiety because of the tardiness of Mam's improvement during more than 10 months. This affects me not less than yourself. She has had the aid of 4 doctors, the occasional attention of 2 others, 4 nurses (2 together for many weeks), 2 masseuses and the constant service of Ethel who is very helpful and fully satisfied the doctors."

We have letters to Dah until 15 April 1905, but no more from him; he died in March 1907. Mam eventually recovered and lived until November 1915, and the last six letters on black-edged notepaper are headed with her own and Holly's addresses:

Robertsbridge

S O

Sussex

9 The Terrace

Hammersmith

W.

An announcement in The Times of 30 May 1911:

"STEPHENS, Major H F on promotion and on appointment to command Kent Fortress R E by the Inspector General of the Forces" was followed on May 31 by the final letter that we have from Mam -

"My dear Holly,

I heartily congratulate you on your promotion. You have given much time and energy to the country. It used to be said that when one's sons had been presented it was usual to have a few yards of extra silk to go to the Drawing Room. There was a time I thought so too but not now.

Much love from Mam"

2.1   Mr and Mrs F G Stephens (Holman's parents) were photographed at their home in Hammersmith Terrace, London W. in about 1900.

2.2   The serious young "Holly" was recorded at about age 12 in 1880.

2.3   Stephens, at the age of 18 was studying in France and Germany.

Chapter 3

Holman Stephens - the formative years at Cranbrook

by Philip Shaw (2001)

Brian Hart's eagerly-awaited book on the Hawkhurst Branch has focused attention on Stephens' early years, in which he experienced both success and failure. Dealing with not only the title subject, but also with some of the social issues in the vicinity, the Hawkhurst Branch encapsulates a wide range of excellent photographs of local towns and villages.

The author deals correctly with common misconceptions regarding the nature of H F Stephens' involvement with the line. Edward P Seaton, a consulting engineer with 20 years experience, was responsible for the design of the route and structures and Stephens was employed by him. To be fair, Stephens never claimed anything else. He was, at the relatively tender age of 22, still a student, but many of the distinctive features and materials used in the buildings on this line were adopted by him subsequently on other schemes. He did, however, claim to have had the responsibility of sole supervision of the works, including setting out the line and was resident at Cranbrook throughout the construction period.

Prior to his arrival at Cranbrook, Stephens' educational achievements had been noteworthy rather than outstanding. After matriculating in 1887, he studied engineering briefly at University College London under the Professor of the faculty, Sir Alexander Kennedy. In 1888 his father, Frederick Stephens, arranged with John Bell, General Manager of the Metropolitan Railway, for him to enter the Company's works at Neasden as a pupil of the Locomotive Superintendent, John Hanbury. Hanbury was a distinguished engineer and had served his apprenticeship under Matthew Kirtley at the "locomotive sheds" of the Midland Railway at Derby. In due course, Stephens pressed for the opportunity of gaining experience in civils work and Hanbury suggested that he approach Seaton, who was working for the Metropolitan on extensive alterations to Baker Street and Portland Road stations. Stephens, who never hesitated to take advantage of family connections, made play of his family's acquaintance with Sir Edward Watkin, Chairman of both the South Eastern and Metropolitan Railways and this was probably enough to persuade Seaton to take Stephens on. The Hawkhurst railway project was an ideal opportunity to gain practical experience.

It was whilst working at Cranbrook that Stephens came across W H Austen. Austen was born at Snodland where his father was a labourer at a paper mill. The family was poor and young William was sent to live with his grandmother in Cranbrook High Street, where he attended school and subsequently obtained a job with Joseph Firbank, the contractors building the line, as a chain-man. Austen was meticulous and quick to learn. He was to remain with Stephens as his personal assistant for the rest of his life and took over the running of the light railway empire when Stephens died in 1931.

The Hawkhurst line was opened from Paddock Wood to Cranbrook on 1st October 1892 and to Hawkhurst on 4th September 1893. After the line was completed, Stephens stayed on for the customary maintenance period and then returned to London with little prospect of any immediate work. He carefully nurtured an acquaintanceship with Sir Myles Fenton, General Manager of the South Eastern Railway, by sending him tickets for Royal Academy exhibitions and gifts of engravings, supplied by his father. He claimed that Sir Myles had virtually promised that if the proposed extension of the Hawkhurst line to Appledore were to go ahead, he would be given the job of supervising the works, but this line was not to be. In May 1894, Seaton proposed Stephens' application for associate membership of The Institution of Civil Engineers. Other distinguished members who put their names to the application included his old tutor Sir Alexander Kennedy, W Wainwright and James Stirling. From then on Stephens was suitably qualified to undertake projects in his own right.

Stephens was back again in the Cranbrook area in July 1895, assisted by Austen, with some work for the Cranbrook Water Company and nearby constructing the Rye & Camber Tramway. The waterworks project did not go smoothly and Stephens was only paid fees of £36 whereas he had claimed £130. He finally left the area in October 1895 and moved to Tonbridge, where he rented rooms at Ashby House, Priory Road. This was to be both home and office until 1900, when the expansion of his engineering practice necessitated the opening of the famous light railway offices at 23, Salford Terrace.

An intriguing development at Cranbrook was a friendship built up with Edward Peterson, the son of the Rector of Biddenden, the Rev William Peterson, and a solicitor with a practice in Staplehurst. Born in 1848 and educated at Cranbrook Grammar School, Peterson is best known for his study of tithes and as 'The Parsons Friend'. According to his obituary in The Times of 7th October 1934, he founded the Tithe Owners Union in 1890 and spent many years of his life defending the status of the clergy and studying their financial problems. His enthusiasm for light railways came about in anticipation of the 1896 Act and he claimed to have clients interested in investing in railway schemes in various parts of the country. Peterson formed a company called the Light Railways Syndicate in July 1895 for the purpose of financing bills or orders in Parliament for proposed new railways. The intention was, that once the necessary authorisations had been obtained, a separate company would be formed for each scheme to raise the capital and the syndicate would receive a fee for its services. A total of seven schemes were formally proposed by the Light Railways Syndicate and its sister company, the Economic Railways Company, formed in 1898, but only one, the Sheppey Light Railway, was built. In all cases, Stephens was to have been the engineer and had a smallish shareholding in the syndicate.

The first proposal put forward was for a light railway serving coal villages in the Clyddach valley near Swansea and in August 1895 Stephens did some preliminary survey work in the area on behalf of one of Peterson's clients. However, this did not get to the application stage and it was not until December 1896 that the first two formalised schemes came before the Light Railway Commissioners.

The Hadlow (Kent) Light Railway and the Gower Light Railway, were followed by the Central Essex Light Railway in 1897. Four schemes were proposed in 1898, the Sheppey Light, the Kelvedon Coggeshall & Halstead and the St Just Land's End & Great Western Junction (two proposals). Peterson's sources of finance, if they ever existed, remain a mystery, but at the enquiry into the Central Essex Light Railway, counsel acting on behalf of Peterson said that he represented "a strong financial group with over a million sterling for investment in light railways". In fact, most of these schemes were of doubtful viability and would have been unattractive investments to all but the most optimistic capitalists. The Syndicate sold its rights to the Central Essex, which would have linked Ongar with Dunmow, to other promoters and claimed a commission.

The Light Railways Syndicate became moribund and was wound up in 1912. Peterson went bankrupt in 1910, claiming that he had been unable to obtain payment of costs and professional charges as a solicitor. The Economic Railways Company had virtually ceased to exist in 1904. In the file at the companies registry there is a letter written by the Registrar of companies to the secretary asking why the statutory return for the previous year had not been filed. A copy of the reply, a sad and poignant ending to the story, is also contained on the file. ".....The reason why no return was made at the commencement of the year is that the company has practically ceased to exist. It has heavy liabilities and its only asset is a light railway order authorising the construction of a line 2 and a half miles in length (Kelvedon to Coggeshall). The compulsory powers for the acquisition of land have run out and a sum of just £1 in the bank. The compulsory powers ran out last November and without such it would be impossible to make the line as at least one of the landowners is decidedly hostile. The directors therefore took no steps towards calling an annual meeting and in fact are allowing the company to fall dormant. It is, I am afraid, never likely to be resuscitated and I do not think that any of the creditors will go to the expense of winding it up."

For Peterson matters were coming to an end, but for Stephens this was only the beginning. Despite the frustration that he must have felt, given the time and energy that he had devoted to Syndicate projects, his infectious enthusiasm for light railway schemes was unabated. First, the Selsey Tramway and then the Rother Valley Railway were keeping him more than busy. His father had provided him with sufficient funds to live on whilst his practice developed. The golden years were yet to come.

3.1   The surveying team was recorded with its instruments. Stephens is adjacent to the theodolite.

3.2   *SER class 118 2-4-0 no. 112 is seen with a special train at Hope Mill on 12th September 1892; the station was soon renamed Goudhurst. Stephens is close to the tender.*

3.3   *The SER offered these services in 1893 and 1894.*

PADDOCK WOOD, HORSMONDEN, & GOUDHURST.—South Eastern.

Fares.			Return.					mrn	mrn	aft	aft	aft	aft	aft				SUNDAYS.	mrn	mrn	aft	aft
1 cl.	2 cl.	3 cl.	1 cl.	2 cl.	3 cl.	Paddock Wood ....dep.		9 7	9 55	1235	2 20	4 48	5 55	6 46	7 55	....	....		8 3	9 7	7 6	8 3
0 10	0 7½	0 4½	1 5	1 0	9	Horsmonden		9 17	10 5	1245	2 30	4 58	6 5	6 56	8 5	....	....		8 13	9 17	7 16	8 13
1 2	0 11	0 6½	2 0	1 6	1	Goudhurst ....arr.		9 23	1011	1251	2 36	5 4	6 11	7 6	8 11	....	....		8 19	9 23	7 22	8 19
Fares.			**Return.**					mrn	mrn	aft	aft	aft	aft	aft	aft				mrn	mrn	aft	aft
1 cl.	2 cl.	3 cl.	1 cl.	2 cl.	3 cl.	Goudhurst ....dep.		8 40	9 35	12 5	1 32	4 15	5 30	6 25	7 20				8 35	9 40	7 30	8 40
0 4	0 3	0 2	0 7	0 5	0 4	Horsmonden		8 46	9 41	1211	1 38	4 21	5 36	6 31	7 25				8 41	9 46	7 36	8 46
1 2	0 11	0 6½	2 0	1 6	1	Paddock Wood 123,120..arr.		8 56	9 51	1221	1 48	4 31	5 46	6 41	7 35				8 51	9 56	7 46	8 56

PADDOCK WOOD, CRANBROOK, and HAWKHURST.—South Eastern.

Fares.			Return.			Paddock Wood ....dep.		mrn	mrn		aft	aft	aft	aft				SUNDAYS.				
0 10	0 7½	0 4½	1 5	1 0	9	Paddock Wood ....dep.		8 52	1010	1235	2 20	4 35	5 55	7 55	....	7 47	9 50	6 28	8 3	....	....
1 2	0 11	0 6½	2 0	1 6	1	Horsmonden		9 2	1020	1245	2 30	4 44	6 5	8 5	....	7 57	10 0	6 38	8 13	....	....
						Goudhurst		9 7	1025	1250	2 35	4 48	6 10	8 10	....	8 2	10 5	6 43	8 18	....	....
....	....	....	....	....	....	Cranbrook		9 16	1034	1259	2 44	4 57	6 19	8 19	....	8 11	1014	6 52	8 27	....	....
						Hawkhurst ....arr.		9 21	1039	1 4	2 49	5 2	6 24	8 24	....	8 16	1019	6 57	8 32	....	....
Fares from Goudhurst.			**Up.**					mrn	mrn	mrn	aft	aft	aft	aft				SUNDAYS.	mrn	mrn	aft	aft
Single.			Return.			Hawkhurst ....dep.		7 48	9 32	1152	1 19	4 0	5 17	7 7					8 27	1030	7 17	8 40
1 cl.	2 cl.	3 cl.	1 cl.	2 cl.	3 cl.	Cranbrook		7 53	9 37	1157	1 24	4 5	5 22	7 12					8 32	1035	7 22	8 45
s.d.	s.d.	s.d.	s.d.	s.d.	s.d.	Goudhurst		8 1	9 45	12 5	1 32	4 13	5 30	7 20					8 40	1043	7 30	8 53
0 4	0 3	0 2	0 7	0 5	0 4	Horsmonden		8 7	9 51	1211	1 38	4 19	5 35	7 26					8 46	1049	7 36	8 59
1 2	0 11	0 6½	2 0	1 6	1	Paddock Wood 123,120..arr.		8 16	10 0	1220	1 47	4 28	5 43	7 35					8 55	1058	7 45	9 8

Chapter 4

100 Years of Light Railways

by Tom Burnham (1996)

The year 1996 is the centenary of the passing of the Light Railways Act, which was intended to provide a simpler procedure for authorising light railways, and less stringent requirements for building and working them. It is under this Act that the K&ESR operates, and it shaped the career of Colonel Stephens, so it is worth taking a look back at how it came about.

We should perhaps start by saying that the Act of 1896 was not the first attempt by parliament to make it easier to build and work minor railways. The Railway Construction Facilities Act of 1864 allowed the Board of Trade (the Government department which was responsible for railways until 1920) to issue a certificate authorising the construction of a railway, provided that the owners of all the land along the route had already agreed to sell, so that no powers for compulsory purchase were needed. This was rarely the case, and so the Act was not often used. Colonel Stephens was one of the few who took advantage of it when he obtained a certificate to regularise the situation of the Selsey Tramway as the West Sussex Railway in 1924.

Again the Regulation of Railways Act of 1868 had included provision for the Board of Trade to issue a licence enabling a railway to be worked as a light railway. Regulations for such light railways were to be laid down by the Board, provided the axle loading was not to exceed 8 tons nor the maximum speed 25 mph. This concession did not remove the need to obtain a private Act of Parliament and so, again, relatively little use was made of it. One line to be built as a light railway under the 1868 Act was the Culm Valley, from Tiverton Junction to Hemyock in Devon, authorised in 1873 and opened in 1876. A few light railways, such as the Wantage Tramway of 1875 and the Wisbech & Upwell Tramway opened in 1883, were even built under the provisions of the Tramways Act of 1870, although this was really intended for street tramways in towns rather than roadside tramways in the country.

Meanwhile, the Board of Trade's inspectors had been protecting the interests of the travelling public by advising the railway companies to adopt ever more rigorous means of ensuring safety. The larger and more prosperous companies were generally willing to comply, but some of the smaller railways, particularly in Ireland, had been reluctant to make what they saw as unremunerative investments. It was on such a line that the Armagh disaster of June 1889 occurred, in which 80 people were killed, the greatest loss of life in a railway accident in the British Isles at that time. In response to the ensuing public outcry, the President of the Board of Trade, Sir Michael Hicks-Beach (1837-1916) dropped the Conservatives' previous opposition to state interference in the management of railways, and the Regulation of Railways Act of 1889 was passed. This Act enabled the Board of Trade to order railway companies to conform to its requirements, in particular regarding the use of the absolute block system for signalling and the provision of continuous automatic brakes on all passenger trains. The latter requirement, incidentally, created difficulties for minor railways with light traffic, as it made it very problematic to run mixed passenger and goods trains. Questioning whether such precautions were appropriate for all railways, one observer wrote that the Act "finally put an end to the possibility of constructing railways in poor districts" and established "the policy of treating the Ravenglass & Eskdale and the Corris Railway as on all-fours with the main line of the North

Western between London and Rugby".

It was, however, the problems of agriculture rather than railways which led to the Light Railways Act of 1896. A slump in the industry had intensified from 1893 onwards, much land had gone out of cultivation, even in usually prosperous counties such as Essex, and the price of wheat had fallen to its lowest level for 150 years. This was due in large measure to overseas competition, as railways and steamships enabled farmers in Australia, Canada or Argentina to sell their produce in the cities of Britain at prices which could not be matched by the home producers. Lord Rosebery's Liberal government needed to be seen to be taking action over the problem; according to The Times (admittedly no friend of the government) a minister had assured his hearers that they had only to vote straight and solid to see the fields once more "wave with golden grain", so expectations were high. Addressing the lack of transport in rural areas would be a sensible approach: in the era of the horse and cart three miles was reckoned as the desirable limit for carting goods to or from the station. Moreover, the existing railway companies were being criticised by farmers for what was seen as unfair preference in charging lower rates for trainloads of imported produce from the docks than for small consignments of individual British farmers, and so measures which tended to break their monopoly would be popular. Following the usual instincts of the politician, the President of the Board of Trade, James Bryce (1838-1922) called a conference on light railways which met for the first time on 6 December 1894. Those present included politicians from both sides of both Houses, with representatives of agriculture, industry and railway companies and a wide range of public and professional bodies. Mr Bryce opened the conference by making it clear what it would not be about: "There is one question which we think it will be entirely unnecessary for you to consider, and which indeed, ought to be regarded as being entirely outside the scope of our conference, and that is the question of anything in the nature of aid by the central Treasury of the country." Having disposed of this issue, the conference listened to several further speeches before appointing a committee of 22 members under the chairmanship of Sir Bernhard Samuelson MP (1820-1905), a Midlands industrialist, to draft a detailed report. The report was presented when the conference re-assembled on 31 January 1895, and advocated cheaper and simpler procedures for authorising light railways together with more latitude to the Board of Trade in waiving unduly onerous requirements for their operation. Minority reports called for more radical measures towards the same ends.

On 25 April 1895, Mr Bryce introduced a Light Railways Bill which sought to implement the committee's main conclusions. The most novel feature was that county councils (which had been set up as recently as 1889) would be charged with considering proposals for light railways in their area and submitting draft orders to the Board of Trade for final approval. There would also be a relaxation of the Board of Trade's requirements for construction and operation which it was hoped might reduce the cost of making railways from the then average of £10,000 a mile or more to £3,500 or even £3,000.

The Bill was naturally criticised by the Conservative opposition as being quite inadequate as an answer to the crisis in agriculture. They - and indeed some of the government's own supporters - doubted whether many light lines would be built without a government subsidy, even at the lower capital costs which might become possible; existing railway companies would see little likelihood of a profit from extensions into sparsely populated areas, while the country landowners to whose public spirit the government had appealed were suffering on the one hand from lower agricultural rents and on the other from the increased death duties imposed by the so-called 'Democratic Budget' of 1894. MPs from rural constituencies in England and Wales were especially annoyed about the lack of subsidies in view of the grants which were already being made for building railways in Ireland and the Highlands of Scotland.

Mr Bryce's Bill was withdrawn before its second reading. Parliament was dissolved shortly afterwards, and at the ensuing general election the Liberal government was replaced by a Conservative administration under Lord Salisbury, in which C T Ritchie (1838-1906) became President of the Board of Trade.

The problems of agriculture and the need for better transport in country areas were still pressing, and one of the new minister's first steps was to visit France and Belgium, accompanied by the Earl of Dudley (the Parliamentary Secretary to the Board of Trade) and Sir Courtenay Boyle (the Permanent Secretary), to make a personal investigation of the construction, working and finance of their light railways. The two countries had very different systems; in France, light railways were of narrow gauge but were otherwise fully-equipped secondary railways, while in Belgium a national system of roadside steam tramways was being developed.

A new Light Railways Bill was brought before Parliament on 20 February 1896, and in view of the government's majority of 150 it was rather more ambitious than the previous attempt. The main feature of Mr Ritchie's Bill was the establishment of a Light Railway Commission of three members (two of whom would serve unpaid while the third would receive £1000 a year) to examine schemes submitted to it, whether by existing railway companies, companies formed for the purpose, and even local councils. The Commissioners would hold a public inquiry if necessary after which proposals which they supported would be submitted to the Board of Trade for final approval. The Board would also determine which obligations as to safety procedures would apply to the new line. The question of finance was addressed by allowing local councils to take shares in light railway companies or to make loans to them, while the Treasury would also make a million pounds available for loans or free grants to schemes which would benefit agriculture or fisheries. There were some restrictions: the Treasury contribution was not to exceed 25% of the total capital, and the free grants were available only if landowners, local councils and other local interests had given all possible help and if the line was to be constructed and worked by an existing railway company. Amongst the other provisions was a clause enabling railways already authorised, to be worked as light railways. An interesting omission from the Bill was any definition of a light railway, although Mr Ritchie said that it would provide both for making conventional branches of existing railways (whether on the standard or the narrow gauge) and for much lighter steam tramways on the Belgian model.

MPs on both sides of the House generally reacted favourably to the Bill although Mr Bryce, the former President of the Board of Trade, drew attention to the differences from his own Bill of the previous year: the creation of the Commission, the powers of local councils to promote or give financial support to light railways, and the possibility of subsidies from national sources. As far as the last point was concerned, he thought that existing railway companies would not build a light railway without a subsidy if they thought there was the slightest chance of getting one so that even the million pounds allocated would be more likely to stimulate than satisfy the appetite for light railways. This last objection was answered by Sir William Hart Dyke, MP for Dartford (and also a director of the London Chatham & Dover Railway, although he did not mention this fact in his speech), who expected the existing railway companies "would be ready to facilitate the reconstruction and working of light lines without regard to state subsidies".

The Bill was carried on its second reading at the beginning of March by 205 votes to 67. A couple of amendments were made during its consideration by the Grand Committee on Trade, including one exempting light railways from passenger duty (a tax on fares other than third class, eventually abolished in 1929). The third reading was passed after a lengthy debate in June, and, having been passed by the House of Lords, the Light Railways act received Royal Assent on 14 August 1896.

The first Commissioners were appointed in October 1896. They were the Earl of Jersey (1845-1915), a former Governor-General of New South Wales, who was Chairman, Colonel G F O Boughey RE (1844-1918), who had served in India, and Mr Gerald A K FitzGerald (1844-1925), a barrister. There was a rush of applications for Light Railway Orders after the Act came into force, with 85 received during the year ended November 1897 and 88 the following year. The first application was from the London & South Western Railway for the Basingstoke & Alton Light Railway, and this was also the subject of the Commissioners' first public inquiry and the first Order to be confirmed, on 9 December 1897. To celebrate its historic status, C T Ritchie was invited to cut the first sod, on 29 July 1898, and the line eventually opened on 1 June 1901.

However, H F Stephens was also among the pioneers, as he was the engineer (although not one of the promoters) of the Hadlow Light Railway, which obtained the fourth Light Railway Order, confirmed on 24 December 1897. It was never built, a situation which was to become all too familiar. A more significant development was that the Rother Valley Railway took advantage of Clause 18 of the Light Railways Act to obtain permission to construct and work its line (which had already been authorised by Act of Parliament) as a light railway. Accordingly, when it was opened to passengers from Robertsbridge to the present Rolvenden station on 2 April 1900, it was the very first railway to operate under the Light Railways Act of 1896.

Subsequent developments in light railway legislation can be summarised briefly. The 1896 Act had established the Light Railway Commission for an initial period of five years, and so the Light Railways Amendment Act was passed in 1901 to extend its term of office. A Light Railway Act of 1912 revised some of the financial arrangements and also allowed the Commissioners themselves to promote a Parliamentary Bill for a scheme which they had rejected as too important to be within the scope of the Light Railways Act. More substantial changes were made by the Railways Act of 1921, which also amalgamated the mainline railways into the familiar four groups. The Act transferred the powers of the Light Railway Commissioners to the Minister of Transport, who was also to be responsible for government grants to light railways instead of the Treasury. There was a clause enabling railway companies to take over light railways compulsorily and also a requirement that the standard charges of a light railway connecting with one of the amalgamated companies were not to exceed those of the amalgamated company, although each mile of the light railway was to be regarded as a mile and a quarter for calculating rates.

Finally, and much more recently, the Transport and Works Act 1992 established new procedures for authorising new railways and other large scale construction projects, and superseded the Light Railways Act with effect from 1 January 1993 as far as England and Wales are concerned. However, there was a final rush of applications before this date, so that at the time of writing the last Light Railway Order is still some way in the future.

To what extent did the Light Railways Act achieve its objectives? One criticism of the Act which has often been made is that it failed to define what a light railway was; one textbook commented that it was impossible "to pick out any features of a light railway to distinguish it from a tramway on the one hand, and a heavy railway on the other; there are light railways indistinguishable from the one and the other. A light railway can only be defined as a railway constructed under the powers of a Light Railway Order". Indeed, of the 548 applications submitted between 1896 and 1914, 279 were for urban electric tramways (including practically all the applications made by local councils). In Kent alone, the electric tramways of Chatham, Dartford, Dover, Maidstone, Sheerness and Thanet were authorised wholly or in part by Light Railway orders.

Again, by no means all of the lines which were approved were actually built; one critic observed that the Act, intended to create light railways, had in practice created Light Railway Orders. And of those lines that were opened to traffic, many were in effect cheaper branches of the main-line companies, rather than the genuinely light railways delivering wagons to individual farms which some enthusiasts had advocated. Nevertheless, many light railways did provide a valuable service to agriculture. Stephens' Sheppey Light Railway for example, had so-called 'farmers sidings' between the main stations, and these sidings soon had to be lengthened to cope with the traffic.

Some local councils took advantage of the Act to support light railways which they believed would benefit the local economy. For example, the two county councils, three rural district councils and Shrewsbury Corporation took a total of £5750 in debenture shares of the Shropshire & Montgomeryshire Light Railway which opened in 1911. Not all were so helpful; in 1932 East Sussex County Council turned down a request from the Kent & East Sussex Railway for financial assistance under the Act. The predicted flood of applications for subsidies by central government did not materialise. One project that did receive a substantial grant from the Ministry of Transport as well as from the local councils was Stephens' North Devon & Cornwall Junction Light Railway, opened in 1925 and always worked by the Southern Railway.

With the benefit of hindsight, it is easy to criticise the Light Railways Act for failing to produce really light railways and for failing to anticipate developments in road transport. However, legislation which created hundreds of miles of rural railways in the early years of the 20th century, and has been used for almost as many tourist railways at the end of the century must be credited with versatility if nothing else. If current proposals for 'microfranchising' as part of the privatisation process come to anything, we may even see light railways created to meet the needs of the 21st century.

4.1   "Terrier" no. 32678 waits outside Rolvenden on the former K&ESR on 14th November 1953 with the 12.20pm mixed train from Robertsbridge. (N.W.Sprinks)

4.2   Rolvenden was photographed on 27th July 1949, the day on which the ticket opposite was issued. Ex-SECR class O1 0-6-0 no. 31048 is about to have its smokebox cleared after a trip to Headcorn. (V.Mitchell)

Chapter 5

The Hub of the Empire

by Michael Davies (1981)

Tonbridge has been on the railway map since May 1842, when the South Eastern Railway reached the town with its line from London Bridge. Later it was to become an important junction on the SE&CR, handling through train services from as far away as Birkenhead and there is little doubt that its strategic location strongly influenced Holman Stephens to establish his practice there in 1895.

Stephens had spent some four years in Kent, mainly on the Paddock Wood & Cranbrook Railway construction, with headquarters in the former town, but by the summer of 1894 his work was near completion and he was seeking fresh employment. Short commissions with the Cranbrook & District Water Company and the Medway Navigation kept him in the locality and the following year he was involved with schemes for railway construction in the Rother Valley, Tonbridge to Hadlow and Yalding and the Rye & Camber, all easily accessible to Tonbridge.

Surviving correspondence indicates that Stephens first took rooms and established an "office" at Ashby House, Priory Road, in November 1895, employing William Henry Austen as his assistant. Austen seems to have first been engaged by Stephens in 1891, whilst he was at Cranbrook and stayed with him throughout his life. eventually to take over the reins in 1931. He retired at the age of 70 upon nationalisation in 1948. In a letter to his father, dated 17th December 1895, Stephens stated (maybe with a touch of customary arrogance!) "my address is Ashby House, Tonbridge, - but Tonbridge is such a small place that the name of the town is sufficient". His telegraphic address throughout the years was simply -"Stephens, Tonbridge station" where else indeed!

During 1896, following the passing of the Light Railways Act, parliamentary work increased enormously and by 1898 he became foremost consultant in light railway planning and construction; a national telephone was installed at Ashby House and very probably at this time he engaged further assistants to deal with clerical work. In due course the accommodation at Ashby House became too small for the growing practice and early in 1900 he rented offices at number 23, Salford Terrace, a pleasing Victorian house a few hundred yards away and close to Tonbridge station. These premises are one of the few parts of old Tonbridge to survive and have changed little externally over the years, even to the iron railings outside, viewed, no doubt, by the East Kent Railway clerks in their basement room, as they compiled the ever-diminishing passenger returns!

Ashby House remained as Stephens' bachelor quarters right up to his death, presided over by his housekeeper, Miss Flo Standen, but business activities were conducted exclusively from Salford Terrace. The Edwardian era saw a steady growth in mileage planned or built by Stephens (there was considerably more of the former) but unlike the major companies, who constructed very little mileage after 1910, Stephens continued to expand and the number of staff at HQ rose into double figures. 1911/12 saw the reopening of the Potteries Shrewsbury & North Wales as the Shropshire & Montgomeryshire, whilst in Kent, work was proceeding on the East Kent, linking various collieries to the South Eastern & Chatham at Shepherdswell. This line opened in stages between 1916 and 1925. The immediate post war years witnessed the final expansion, with the construction of the Ashover, North Devon & Cornwall Junction, Weston Point and the acquisition of the Snailbeach. In 1923, Tonbridge became responsible for the management and engineering of the Festiniog and Welsh Highland Railways, operating some 36 miles of 2 foot gauge line in a remote part of North Wales. Thus between 1925 and 1931, Salford Terrace administered some 150 miles of line, together with around 70 locomotives and attendant rolling stock. Fortunately for the historian, some former members of the staff, most now sadly departed, recorded their memories of day to day life under the legendary Colonel, and it is possible to portray a fairly accurate account of activity there from around 1914 until closure in 1948.

A visitor to 'number 23' in 1925 would have been confronted with a board outside the front door proclaiming, in gold letters, that the premises housed the offices of the Kent & East Sussex, East Kent, West Sussex, Snailbeach, Shropshire & Montgomeryshire, Weston Clevedon & Portishead and Festiniog & Welsh Highland Railways. The premises themselves consisted of a basement and three floors; the basement could be reached by steps directly from the pavement, crossing a narrow strip of grass (the front garden!) or by stairs from the ground floor. Here, there was one main room looking out across the garden to the pavement wall, its two occupants, W Wills and his assistant, dealt with the affairs of the East Kent. In addition, there was a plans storeroom in the basement area, a blueprint washing and drying room and two store rooms for the filing of correspondence from all lines.

The principal room on the ground floor was at the front of the house, with access off a passage on the right of the front door. This was occupied by J A (Arthur) Iggulden, together with his principal clerk, George Willard and two assistants. Arthur Iggulden was Clerk to the Kent & East Sussex, East Kent, Festiniog and Welsh Highland; Audit Accountant to the Shropshire & Montgomeryshire and Festiniog and Welsh Highland and Secretary to the Shropshire Railways Company. The next door off the passage led to the back room, or inner sanctum, where the Colonel presided and which overlooked the rear of the premises. Stephens' office contained his huge, roll top desk and chair; in the drawers, his fabulous pass collection, which he always showed to visitors; on the top an elaborate writing set - a present from the Canadian National Railways. Elsewhere in the room, his drawing board and bookshelves lined with bound volumes of the proceedings of the Institute of Civil Engineers. On the walls, a dark rose wall paper with floral design, brown paint and photographs of locomotives around the room; the floor covered with brown linoleum. On the back of the door hung his customary Burberry coat. In the last year of his life, when he was desperately ill, the opening of the door produced a 'clunk' as a hard object in the pocket struck the woodwork. Could this, as at least one member of the staff believed, have been his service revolver?

All rooms at Salford Terrace originally had coal fires and it was the duty of the junior clerks to bring coal or carry ashes to their respective areas in the basement; curiously, female cleaning staff were never allowed on the premises and no doubt to ease the workload, gas fires were installed about 1920. A staircase led upwards from outside Colonel Stephens' door to the first floor landing, whilst the ground floor passage terminated with a door leading to a washroom and toilet. The upper floors were of identical layout, each with a large front room occupying the full width of the house and a somewhat smaller room at the rear. Internal communication was by means of a railway-type telephone, with bell codes for each individual. There was also a private telephone line to Tenterden and Rolvenden.

The front room on the first floor was the general drawing office and civil engineering department, the principal occupant of which was W H ("Billy") Austen, who covered the 'outdoor administration' for all lines. He was assisted by W H ("Bungy") Corke, the other occupants being K&ESR stores Superintendent, Fred Willard and Albert Osborne, the general clerk to the West Sussex Railway, who also assisted in the drawing office. Osborne was also the Colonel's batman during the Great War. The back room was the preserve of John Ashworth, the Colonel's civil engineering assistant for all lines, whose services were terminated after Stephens' death and the collapse of the Southern Heights scheme.

Finally, to the second floor, where the front room was occupied by Cyril Hewitt and his assistants, Archie Judd, John Elcombe and another clerk. Hewitt was Secretary to the Shropshire & Montgomeryshire and Snailbeach also chief clerk to the Weston Clevedon & Portishead. Elcome was Secretary to the West Sussex line. The back room was the K&ESR audit office, occupied by the audit clerk, Tommy Edwards and a rates and general assistant. The total staff numbered around 17 at this time, a number which remained fairly constant until the outbreak of the Second World War.

Sometime after 1920, Stephens purchased the freehold of the Salford Terrace offices and on his death in 1931 it was sold to W H Austen, to ensure their continued tenancy, each of the representative railways paying an annual rental to cover the maintenance of the property. With the nationalisation of the Kent & East Sussex and East Kent in 1948, only the Snailbeach remained, as the other lines had closed by the outbreak of war, although civilian goods traffic on the Shropshire & Montgomeryshire continued to be handled throughout the war years, despite the fact that to all intents and purposes the line had been taken over by the military in 1941.

Clearly this was insufficient to maintain the offices and on 7th June 1948 there came to an end half a century of light railway history and administration. Of the dozen or so remaining staff, six elected to be transferred to the Southern Region and W H Austen retired. Several lorry loads of papers, plans and other material were sent for pulping, although some were rescued by British Railways archives and by well wishers. Today, the offices are occupied by a firm of architects - the basement; a hairdressers, the nameboard with its gold lettering, long disappeared.

No account of Salford Terrace would be complete without a reference to some of the incidents which helped to contribute to the atmosphere of this unique establishment and for much of this information we are indebted to the late Arthur Iggulden, who worked there from 1914 until closure. Iggulden recalled that Stephens loved to please his friends and acquaintances by sending them free passes for his lines or with gifts, mainly of a culinary nature. Amongst these was Rudyard Kipling, who lived at Batemans, near Etchingham. In January 1925, Kipling wrote to Stephens, "the faithful pass has duly arrived and though I am not likely to use it, I am always grateful that you remember me, though after the last month or six weeks I have got an idea that it would be more to the point if you had given me a free seat in a motor boat, punt or barge from Robertsbridge to Paddock Wood!"

Food would arrive at Salford Terrace in large quantities; at one period a butcher at Llanidloes, noted for his Welsh lamb, would despatch a half a dozen legs to Tonbridge, which would, on arrival, be despatched by parcel post according to Stephens' directions. Similarly, there was an arrangement with the station agent at Crew Green, on the Shropshire & Montgomeryshire to send salmon to Salford Terrace; stags heads and lobsters were sent down from a contact in Oban.

Stephens was frequently away from the offices visiting parts of his railway empire but immediately on his return, be it day or night, he insisted on being briefed on events that had occurred during his absence. A terse telegram to Iggulden's Tonbridge home worded "Arrive Tonbridge 10 pm" would necessitate his return to the office for consultation, maybe into the small hours of the following morning. There was little social contact between Stephens and his staff, the only outing being a dinner at the Criterion Restaurant, followed by a visit to the Lyceum theatre, on 4th February 1916, probably to mark the occasion of Stephens' return to full-time railway work after he gave up his military commitments.

Although Stephens kept on his rooms at Ashby House until his death, he frequently stayed for extended periods at the Lord Warden Hotel, Dover, and, in fact, he died there in October 1931. His usual routine was to catch an early train to Tonbridge, call in at the office and then make his way to Ashby House. In the meantime, one of the Salford Terrace clerks would call at Catley's cafe nearby, collect a specially prepared breakfast and carry it across the road to Ashby House. After this, work would commence for the day.

During the general strike of May 1926, Stephens found himself marooned on the K&ESR, but fortunately his own staff remained loyal. For many years he had rented rooms from a Mrs Reeves in Station Road, Robertsbridge, although nobody could remember him occupying them after 1914. However, during the strike period they proved to be a real boon and became a temporary headquarters, with Iggulden going over there daily on his motor cycle to convey messages. Certainly working at number 23 was no sinecure; pay rates were below those of the main line companies, overtime was expected and not paid for and it was quite out of the question for a member of the staff to join a trade union.

Nevertheless, faithful service was rewarded by generous tips and in the case of four staff members, they shared equally in his estate of some £30,000 at his death, there being no surviving relatives. It is fortunate that some of the most important archive material, including the Colonel's pass collection have survived and some may be seen in the Colonel Stephens Railway Museum at Tenterden.

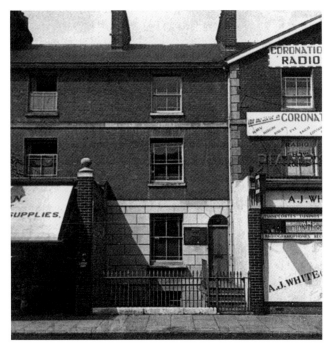

5.1   The board to the left of the front door of 23 Salford Terrace, Tonbridge, listed the companies controlled from there in 1937.

5.2   *J A (Arthur) Iggulden was photographed in 1931.*

5.3   *R V Fuller was recorded at Colonel Stephens' desk in about 1934; compare this picture with the one on the back cover of this volume.*

5.4   Stephens circulated other railways with requests for free passes for himself and W H Austen. His own empire was somewhat overstated, with railways that had not been built, such as The Gower.

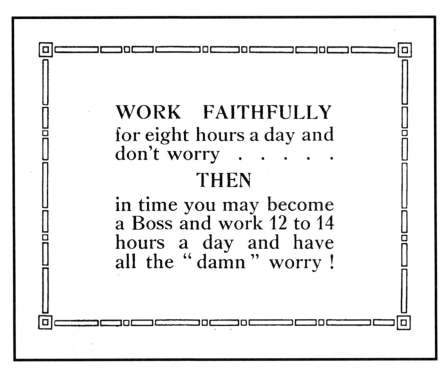

WORK   FAITHFULLY
for eight hours a day and
don't worry . . . . .
THEN
in time you may become
a Boss and work 12 to 14
hours a day and have
all the " damn " worry !

Chapter 6

The Hadlow Light Railway

by Tom Burnham (1986)

Colonel Stephens' office at Salford Terrace, Tonbridge was, of course, remote from any of the railways he managed and control had to be exercised by pithy memoranda and periodic flying visits. However, if the Hadlow Light Railway, for which he acted as Engineer, had been built as planned, K&ESR locomotives would have run to Tonbridge.

The first proposal for a railway to serve the area north east of Tonbridge appears to have been the unlikely sounding Tonbridge Wells, Snodland & Edenbridge Suspension Railway, mooted in 1825. In about 1836, some residents of West Peckham petitioned the House of Lords in favour of an extension of the South Eastern Railway to the village. An Act of Parliament was obtained in 1863 for a Hadlow Railway, which was to have left the Otford to Maidstone line of the London, Chatham & Dover Railway (authorised in 1862 but not completed until 1874) at Ightham, about 1 mile west of Borough Green station, and run some 5½ miles to terminate in "a Cherry Orchard in the Occupation of Messieurs Kenward and Barnett" in Hadlow. The line was to have been financed by local millowners and by the contractors who would have built it. However, although notices were issued to landowners in 1866, the financial crisis of the same year put paid to the scheme, and in 1876 when the Parliamentary powers were formally abandoned it was noted that the former Secretary had not been heard of since appearing as a witness in the Titchborne case while the solicitor for the promoters, who had put up the money for the Parliamentary expenses, had been made an outlaw.

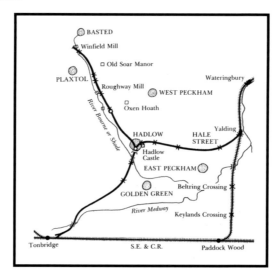

Matters rested thus for another twenty years, when, taking advantage of the recently passed Light Railways Act of 1896, plans were prepared for a Hadlow Light Railway of standard gauge to serve the district between Tonbridge and Ightham, an area then as now devoted mainly to fruit growing, hop gardens and the dairy trade. Starting from the goods yard of the South Eastern Railway station at Tonbridge, it would have left the town not far from the present Angel Centre, with a level crossing at Botany, and crossed the river Medway by means of a 10 ft high bridge with a span of 70 ft. The line then ran to the south of the main road, with two public road level crossings and a road overbridge, to Hadlow (3¾ miles), then a village with a population of some 2500, two breweries (Kenward & Court Ltd, and Henry Simmons' Style Place Brewery) and the Mid-Kent Jam Factory Ltd. Public transport was supplied by George Castle's horse omnibus to and from Tonbridge station four times a day and by daily carriers' carts to Tonbridge and Maidstone. At Hadlow, the line would have divided. One branch ran somewhat to the north of East Peckham to rejoin the SER at Yalding on the Paddock Wood to Maidstone line. This was an easily graded line, again 3¾ miles long, with seven level crossings, two of which, at Hadlow and near Hale Street, were over relatively busy roads.

The other branch ran northwards along the valley of a stream known as the Bourne or Shode, past the village of Plaxtol (with a population of about 1000) to terminate near Winfield Mill, a mile or so south of Basted and about 3¾ miles from Hadlow. Although all that is left of Winfield Mill today are some derelict sluices and broken masonry buried in the woods, at the turn of the century it was a thriving flour mill turned by a great water wheel and in the ownership of Mr. James Smith Bellingham. In the days when water power was of importance, the little river was a hive of activity. Beside the Winfield flour mill, the line would have served the Roughway paper mills of Richard David Turner & Co, then engaged solely on Government work and now occupied by WBC Packaging Ltd. No doubt it was also hoped to attract traffic from the Basted mills where paper for stamps was made, and possibly also from local stone quarries. This branch had considerably heavier earthworks and steeper gradients; up to 1 in 87. An application was made to the Board of Trade for a Light Railway Order in December 1896. The promoters were the Light Railways Syndicate Ltd., represented as usual by E W I Peterson, a solicitor of Lincoln's Inn Fields and Cranbrook, and the Engineer was H F Stephens.

Commenting on the plans in its issue of 21 November 1896, the Tonbridge Free Press stated "it is gratifying to see that no time has been lost in carrying the scheme on toward completion It is not probable that all the sections of the railway will be taken in hand at once, but there is no reason, unless some unlooked-for opposition arises, why the line from Tonbridge to Hadlow and Plaxtol should not be opened in the course of the next 12 months." In hindsight it is significant that the same issue of the paper also carried a report of the passing of the Locomotives & Highways Act, allowing motor cars to travel at up to 12 mph, and of the first London to Brighton run celebrating this event.

Although unrecognised at the time, it could be argued that this marked the beginning of the end for the local country railway! Undeterred by such premonitions, the promoters pressed on. Although Tonbridge Urban District Council had entered a formal objection to the scheme, to enable them to be represented at the public inquiry, a resolution was passed at Mr. Peterson's request in March 1897 to the effect that the district was in great need of improved facilities and that the UDC supported the line subject to its objections being resolved. However, no action was taken on a suggestion that the Council actually subscribe towards the line.

The estimated cost of land and construction was £49,045 or £4240 per mile. The Board of Trade noted that the cost of earthworks on the Tonbridge to Hadlow section appeared to have been underestimated, as the volume of embankments considerably exceeded that of cuttings and only the latter had been allowed for. The £1270 per mile estimated for permanent way appeared a rather low figure. The public inquiry by the Light Railway Commissioners into the application was held at Tonbridge on 27 April 1897. The Tonbridge UDC complained that parts of the line were on land liable to flooding and the waterways proposed to carry the excess water were inadequate and that the level crossings would be dangerous. The promoters agreed to alter the alignment through the flooded areas and to a clause in the Light Railway Order enabling the Board of Trade to require more or larger flood relief openings to be provided. The company agreed to cause a bell to be rung when a train was approaching the level crossing at Botany and to provide a footbridge at least 5 ft wide at a footway crossing much used by school children. Three level crossings were to have gates (and keepers, unless the Board of Trade agreed otherwise) and there were to be 5 or 10 mph speed restrictions at ungated crossings. The UDC asked that the company be required to provide a station near the Hadlow Road in the north of Tonbridge; Mr. Stephens agreed to construct this station but the Commissioners decided that it could be left to the company to select the most convenient site. Sir William Geary, owner of the Oxen Hoath estate, objected to the effect on his property and was rewarded by a requirement that the company should provide a station and sidings for cattle and goods traffic at Mount Pleasant for his use. Other objections were raised by local landowners, complaining about their land being split up by the line, Col. James Clayhills of Hadlow, who was concerned about the level crossings in the village, the SER and the National Telephone Company.

The Commissioners advised that the Light Railway Order should be granted and this was done on Christmas Eve 1897. In addition to the requirements indicated above, it stipulated a maximum speed of 25 mph (15 mph for tender locomotives running tender first) and a maximum axle load of 10t. Traction could be steam or, with the Board of Trade's approval electric, and the company could by agreement with the SER use the station and sidings at Tonbridge and the line between the up and down distant signals at Yalding. The rails had to weigh at least 56lb per yard and platforms were to be provided at stations unless all the carriages used had "proper and convenient means of access." There was, however, "no obligation on the Company to provide shelter or conveniences at any station or stopping place other than at Hadlow Junction." Passing stations were to have home signals and also distant signals where visibility was less than ¼ mile and there were to be junction signals at junctions. The authorised capital was £70,000 in £1 shares (to which the SER was entitled to subscribe) plus powers to borrow up to £23,000. Three years were allowed for compulsory purchase of land and 5 years for completion of the works. The first directors of the Hadlow Light Railway Company were to be three directors of the Light Railways Syndicate Ltd, and one other person to be nominated by them.

The company seems to have had at least some measure of existence, as we find William Stow, a Hadlow coal merchant, listed in local directories as Secretary to the Hadlow Light Railway, in addition to being manager of the Medway Navigation Co (Mr. Stephens was the Engineer of the latter company for a couple of years). However, no great progress can have been made as in November 1900 the Hadlow Light Railway, now with an office at H F Stephens' Salford Terrace, Tonbridge headquarters, applied for an extension of time to build the line, on the grounds that "their negotiations with the South Eastern Railway Company, as to an agreement to work the light railway, were temporarily stopped during the proceedings concerning the amalgamation of that Railway with the London, Chatham & Dover Railway, but that it is anticipated that within the next six months some definite arrangement may be made with the South Eastern Company which will enable the company to raise the capital required for this light railway." A revised estimate of £62,271 was submitted; the Board of Trade commented that it still ignored the cost of a total of 133,400 cubic yards of embankment, but it did allow £400 for stations on each of the three main branches - not a very generous sum even in 1900!

As no pertinent objections were received, no local inquiry was held and the Hadlow Light Railway (Amendment) Order was made on 4 October 1901. It extended the periods for acquisition of land and construction to 5 and 7 years respectively (i e to December 1902 and 1904), it allowed an axle load up to 14 tons if the rails weighed not less than 60 lb per yard and it increased the authorised capital to £75,000 and the borrowing powers to £25,000. Perhaps the most interesting feature of the Order from our point of view is that it empowered the Hadlow Light Railway to enter into agreements with the Rother Valley Railway to construct and work the line. It conjures up an intriguing picture of, say, No. 3 "Bodiam" puffing into Tonbridge with a train from Plaxtol or even hurrying down the main line to Headcorn or Robertsbridge on its way to Rolvenden for overhaul.

As a final postscript to the story, the SE&CR opened Beltring & Branbridges Halt in September 1909, affording slightly more convenient rail access to the villages of East Peckham and Hale Street.

6.1   The quiet country station at Yalding would have become a junction. This northward view is after the rebuilding of 1893.

Chapter 7

Some 'Stephens' Lines that might have been

Central Essex Light Railway, Hedingham & Long Melford Light Railway, Kelvedon, Coggeshall & Halstead Light Railway and Long Melford & Hadleigh Light Railway.

by Stephen Garrett (1981)

It has been considered that the Light Railways Act 1896 came twenty years too late. It was intended to make it easier for railways to be built in those areas still without rail transport by permitting lighter permanent way, steeper gradients, sharper curves and less stringent signalling, fencing and accommodation requirements though at the expense of lower permitted speeds. In appropriate cases there was even the possibility of Treasury grants or loans to encourage such enterprises. Unfortunately the severely depressed state of agriculture in the country areas combined with the far more profitable alternative areas for investment in the City to prevent the Act producing more than a mild surge of light railway developments. Those lines that were built found it hard to survive the unforeseen competition from the roads that came with the development of the lorry, bus and car.

For Holman Fred Stephens, however, the Light Railways Act was well timed. With the experience of engineering and supervising the building of the Cranbrook & Paddock Wood Railway between 1890 and 1893 and his subsequent work in planning the Rother Valley Railway he was well qualified to undertake the design and construction of the sort of economical railway envisaged by the Light Railways Act. As a result, between 1897 and 1900 his services were sought in planning lines as far flung as Land's End, the Gower Peninsula, the Isle of Sheppey, Selsey, Orpington and Faversham as well as continuing his work on the Rother Valley line and serving as Engineer to the Upper Medway Navigation. As if all this were not enough to keep him occupied he became closely involved in a series of schemes which, had they succeeded, would have produced a substantial chain of light railways across Essex.

Strangely, the origin of Stephens' involvement with Essex appears to have been on the Cranbrook & Paddock Wood Railway. From 1890 to 1910 a solicitor, Edward W I Peterson, was practising in the neighbourhood of Staplehurst and it is to be presumed that this is how he and Stephens became acquainted. The result of this acquaintanceship was the involvement of Stephens in a body known as the Light Railway Syndicate, incorporated in 1895, and in a related concern, the Economic Railways Company, incorporated in 1898. Peterson was Solicitor to the Syndicate and a director of the Company. Stephens held a substantial share in the Syndicate but was only a nominal shareholder in the Company although one of its initial subscribers. Nobody else held shares in both companies; the majority of the shareholders in the Syndicate were from the London area whilst most of the Company shares were held by residents of Bath and its vicinity. These two concerns were not solely interested in Essex; the Syndicate was the instigator of the Sheppey Light Railway and various other lines whilst the Company waged a protracted and ultimately unsuccessful contest with the Railway Development Company for the right to build a light railway in furthest Cornwall. However, it was in Essex that the Syndicate and the Economic had their highest hopes.

The Great Eastern Railway and its predecessors had never been particularly responsive to requests from local communities for branch lines unless the building of such a line would keep a competitor out of its 'sphere of influence'. As a result there were substantial areas of rural Essex without easy access to rail transport and it was to these areas that the Light Railways Act drew the attention of Peterson and Stephens. The presence of an independent line, the Colne Valley Railway, in the heart of this territory may have served as an encouragement though the fact that this concern had gone into receivership as early as 1874 should perhaps have served as a warning instead.

There were two schemes proposed by the Light Railway Syndicate. The first was a Central Essex Light Railway running from Ongar, at the end of the Great Eastern line from Epping and Stratford, to Great Dunmow where the Great Eastern line from Witham to Bishops Stortford would be crossed and then on to Great Yeldham on the Colne Valley Railway. The second scheme was for a Hedingham & Long Melford Light Railway which would have continued the Central Essex from Yeldham to Long Melford on the Great Eastern line from Marks Tey to Bury St Edmunds with an alternative route from the Central Essex some two miles short of Yeldham sweeping south to Sible Hedingham and thence north to rejoin the direct route to Long Melford at North End. In the event, when the public enquiry into these proposals was held, the direct route between Yeldham and North End was dropped altogether.

Linked to the two Syndicate schemes was the Kelvedon, Coggeshall & Halstead Light Railway promoted by the Economic. This would have left the Great Eastern main line to Colchester at Kelvedon and headed north through the ancient but reduced town of Coggeshall to join the

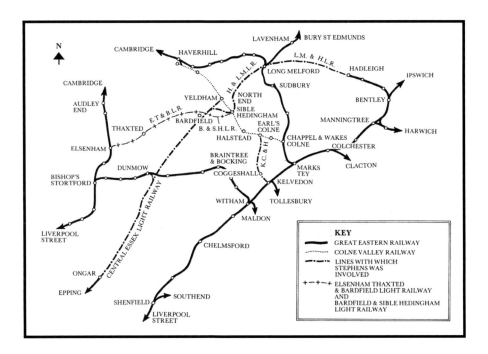

Colne Valley Railway close to Earls Colne. From here running powers were requested over the Colne Valley line not just to the textile town of Halstead but over a further six miles to link up with the Syndicate lines at Sible Hedingham and Yeldham. Nor was this the full extent of Stephens' involvement in the area for he and Peterson were both employed in the promotion of a Long Melford & Hadleigh Light Railway proposed by local interests to link Long Melford and the Great Eastern branch from Bentley to Hadleigh. Had all these schemes come to fruition there would have been an independent line of rails some 57 miles in length from Ongar to Hadleigh with a 15 mile branch over the Colne Valley line and via Coggeshall to Kelvedon.

That these schemes did not proceed as intended was due in part to the intervention of yet another scheme in the area. This was the Bardfield & Sible Hedingham Light Railway which was an extension of a proposed Elsenham Thaxted & Bardfield Light Railway. Originally promoted as a 2' 6" narrow gauge railway by local interests who had despaired of interesting the Great Eastern in the area; this proposal had been promised a Treasury Grant if satisfactory arrangements for working the line could be reached with the Great Eastern. The plans had then been altered to standard gauge and while negotiations proceeded with the Great Eastern this extension to Sible Hedingham had been mooted. The problem for Peterson and Stephens was that the Bardfield & Sible Hedingham cut right across their route from Dunmow to Yeldham. It is certain that the deletion mentioned earlier of the direct route from Yeldham to North End was a result of concentrating the Syndicate's resources on a route to Sible Hedingham to fight off the Bardfield & Sible Hedingham proposals.

The sequence of events in all these proposals was as follows. The Central Essex application was made in November 1897, the Hedingham & Long Melford, Bardfield & Sible Hedingham and Kelvedon, Coggeshall & Halstead applications were made in May 1898 and the Long Melford & Hadleigh application was made in November 1899.

The Kelvedon Coggeshall & Halstead was an early casualty. Few objections were raised against the first two miles from Kelvedon to Coggeshall except from the owner of most of the land affected but beyond Coggeshall little was found in favour of the scheme. The Essex County Chronicle summed up the vehement opposition of the Colne Valley Railway in these words: "It sought to tap the Colne Valley Railway at the most vital part of their system and rob them of the little - the very little - which enabled them to pay their preference shareholders ... It was a London-promoted enterprise and a predatory enterprise." In vain did Mr Gollen on behalf of the scheme urge that far from taking traffic from the Colne Valley it would in fact increase trade in the area to the benefit of both concerns. The Colne Valley's main source of traffic was from Courtaulds' mills at Halstead and it could clearly see that a more direct route to London would have a drastic effect on its freight receipts.

The view of the Enquiry was that no public advantage had been proved for the line beyond Coggeshall and since this portion of the neighbourhood was at no point more than three miles from a railway there was no need to sanction more than the length of line between Kelvedon and Coggeshall. A Coggeshall Light Railway Order was duly granted in 1899 with three years given to complete the line. There is no indication that any serious effort was ever made to exercise the powers under this order and no application was made for an extension of time when these ran out.

Cut off from the main scheme and with little prospect of more than a very modest local traffic it is not hard to see why no effort was made to persevere with the Coggeshall Light Railway.

The Enquiry into the Central Essex and the rival Hedingham schemes was more complicated. For the greater part of the Central Essex the Commissioners recognised that there was a real need for rail transport through the Rodings and between Dunmow and Bardfield. Beyond Bardfield there was clearly no need for three separate schemes in such close proximity. The Hedingham & Long Melford scheme, though fervently supported by a local brick manufacturer, Mr Gentry, had little to commend it between Hedingham and Long Melford whilst its initial course from the Central Essex to Sible Hedingham was so closely duplicated by the Bardfield & Sible Hedingham as to be rendered redundant; each line in fact accused the other of plagiarising its plans. An equally important point was that the Colne Valley would not permit access to its lines, Stephens would not build a bridge across the Colne Valley line and the Commissioners were naturally reluctant either to force the Colne Valley to accept the Hedingham & Long Melford on its lines or to permit the two lines to cross on the level. The Hedingham & Long Melford was therefore rejected in its entirety.

To resolve the problem of the proximity of the Central Essex and the Bardfield & Sible Hedingham an ingenious compromise was reached by the Commissioners. The Central Essex would end at Bardfield, the Bardfield & Sible Hedingham would be approved subject to the satisfactory conclusion of negotiations between the Elsenham Thaxted & Bardfield and the Great Eastern while the Central Essex would be given running powers between Bardfield and Sible Hedingham though not over the Colne Valley to Halstead and Haverhill as the Central Essex had audaciously requested.

The plans of the Light Railway Syndicate were obviously coming unstuck. Although the Sible Hedingham enquiry was held in 1899 it was not until 1901 that a Central Essex Light Railway Order was granted. This was because of the difficulty of reaching an agreement between the Elsenham Thaxted & Bardfield and the Great Eastern. It would seem though that Stephens was not entirely discouraged as his plans for the Long Melford & Hadleigh, deposited after the rejection of the Hedingham & Long Melford appear to have anticipated success in linking Hedingham and Long Melford at some date in the future. It is difficult to explain otherwise the reason for Stephens placing his passenger terminus for the Long Melford & Hadleigh to the west of Long Melford Station and thus necessitating a bridge over the Great Eastern line before heading eastwards to Hadleigh. This seems to have been a great extravagance for a light railway which was to have a goods connection to the Great Eastern on the eastern side of Long Melford Station anyway. How Stephens justified this to the local promoters of the line or whether they too had intentions of building a link to the Central Essex will probably never be known. The enquiry into the merits of the Hadleigh scheme was held at Long Melford in March 1900.

There were a number of objections from landowners but these mostly related to details and were met by promises of deviations and adjustments. The Great Eastern made a number of objections to the form that junctions should take at Hadleigh and Long Melford and also alleged that the new line would attract traffic away from their own. Since the whole point of the line was to provide a convenient link between two Great Eastern lines it is hard to see how the Great Eastern could have lost by such a proposal. There were also objections from the local population, not to the principle of a railway but to the fact that it would only be a light railway. The Commissioners were pleased to recommend that the scheme be approved and the Long Melford & Hadleigh Light Railway Order was duly granted in 1901. Unfortunately that is as far as the scheme ever got. Whether the costs proved beyond the means of the promoters or they lost heart for some other reason does not appear on the records. The five years for the purchase of lands passed without any application for the extension or revival of powers.

Before returning to the progress of the Central Essex it is instructive to compare the Long Melford & Hadleigh, a locally promoted venture, with the schemes prepared by Stephens for the Syndicate and the Economic. All schemes bore his hallmark of following contours where he could but plunging with a minimum of earthworks over those contours that could not be avoided without undue expense; fortunately Essex is not a county of great heights or depths, though by no means as flat as many appear to believe. In other respects there were major differences between the schemes. With the Long Melford & Hadleigh, objections were met by deviations and even the building of bridges where level crossings aroused concern. With the other schemes there was far less willingness to compromise and objections were resisted rather than accommodated. In each scheme, except the Long Melford & Hadleigh, Stephens requested a maximum speed of 35 mph and to be exempted from the use of continuous brakes on trains of three or fewer carriages; the Commissioners insisted on 25 mph and continuous brakes. Above all the Commissioners repeatedly complained of the high estimates of capital required for the schemes for the Syndicate and the Economic, a point also made by the Colne Valley and other objectors. A passage in the report on the Long Melford & Hadleigh draws a comparison with the other schemes: "The Capital proposed is ... about £7000 per mile. This is a remarkable difference from the former proposals as to the capital of lines with which Mr Stephens is concerned. For in this case the Capital is only about £1250 per mile in excess of the estimate whereas in former cases the excess asked for has been as much as £4000 per mile."

So by 1901 Orders has been granted for the Central Essex as amended, for the Coggeshall and for the Long Melford & Hadleigh. Chronologically the next event seems to have been the disposal by Stephens of 476 of his 526 shares in the Light Railway Syndicate to a New General Traction Company about which little else is known. This happened in 1902 and it seems that Stephens was losing interest in Essex or at least taking a more realistic view of the chances of these schemes than his fellow shareholders. Besides his 50 remaining shares in the Syndicate he also held one share in the Economic whose assets were reported in 1903 by Peterson as the possession of ". . . a Light Railway Order authorising the construction of a line 2¼ - miles in length. The compulsory powers for the acquisition of lands have run out and a sum just over £1 in the bank." The Economic was dissolved the following year. Although Stephens retained his shares in the Syndicate until its end he appears to have played no further active part in its affairs. The Central Essex Light Railway was, however, far from dead.

In 1905 the powers for the Elsenham Thaxted & Bardfield lapsed. The promoters had been unable to meet the conditions laid down by the Great Eastern though a modified scheme was eventually built as far as Thaxted in 1911. To get the Great Eastern to build and work the line the local promoters had to provide the Great Eastern with the Treasury Grant and half the costs of construction as well as agreeing to forego any return on their investment. With such terms it is not surprising that the original scheme foundered.

For the Central Essex the failure of the Elsenham Thaxted & Bardfield cleared the way to apply for the Bardfield & Sible Hedingham powers. The Central Essex (Amendment) Light Railway Order 1905 gave these powers to the Central Essex as well as granting an extension of time. By now the line's Engineer was F Leslie Jeyes.

A further extension of time was sought and granted in 1907 but no progress was made and Peterson was back to request a further extension in 1908. He explained that in 1907 he had expected investment from a group who had failed to obtain consent to build a line in the Cape Colony. They had found it more profitable to put their money on deposit but now "certain persons" had come forward to build the line and he was assured of their good faith. Correspondence between the Colne Valley Railway and its solicitor at this time reveals that they had no expectation of the Central Essex succeeding but that if it went ahead they must be prepared to take on the working of the line rather than let it fall into the hands of the Great Eastern. The identity of the "certain persons" never was revealed but the Commissioners granted an extension to 1910. The engineer at this time was George Attwood.

It is at this stage that Stephens and Peterson leave entirely, for in 1910 Peterson was adjudged bankrupt and in 1912 the Light Railway Syndicate was voluntarily liquidated. In 1911, though, a fresh group of promoters had taken the reins of the Central Essex and with S W Yockney as their engineer successfully sought a further extension of time to 1912. The Commissioners would probably have let the Central Essex powers lapse in 1912 but for news that a contractor, not named, was delivering plant to the site and preparing to start work. What became of this contractor is not clear, for in 1913 Sir Douglas Fox & Partners appear on the scene as new contractors with a request for a further extension of time to allow for an application for a Treasury Grant. In 1914 it is the turn of Mr E J Wills, Director and Acting Secretary, to apply for and gain a further 12 months. In the meantime landowners and the Essex County Council whose lands and roads respectively have by now been blighted for some 14 years by the scheme are beginning to complain.

In 1915 events took a final and bizarre turn. Describing himself as Chairman of the Central Essex Light Railway an application is received by the Light Railway Commissioners from R C Temple Bt. not only for an extension of time but also for powers to extend the Central Essex from Yeldham (sic) to Long Melford, thence via Lavenham to Haughley where the Mid-Suffolk Light Railway would be acquired and extended to Halesworth where in turn the Southwold Railway would be acquired and converted to standard gauge thus bringing the Central Essex from Ongar to the sea at Southwold, some 113 miles in all. The Commissioners do not seem to have been impressed despite the subsequent submission by Temple of a letter solicited from the War Office saying that under certain circumstances the line might have military value. Two months were granted for a proper application to be made. When Temple returned in June to seek a further extension of time it was refused.

Even then the ghost of the Central Essex lingered a little longer. In 1919 a proposal was made for a Braintree & Marks Tey Light Railway which would have passed through Coggeshall and the same promoters put forward an Ongar & Shenfield Light Railway. The following year a Mid-Essex Light Railway was proposed over that portion of the Central Essex between Ongar and Dunmow by a group known as the Essex Light Railway & Property Company. These schemes were, however, essentially dependent on obtaining Treasury Grants and got no further than the application stage.

Today the Colne Valley Railway has itself disappeared with the exception of the short section preserved around the rebuilt Castle Hedingham Station. The Hadleigh Branch has gone and both Dunmow and Long Melford have lost their railways. At Ongar the line from Epping hangs on by the skin of its teeth. Would Stephens, at one time apprenticed to the Metropolitan Railway, have seen any irony in the fact that the one station to have survived on the route of the Central Essex is now served by London Transport?

7.1   Long Melford would have become a major junction in East Anglia. The deserted station is seen in May 1961; it closed in 1967.

7.2   Ongar would have been transformed to a through station. It became London Transport property in 1949, was electrified in 1957 and closed in 1994. Revival began about 10 years later.

7.3   Thaxted was the simplest of stations, with minimal platform height and very light rail. It closed to passengers on 15th September 1952, although freight continued for a further nine months.

Chapter 8

William Rigby –Contractor to the Colonel

by Tom Burnham (2001/2)

The influence of the railway contractor, the archetypal self-made nouveau riche of the mid-Victorian novel, has been insufficiently recognised. A few, like Thomas Brassey, have been rescued from oblivion by their biographers, but most of the men responsible for building our railways remain unknown to the general public and the railway expert alike.

William Rigby had a career as an independent contractor which lasted from the mid-1880s to just after the Great War. In this era most of the great trunk railways had already been built, but there was plenty of work for contractors in building feeder lines - including those authorised under the Light Railways Act of 1896 - and in rebuilding the existing main lines to handle heavier and faster traffic. Rigby is of particular interest to us, as he was involved with Colonel Stephens for some of this period, not only as the builder of railways of which Stephens was the engineer (including part of the K&ESR), but also in the promotion and management of others, including the Shropshire & Montgomeryshire Light Railway, of which he was Chairman for many years.

His career also illustrates the network of personal contacts between railway managers, directors, financiers, engineers and contractors that influenced the development of Britain's railways in the pre-grouping era.

William Rigby was born in Addiscombe Road, Croydon, on 23 January 1850. His father, also named William Rigby, was born in Lowton, Lancashire in 1811. He had married Elizabeth Oliver (born in 1814 at Beechburn, County Durham) and had migrated gradually southwards by way of Leeds and Chesterfield, arriving in Croydon shortly before William junior was born. William Rigby senior remained in Croydon, moving house from time to time to accommodate his growing family, until his death on 6 December 1884, a few years after his wife, Elizabeth (11 March 1879). William Rigby senior was a contractor, although he is not known to have carried out railway work. However, the young William Rigby may well have heard stories about trains from his uncle Cuthbert Oliver, a foreman on the railway, who used to visit the house.

William moved to the East Midlands, perhaps taking advantage of connections from the period when his father had worked in the area. By 1871, he had become a contractor's clerk, and was boarding in Whitwell, Derbyshire, a village near Worksop. On 18 August 1873 he was married to Emma White, the daughter of a Barnsley callenderer, at St George's church, Sheffield, by the curate, Rev Thomas Rigby. It is uncertain whether Rev Rigby was a relation, although it may be significant that William was stated to be a resident of the parish. The couple returned to Whitwell, where their daughter, Margaret, was born on 28 October 1873.

William Rigby soon became a railway contractor in his own right, with an office at the Corn Exchange in Potter Street, Worksop, and a country house at The Aviaries, on the Clumber Park estate, where the establishment included a cook and kitchenmaid. Together with the rest of the estate, The Aviaries is now in the care of the National Trust. Rigby was evidently successful, as in 1881 he was one of two people who each guaranteed a £3000 surety for the completion of the Blakedown viaduct near Kidderminster on the Great Western by its contractors, Abram Kellett and Samuel Bently. But the Rigbys did not have long to enjoy this prosperity together, for Emma died of pneumonia on 22 October 1880 aged only 33, leaving William to bring up Margaret. Perhaps because of this unhappy event, the family had by 1885 moved to Calverton House, Calverton, north of Nottingham, where in due course they were joined by William's unmarried eldest sister, also named Margaret.

No details have come to light of the contracts which William Rigby undertook in these early years of his career, although we may suppose that they were in and around the East Midlands. The first independent contract of which we have particulars is that for the construction of the Scarborough, Bridlington & West Riding Junction Railway. Despite its lengthy title and the company's original ambitions, the line as built (Railway No. 2 of the original Act) extended 13¾ miles from Market Weighton to Driffield. A contract for the construction of the line was signed on 12 May 1887, and Rigby began work shortly afterwards. Although the railway was to be worked by the North Eastern Railway, that company did not contribute to the capital, and one of the conditions of the agreement with Rigby was that he should apply for 9000 £20 shares (later reduced to 6000). In some cases he was able to resell his shares immediately - Henry Tate, the sugar magnate and founder of the Tate Gallery, was the largest purchaser - but he kept a considerable number himself. No doubt as a result of this fact, Rigby seems to have been quite closely involved with the management of the company. He was in attendance at most of the meetings of the board of directors during construction, and he offered to contribute £500 towards the cost of an Act to abandon Railway No. 1 authorised by the original Act, amongst other purposes. This would have enabled the Parliamentary deposit to be returned. During this time, Charles Grey Mott became chairman of the company. He had been a director of the Great Western Railway since 1868, and sat on the boards of other railways, including the Mersey Railway and the City & South London.

The work, which included some heavy cutting through the chalk near Enthorpe, was eventually completed. Board of Trade approval to open the line to traffic was given on 2 April 1890 and the NER began its service on 1 May 1890. Much of the plant Rigby had used for the contract (including no fewer than nine locomotives) was advertised for sale by auction on 21 May 1890, although some equipment was retained for use on other jobs.

When the Driffield line opened, Rigby had already been instructed to start work on his next project, the 7-mile Newcastle Emlyn Extension Railway in West Wales, for which he had tendered £53,500. The contract was with the Great Western Railway, and so, no doubt much to his relief, Rigby was not required to help with finance. He was, however, required to provide two sureties of £4000 each, and these were his brother, Thomas G Rigby, and William Burnett. The railway continued the Llandyssil branch of the former Carmarthen & Cardigan Railway (opened in 1864) along the valley of the Teifi river, and today the narrow-gauge Teifi Valley Railway occupies part of its trackbed. In 1892, problems arose when it was found that clay from some of the cuttings, which the GWR engineer had expected to be suitable for embankments, was not stable. The GWR had to purchase additional land to accommodate the wider embankments, and also 2500 cubic yards of heavy copper slag were purchased to weight the slopes of the Henllan cutting to prevent landslips. The railway eventually opened on 1 July 1895.

Rigby's next contract took him to the South East, and set a course for the second half of his working life. The Bexley Heath Railway had been promoted chiefly by local landowners and comprised an 8¼ mile loop off the South Eastern Railway's North Kent line, from Blackheath to Crayford Creek Junction. Rigby was awarded the contract to build the line for £173,000 (of which £26,980 was to be taken in Bexley Heath Railway Company shares) and he started work in May 1891. The railway company had had to buy a house named Swiss Cottage adjacent to the line at Blackheath, and Rigby moved there at the start of the contract. He resided there until about 1897, when he moved to 2 Vanburgh Fields, Blackheath.

We have an unusually good idea of how the Bexley Heath Railway was built, as a local photographer, A H T Boswell, recorded each stage of construction, from the first rough 'overland' route with its horse-drawn tipping wagons, right through to the landscaping of the embankments and the erection of signs at the stations. A steam excavator which arrived on the site in September 1891 was a favourite subject for his lens. We are also fortunate in having some recollections of William Rigby from one of his navvies on this contract, 'Punch' Hollands, who stayed on after the line was finished to become a ganger on the South Eastern Railway, and was interviewed by Dr E A Course in the 1950s. Rigby was remembered as a fair employer, despite the remarkable invective which he used on the navvies, and as having a memorable set of whiskers.

His language was understandable, as the Bexley Heath Railway was not built without difficulty, and was not completed on time. The earthworks were in a mixture of sands and clays, and banks were prone to collapse, at least when graded to the angle specified by the long-serving Engineer of the SER, Francis Brady. But at last the line was ready for its final Board of Trade inspection, on 7 April 1895, when Brady, Rigby and a Mr Gray, who was Rigby's chief engineer for the contract, were among the party who embarked with Major Marindin in a train of special saloons at Blackheath station for a tour of the new works. The local paper was then able to report that "after sticking to his task with dogged determination, Mr Rigby has at length surmounted all difficulties." The railway was opened on 1 May 1895, and was worked by the SER. Six locomotives and other plant used for the contract were sold by auction at Welling on 3 May 1895.

Completing the task was one thing; being paid for it was another. Rigby was financially stretched by this contract and is said to have been on the verge of bankruptcy at times. In 1892, for example, he was unable to meet calls on some Scarborough, Bridlington & West Riding Junction shares, and had to agree to pay 4% interest until the outstanding balance was settled. The Bexley Heath Railway Company was in little better shape and Rigby had been obliged to accept part of his payment in debenture stock. After the line opened, the SER had to lend the local company £6000 to enable it to meet Rigby's final claim. As the Secretary of the Board of Directors of the SER rather dryly minuted, "rightly or wrongly Mr Rigby has taken it for granted that from the fact of the South Eastern Company being represented by Directors on the Bexley Board, that the South Eastern Company, who are in possession of the Line, would see that he was paid for the work so done... if the amount is not paid Mr Rigby would be entitled to obtain the appointment of a Receiver... and there can be no doubt that [he] would immediately avail himself of this remedy."

Rigby had certainly brought himself to the attention of the SER's officers and directors, and they seem to have determined to find him work so as to avoid the need for action which might bring down the shaky finances of the Bexley Heath Railway. In February 1896 it was agreed to ask him to carry out improvements at Ore station, and a steady stream of work followed for almost the next 25 years, to the mutual advantage of the parties. Much of this was not formally tendered, but was done either on a schedule of prices or on the basis of cost plus 10% profit. The SER was steadily modernising its facilities at this time, widening the main line as far as Orpington to four tracks and putting in new sidings and other improvements at many other places. These piecemeal jobs, with inevitable uncertainties and often the need to work while traffic continued, were less attractive to the larger firms. For example, Rigby carried out widening near Waterloo station, for which the well-known contractors J T Firbank and Walter Scott & Co had declined to tender.

We have seen how William Rigby developed his career as a railway contractor, and how his work on the Bexley Heath Railway led to a mutually beneficial relationship with the South Eastern Railway.

In addition to using him to make improvements to the line, the SER found that Rigby was also a useful man to have on tap to handle emergencies. Following the 1896 landslip adjoining Martello Tunnel near Folkestone, it was decided to open out at least part of the tunnel, and Rigby was set to work even before the eventual extent of the changes had been decided.

On its side, the SER took steps to ensure that Rigby had a steady flow of work. In 1896 the railway's finance committee advanced him £5000 to order three Goliath steam cranes and other machinery for the pier extension and other works at Folkestone Harbour, the agreement for which was not signed until nearly two years later.

A contract for which the niceties had to be observed was the replacement of the St Andrew's archway in Hastings by the Queens Road bridge. The borough council was paying five sixths of the cost, so tenders had to be invited and formally opened. William Rigby's was the lowest, although all were more than the original estimate. The road had originally passed through the high embankment of the railway from Hastings to Ore by a gloomy tunnel no more than 19 feet in width. This had become an obstruction to traffic and was to be replaced by a high, wide bridge with fluted iron columns. The bridge was built without undue disruption to either road or rail traffic, by means of interlacing the tracks across it. However, when the bridge had been completed and the embankment under it was about to be removed, it began to collapse, so that the road had to be closed until the work was finished.

In 1898, it was decided that Rigby, who was then putting in the new sidings at Hither Green, would be employed for the St.Johns to Orpington widening, so that he could move his plant directly from one contract to the other. The decision was taken when plans, estimates and contracts had yet to be drawn up. The widening contract was at first associated with no more than the usual accidents, such as the collapse of a newly excavated cutting near Orpington in January 1902, killing a workman named Brown on the spot and injuring another. A party from the Geologists' Association of London visited the new tunnel at Chislehurst in the following June. London Clay was exposed at the north end of the tunnel, while at the south end was an open cutting seventy feet deep in the Oldhaven Beds (sand and flint pebbles).

With the benefit of hindsight, it will be recognised that these were unstable materials, and in August 1902 a length of the old tunnel partially collapsed, completely disrupting services on the SER main line. An inspection by Sir Benjamin Baker, the eminent consulting engineer, showed flaking of brickwork in the old tunnel and signs of abnormal pressure in the parallel section of the new one. It was decided to provide an invert (a solid floor joining the side walls of the tunnel beneath the tracks) for certain lengths of both the old and new tunnels, in order to distribute the weight over the foundations and stop the side walls moving inwards. An army of men worked day and night to complete the work as soon as possible, to enable the line to be reopened. The construction of the new connections between the SER and London, Chatham & Dover lines near Bickley was also accelerated, to give greater possibilities for diversions while the SER line remained blocked. The down Bickley-Orpington loop was brought into use on 8th September 1902, the up connection on 14th September, and the Chislehurst-St Mary Cray loops (in both directions) on 19th June 1904.

The Bexley Heath Railway was also indirectly responsible for Rigby becoming acquainted with Holman F Stephens. The secretary of the Bexley Heath company, William B Pritchard, a partner in the solicitors Dollman and Pritchard, and Richard Jones, of East Wickham House, Welling, one of the Bexley Heath directors, were among the promoters of the Orpington Cudham & Tatsfield Light Railway and persuaded Rigby to join them. Stephens was the engineer of the proposed railway, and although he was not much involved with its promotion, he would have met William Rigby at the public inquiry at Orpington on 2nd March 1899. Both gave evidence, Rigby stating that he envisaged no problem in raising the necessary capital, and that Alfred Willis, general manager of the SE&CR, had agreed that his company would work the line if it were built.

One consequence of the meeting was that Rigby became involved with Stephens in the Light Railway Syndicate, the company formed to promote and build light railways. William Rigby was the contractor for the Sheppey Light Railway, which was the only light railway the Syndicate promoted which was actually built. To assist with the construction of the railway Rigby hired 'Terrier' No 71, *Wapping*, from the London, Brighton & South Coast Railway for £2 a day. It is an interesting coincidence that this engine was later bought by the K&ESR, where it became No 5 *Rolvenden*.

Another consequence was the extension of the Rother Valley Railway to Tenterden Town and then Headcorn. William Rigby extended the RVR from its original terminus (the present Rolvenden station) to Tenterden Town in 1902 to 1903, the work being done under powers granted to the Cranbrook & Tenterden Railway. In March 1903, the RVR signed a contract with William Rigby and William Burnett to build the Tenterden to Headcorn extension for £51,100 and to strengthen and relay the original RVR line for £31,250 (less £6000 credited for old materials recovered). A condition of the contract was that Rigby and his partner took a total of not less than 500 of the original unissued shares of the RVR at their nominal price of £10 each.

Some excavation in rather unstable ground was required between Rolvenden and Tenterden, and again north of Tenterden - including the short Shoreham Lane Tunnel. Later experience suggests that H F Stephens may have been unduly optimistic in estimating the slopes that could be supported by the material encountered on Tenterden bank, as much remedial work has been required. A fatal accident while building the line near St Michaels throws light on the usual working practices of the period. An unsecured baulk of timber fell from a wagon and stove in the bunker of Hunslet 0-6-0ST *Sutton* which was propelling it, killing one man and injuring others.

The local press suggests that pilfering of stores was a problem, as it no doubt was elsewhere.

On one occasion in the winter of 1904, P C Byerley found one of the navvies walking along the line carrying half a hundredweight of coal in a sack. It was found that this had been removed from the contractor's dump, and Mr Coombes, Rigby's local representative, had to attend the Tenterden police court to plead for leniency. The Headcorn extension opened for public traffic on 17th May 1905.

Light railways formed only a small part of Rigby's work at this period. Widening and new traffic facilities for the South Eastern & Chatham Railways Managing Committee continued, including the reconstruction of Folkestone Harbour, which was eventually completed in July 1904, the final stone being laid by the French Ambassador.

Rigby also obtained contracts for two extensions of the City & South London tube railway. These were from Stockwell to Clapham Common, opened in 1900, and from Moorgate Street to Angel, opened in 1901. As we have seen, Rigby was acquainted with C G Mott, the chairman of the City & South London, from his Driffield days. William Rigby & Co had offices at various times in Pascoe Road, Lewisham, and also in London, first at 15 Denman Street, SE, and then at 8 Laurence Poutney Lane, off Cannon Street. About 1900 there was also an office at 274 City Road, EC, no doubt in connection with the City & South London extensions.

In 1904, Rigby himself moved from Blackheath to the 'stockbroker belt', when he purchased Ewhurst Place, near Cranleigh in Surrey, from its builder, Colonel Thomas Warne Lemmon. Built about 1880 of local stone with castellated walls, the house survives today as part of a boarding school. The nearest station to Ewhurst Place was Cranleigh on the Horsham to Guildford line of the London Brighton & South Coast Railway which offered a rather inconvenient route to London.

Plans to make the district more accessible by building a railway from Holmwood to Cranleigh via Ewhurst had been put forward in 1884 and 1897 but came to nothing. Neither did a proposal for a Surrey & Sussex Light Railway - engineer H E Stephens - which reached the stage of submitting plans to the Board of Trade in about 1902. This envisaged a total of 25 miles of light railways from Cranleigh to Ockley via Ewhurst Green, and from Cranleigh to Selham (on the LB&SCR Midhurst branch) via Northchapel and Lurgashall. It is hard to imagine the then sparsely populated agricultural district south of Cranleigh supporting even a light railway. The last railway scheme for the area, which was discussed in 1905 was for a Holmwood, Cranleigh, Midhurst & Havant Railway, envisaged as the central section of a more direct main line from London to Portsmouth. The engineer of this project was again H F Stephens, but it is seems unlikely that William Rigby did not take a keen interest behind the scenes.

Rigby was still a significant shareholder in the Scarborough, Bridlington & West Riding Junction Railway, and was elected a director of the company in November 1905, following the death of its long-serving chairman, C G Mott. Rigby's partner, William Burnett, was already a director, having been appointed at the 1896 annual meeting. Although, as we have mentioned, the line was worked by the North Eastern Railway from the outset, the company was not taken over by the NER until 1914. Protracted negotiations had been necessary to secure the best terms for the shareholders, and Rigby had to attend further meetings in 1915 and 1916 to bring the affairs of the company to a conclusion. In the pre-Great War period Rigby also served for a time as a director of the Dominion of Canada Trust Corporation Ltd.

Rigby had continued his acquaintance with Stephens despite the failure of the Light Railways Syndicate to achieve the hoped-for results. In 1908, Stephens, together with the 4th Earl of Bradford (1845-1915) and William Rigby applied for a Light Railway Order for the reconstruction of the derelict Potteries Shrewsbury & North Wales Railway as a light railway, the Shropshire & Montgomeryshire. It was stated that Rigby would undertake the rebuilding, but in fact the company eventually signed a contract for the work with a partnership of H F Stephens himself and Francis Claughton. Rigby was no doubt able to offer advice, but it would be interesting to know whether he was involved in a practical capacity, for instance by the loan of equipment or personnel.

Rigby was a director of the Shropshire & Montgomeryshire Light Railway from the first recorded meeting of the board, and was elected chairman on 26th March 1909 in succession to the Earl of Bradford. Attendance at meetings involved Rigby in less travelling than might have been expected, as they were not held in either of the counties the line served, but at 11 Ironmonger Lane, London EC, the offices of the accountants W B Peat Ltd. (later Peat Marwick Mitchell & Co).

William Rigby's last involvement with a railway engineered by H F Stephens was the East Kent Light Railway. Like most aspects of the early history of the East Kent, the details are obscure and poorly documented. The contract for building the EKLR was awarded to the Kent Contract & Finance Company, an associated company in the group controlled by Arthur Burr. However, it appears that at least some of the actual construction was subcontracted to William Rigby.

During the Great War, Rigby was involved in work at Woolwich and Plumstead, probably in connection with the expansion of the Royal Arsenal. New sidings and a new connection to the SE&CR North Kent line were laid to handle the greatly increased munitions traffic. Another wartime contract was a siding for the Dover gasworks (estimated at £1150 including signalling) and completed in September 1917. After the war, there were a couple of further contracts for the SE&CR, in particular reconstruction of the line through Folkestone Warren which had been closed ever since a bad landslip on 19th December 1915. Once approval had been given by the interested Government departments, the work, which was estimated at £45,750 and involved a great deal of cutting, filling and earth-moving, was completed quite quickly. The line between Folkestone and Dover was reopened to traffic on 11th August 1919. There was also some work for the Port of London Authority. He then enjoyed retirement for a few years, but in 1928 he sold Ewhurst Place to a neighbour, Donald Morton, and moved to New Milton, on the Hampshire coast. His retirement from the Shropshire & Montgomeryshire board on grounds of ill health was reported at the meeting on 10th April 1929, and he died on 30th May 1929. His estate was valued at the surprisingly modest sum of £1589. His widow, Adelia Rigby (he had eventually remarried) moved to the Green Lane Riding School in New Milton after his death. This was kept by William Rigby's niece, Margaret Wynne, who as a small girl had visited Rigby when he was still living in Blackheath. Adelia Rigby died on 18th May 1940.

The table below lists locomotives which William Rigby is known to have owned and used on his contracts. Moving locomotives from one job to the next was the exception rather than the rule, and locomotives and other items of plant were generally sold off at the end of the contract. The list includes only one engine which Rigby bought new - named *Margaret* after his daughter. Other locomotives were hired, such as the Terrier used on the Sheppey Light Railway contract.

The list is certainly not complete - for instance at least two engines were used on the Headcorn extension of the K&ESR.

	0-6-0ST	Fox Walker & Co	1875	271	Built for Whitland & Cardigan Rly, later GWR 1386, purchased 1911 via Bute Works Supply Co for East Kent contract. Later EKLR No 1
ROYAL ENGINEER	0-4-0ST class D	Manning Wardle	1876	602	Purchased by Rigby from Admiralty (Chattenden Naval Tramway)
SUTTON	0-6-0ST	Hunslet	1877	187	Purchased by Rigby 1898. Used on various contracts to 1905, last being RVR Headcorn extension. To WD by 1916
JESSIE	0-6-0ST class K	Manning Wardle	1877	641	Now preserved on the Bluebell Railway as SHARPTHORN
SUSSEX	0-6-0ST	Hunslet	1879	221	Purchased by Rigby c.1895
MIDDLETON	0-6-0ST class K	Manning Wardle	1879	725	Used on Folkestone Harbour contract. Sold to SE&CR 1904
WYE	0-4-0ST	Hunslet	1887	420	Purchased by Rigby Feb 1902
CANADA	0-4-0ST	Hunslet	1890	525	Purchased by Rigby from Eckersley Godfrey & Liddelow (contractors for Canada Dock, MDHB), 1893. Used on Bexley Heath Railway. Sold to Bott & Lewis Jones(contractors) c.1895
FYLDE	0-6-0ST	Hunslet	1891	528	Purchased by Rigby c.1892. Used on Bexley Heath Railway Sold c.1895
LOUISE	0-6-0ST class M	Manning Wardle	1894	1245	Purchased by Rigby after 1896 Used on St Johns-Orpington widening. Sold to APCM Burham works (ECCLES) 1911
MARGARET	0-4-0ST	Hunslet	1900	735	Purchased new by Rigby Later sold to Hudsons Ltd. (refuse contractors) Crayford

8.1 Construction of a temporary bridge was undertaken at Pickford Lane, close to Bexleyheath station.

8.2 A massive steam navvy was in use near Barnehurst in 1892.

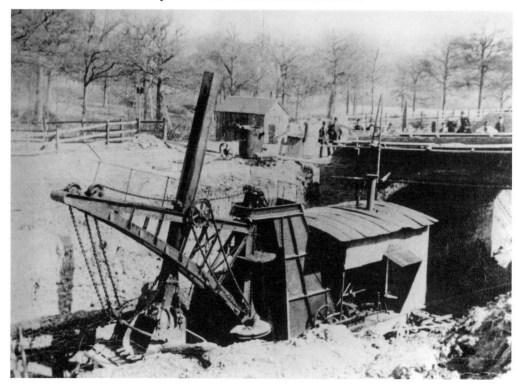

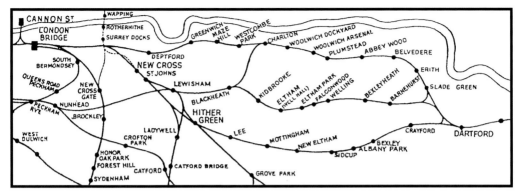

8.3   Route map of Southeast London with the River Thames at the top.

8.4   An eastward view of Bexleyheath station was the subject for an Edwardian postcard.

Chapter 9

Early Days of the Sheppey Light Railway

by Tom Burnham (1987)

The Sheppey Light Railway was always worked by the main line company with comparatively conventional rolling stock and so has received less attention than some other Colonel Stephens' railways. This is a pity as in other respects it had many typical features; the corrugated iron stations in cricket pavilion style, the light earthworks resulting in short but sharp gradients (even in distinctly flat country), the frequent level crossings, the farmers' sidings and the association with bright hopes for future development and prosperity that never quite materialised. Even the people involved are familiar; the team of E W I Peterson, the Cranbrook solicitor as promoter, H F Stephens as engineer and William Rigby as contractor was associated with several light railways and still more abortive proposals.

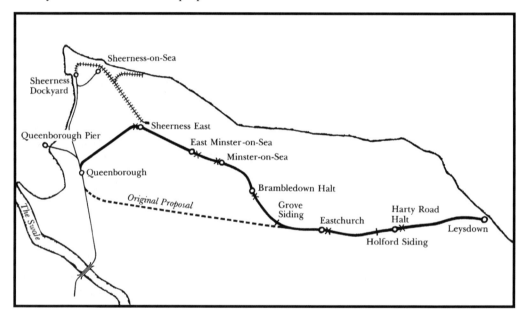

Although the western end of the Isle of Sheppey was served by the Sittingbourne & Sheerness Railway as early as 1860 and this had brought about a limited amount of development at Queenborough and Sheerness, the greater part of the island remained agricultural. Minster, indeed, had declined greatly since the days when it was the site of a rich abbey. The Light Railways Act of 1896 provided the opportunity to extend the railway to serve the rest of the island at reasonable cost and local landowners were naturally interested in taking advantage of it, especially Lord Harris and Colonel F Holford. Lord Harris (1851-1932) of Belmont Park, Faversham, owned much of the land in Kent, including some in Minster. Colonel (later Sir) George Holford (1860-1926) was the son of millionaire, Robert S Holford, who had built Dorchester House in Park Lane, a private palace of monumental grandeur, eventually demolished to make way for the Dorchester Hotel. Colonel Holford's holdings of more than 16,000 acres included land in Eastchurch.

H F Stephens' involvement began in 1896, when he wrote to his Father:- *"I have a letter of introduction from Lord Medway to Lord Harris re a proposed line in the Isle of Sheppey. You know so much better than I do how to manage these things, how shall I address Lord Harris? I write, My Dear Lord Medway, because I know him, but I don't know Lord H. Shall I say, Sir!! or, My Lord?"*

Lord Medway had long been an advocate of the Paddock Wood to Hawkhurst Railway, for which Stephens was the Resident engineer. However the letter was addressed, it appears to have been effective, as in 1897 a draft Light Railway Order was submitted to the Board of Trade by Stephens from the "Engineers office" of the Sheppey Railway at Tonbridge. The planning and promotion of the railway was carried out by the Light Railway Syndicate Ltd, a company formed in 1895 in which Stephens owned a minority shareholding and acted as its engineer, although he was not a Director. Some of the proposals seem to have caused concern to the Board, as a memorandum states:- "In the schedule of the draft order there is a novel proposal by the ingenious young engineer of this line, Mr Stephens, that no train not exceeding three passenger carrying vehicles need be provided with continuous brakes. This is not very well worded, but as they wouldn't want to run trains consisting of three vehicles only, it evidently is meant to apply to trains of any number of vehicles but on which there are not more than three passenger vehicles. This is ingenious and I have given some thought to it, but I hardly think it is to be recommended".

The estimated cost of the line, without stock, was £43,852 and the fact that the capital given in the draft order was £60,000 plus £20,000 in loans also caused the Board some concern: "The capital fixed by these promoters always seems to me to be excessive and in this case it seems rather more excessive than usual". Following these exchanges, a Public Inquiry was held at Queenborough Town Hall on 29th April 1898. The Light Railway Commissioners present were the Earl of Jersey, Mr G A R Fitzgerald and Colonel Boughey, whilst the promoters were represented by Mr H C Gollan, Mr E W I Peterson and Mr H F Stephens. A deviation of the line to run via Minster instead of the straight line from Queenborough to Eastchurch originally envisaged was proposed by the local authorities and accepted by the promoters, increasing the length by just under a mile and the estimated cost by £8,571. The Manager of the Colne Valley Light Railway, Mr G Copus, who Stephens may have met when he was planning a whole network of light railways in Essex and Suffolk, gave evidence based on the traffic on his line and expected it to be higher on the Sheppey line. It was stated that a Mr Barton Hallett had entered into a contract for the purchase of the Leysdown estate to lay it out as a seaside resort; clause 60 of the draft order which empowered the Company to build a hotel at Leysdown was, however, considered to be outside the powers of the Commissioners. The only objector was Mr T Goodwin of Harp's Farm whose pond would be destroyed by the line; this objection was withdrawn on suitable compensation being arranged.

Following this enquiry, a revised light railway order was approved on 3rd April 1899. It imposed a maximum speed of 25 miles per hour, with 10 miles per hour on curves of less than 9 chains radius, (although in fact there were none) and within 300 yards of ungated level crossings; for tender locomotives working tender forward the limit was 15 miles per hour. Stephens had wanted to run at 35 miles per hour but the commissioners evidently saw no reason to deviate from their usual practice. A rather ominous clause read "there shall be no obligation on the Company to provide shelter or conveniences at any station or stopping place", although it had been stated at the Inquiry that it was intended to provide shelter at all stations.

Construction of the line was undertaken by William Rigby and Company who was associated with a number of Stephens' projects, including the Headcorn extension of the K&ESR. There were no cuttings or embankments of more than 10 feet and so by 21 June 1901 the works were ready for official inspection by Major Pringle.

The line started from a bay platform 300 feet long on the up side of the line at Queenborough, where a small signal cabin had been erected to operate the home and starting signals. It then ran across marshes to Sheerness East (1m 40c) where there was a 200 feet long platform, without shelter, and a small goods yard. Sheerness East was in fact about a mile from Sheerness, from which it could be reached (between 1903 and 1913) by the cars of the Sheerness & District electric tramways, whose shed and power station was next to the light railway station. The line continued over the Scraps Gate road ungated level crossing (2m 17c) to East Minster-on-Sea (2m 44c) with a 60 feet long platform on a 1 in 79 gradient and a small shelter. This halt was "used only on specified occasions" at opening, but was brought into regular use in 1902.

The next station, Minster (3m 10c) had a 200 feet long platform with a shelter and urinal and some sidings. Passing Stickfast Lane ungated crossing (3m 57c) the first of the 'farmers' sidings' was reached at Brambledown (3m 79c), then Newhook Farm crossing (4m 16c) and Grove Siding (4m 73c). The passing station Eastchurch (5m 47c) had a loop, but only one platform, 200 feet long with a small shelter, two ground frames, one at each end of the station and up and down home signals. Major Pringle commented that if it were intended to pass passenger trains there, a second platform would have to be provided. There were then two more farmers' sidings, Holford Siding (6m 52c) and Harty Road (7m 7c) and two more gated crossings, Mustards Road (7m 48c) and the curiously named Frogs Island (8m 6c) before Leysdown (8m 52c). Here also was a 200 feet long platform, with a rather larger shelter than elsewhere and a 6-lever ground frame working a home signal, the loop and goods sidings, one of which served a loading bank. A water tank was provided, supplied by a wind pump direct from a well. Reputedly, when the well was being drilled, the bit ran into a layer of hard rock not far below the surface which diverted it sideways. No water was found at the expected depth, but the reason was only discovered when the bit emerged above ground some distance from the well.

The goods sidings at the stations could hold about 20 wagons, but those at the farmers' sidings were only long enough for three. The single track was laid with second-hand SE&CR rails, fishplates, chairs and fastenings on half round sleepers. Major Pringle thought the ballast was short in quantity outside the ends of the sleepers.

The line was worked on the train staff and ticket system in two sections; Queenborough to Eastchurch used a triangular brass bar painted red as the staff and Eastchurch to Leysdown had a circular brass bar painted green. There were no block signalling instruments, but a telephone was provided at each station and there were warning bells at the gatemen's huts at gated level crossings. Ungated level crossings had cattleguards and a feature then regarded as novel was the provision of warning boards (white with black '10') to indicate speed restrictions at level crossings and sharp curves.

The Sheppey Light Railway was leased and worked by the SE&CR whose service timetable stated "This new railway, which extends from Queenborough to Leysdown will be opened for passengers and goods traffic on Thursday, August 1 1901 and will be worked by a local service to and from Queenborough". This comprised four passenger trains each way daily (including Sundays) taking 35 minutes for the journey of nearly 9 miles, plus a return goods working on weekdays. From 1 November 1901 to 31 March 1902, Eastchurch to Leysdown was closed to passenger traffic and the service was revised with only four trains each way, the first down and last up being mixed passenger and goods, while there were only two trains on Sundays.

Tickets issued were for local journeys only, passengers for further afield being obliged to re-book at Queenborough. The design was rather like a tram ticket and the third class fare was 9d for the full single journey (first class passengers to hold two third class tickets).
On 8th August 1901 Stephens wrote to his father, *"My little Sheppey Railway was opened for traffic on 1 August but it is too early yet to say how the traffic will turn out. The SE&C Railway are working the line so that I have not much to do with the arrangements as I am only Engineer"* One result of this was that the SE&CR had to issue a locomotive pass to Stephens' assistant, W H Austen, described as an "Inspector", allowing him to travel on the engine over the light railway until the end of 1901. An official opening ceremony attended by many local dignitaries took place on 9th August.

To work the lines, the SE&CR provided two small 2-4-0T locomotives, nos 518 and 523 which had been rebuilt in 1865. The usual train was a set of three ex-LC&DR six wheelers, which had been rebuilt with gangways between carriages and the third class accommodation in saloons.

The opening of the line encouraged attempts to develop Sheppey as a resort. At Minster, Frederick Ramuz bought about 1000 acres of the derelict farmland and attempted to sell it in plots to Londoners through the Land Company and the Minster Development Corporation as "one of the finest, if not the best marine estate ever acquired by us or any other company for sale in plots to the general public" The Land Company even organised special through trains from London in the hope of encouraging sales. Similarly, The Sheerness & Leysdown Estates Co managed to sell plots of land in 1903 and proposed the construction of an hotel and golf club at Leysdown. Development was, however, very slow and when much later it did come, it was too late to bring any appreciable traffic to the light railway. The Railway's period of nominal independence was brief, as in August 1902 an agreement was reached with the SE&CR to purchase the line for £65,000 and powers for this were included in the Acts of 1903 and 1905. The new owners lost no time in improving their acquisition; traffic was being turned away at Harty Road and Brambledown, so in 1903 the sidings were extended. The stations were also improved; concrete platform walls replaced Stephens' old sleepers, the wooden trellis fences were replaced by iron railings and wooden lamp posts by elegant twisted iron columns.

Following experiments on the line with two small petrol railcars, the SE&CR acquired a number of steam railcars. Car No. 1 was delivered on 16th January 1905 and after trials in Deal area, entered service on the SLR at the beginning of March. The title "Sheppey Light Railway" was painted above the windows at first, but was soon removed. The car seated 56 passengers in two third class saloons; a six-wheeled 3rd class carriage was kept at Queenborough and could be added if necessary. The train stopped at East Minster only "in event of passengers requiring to alight or join the car" and one disadvantage was apparent in the provision of a separate goods train in place of the former mixed working. As if to maintain the Stephens connection, a second-hand 'Terrier' tank was purchased from the LB&SCR to handle this. A report at the end of

March stated that the railcar had given entire satisfaction, had fully met the demands of traffic and that there had been a worthwhile saving in coal.

By the beginning of May 1905, short platforms had been provided at the farmers' sidings at Brambledown and Harty Road and it was arranged that the railcar would halt as required during daylight. The service timetable noted that "the car will also call at these platforms occasionally after daylight, but only by special arrangement being made beforehand with the stationmaster at Queenborough and at passengers own risk. Passengers requiring to join or alight at these platforms after dark will be required to have a man at the platform with lamp to indicate to driver where he is required to pull up".

Further developments on the SLR are really beyond the scope of this chapter. The railcars were withdrawn in 1912. The First World War saw the aerodrome at Eastchurch develop into a major source of traffic, both as passenger and goods, which brought the only regular through trains. After the War, traffic declined even though Leysdown achieved limited success as a resort. The passenger sections of the steam railcars were rebuilt into articulated push and pull sets, which provided passenger services until the inevitable closure in December 1950. Today only a few traces of the line remain.

9.1   *The opening of the Sheppey Light Railway was recorded at Leysdown on 1st August 1901.*

9.2 *The SR for a long time operated the branch with two former SECR railmotor bodies mounted on a special common bogie. The engine is ex-SECR class R1 0-4-4T no. A697.*

9.3 *Eastchurch had a goods loop and two sidings. It was the terminus of the line for a short period initially.*

9.4   The Leysdown terminus was provided with Stephens' standard corrugated iron building.

Chapter 10

Reflections on the K&ESR's Pickering Steam Railcar

by Brian Janes (2002)

In 1905 the railway technical press was filled with the latest development in economical transport - the steam rail motor (later called railcar). *The Locomotive* in that year carried news of a new railcar every month. Most of these were bogie carriages with a small engine conventionally built on the same chassis. Originally envisaged to increase frequency and reduce costs on routes that competed with the then current arch enemy - the electric tram - there were exceptions. Tucked away at the end of an article on the latest batch of rail motors in *The Locomotive* of March 1905 there was a description of an experimental machine designed to be used on rural light railways. And she was very different from all the others too; a four-wheeled engine owing far more to road steam lorry practice than the blending of conventional locomotives and carriages that the others represented. Holman F Stephens was again innovating to try and keep down the cost of operating a rural light railway, and the Kent & East Sussex now acquired its 6th item of motive power when delivery was effected in March 1905.

The railmotor craze had started a year or two earlier. Soon after his appointment as General Manager of the London and South Western Railway, Sir Charles Owens came to the conclusion that material economies might be effected by running a powered single coach where the traffic did not call for a train of six or seven 4 or 6 wheeled vehicles hauled by an ordinary locomotive. The line from Fratton to East Southsea, the joint property of the London and South Western and the London, Brighton and South Coast companies was selected for the purpose of an experiment. In 1902 Duguld Drummond the chief mechanical engineer of the LSWR was requested to "take the subject into consideration" (nobody TOLD Drummond), and to devise a rail motor. The design produced at Nine Elms Works was ready for use in the following April and the first of two cars began regular working in June 1903. Even before this the Great Western Railway asked to copy the design. This was agreed and the GWR made the very sensible decision to substantially enlarge the boiler unit. Both railways immediately claimed a very appreciable reduction in the cost of haulage, without "the withdrawal of any accommodation required by the public". The other railways poured out designs over the next three years with very mixed success. Some persisted and met with modest success continuing services until World War I, but others quickly succumbed to poor performance and/or passenger discomfort. Only the GWR and the Lancashire and Yorkshire really persisted beyond this.

Matching the Railmotor craze at this time was the enthusiasm on the road for the steam lorry and, in particular, the then modern relatively lightweight 'Undertype' lorry with high speed geared engines and vertical boilers. Historic trials in Liverpool in 1899 and 1901 had proved the economy and practicability of the steam lorry, and a seminal book published in 1906 claimed "During the past fifteen years considerable progress has been made in high- speed engines, and reliable data are now available which prove beyond all doubt that this class of engine can be relied on-prophecies to the contrary notwithstanding-and that greater signs of wear in a given period are not more observable than in ordinary slow-running engines. The advantages of 'high speed' (in economical use of steam and power/weight ratio) are practically acknowledged by the majority of makers who run their engines as fast as they consider prudent."

The Sentinel lorry of the period had a classic undertype configuration with a compact tube boiler mounted ahead of the front axle, an engine having cylinders with 6in bore and 10in stroke slung amidships under the framing. It attained engine speeds of 300 revolutions per minute geared down through a chain drive to the rear wheels. Such speeds allowed a far more lightweight unit than railway locomotive type mechanisms but they tended to be more complicated and needed sophisticated gearing and lubrication, with all the moving parts running in a bath of oil.

There was another problem too. The early years of the twentieth century saw many makes of undertype steam wagons come and go; and with hindsight all of them suffered from inefficient boilers. Many went well enough when supplied with sufficient steam but on hills they stalled because of the inability of their boilers to produce the required volume of steam quickly enough. Locomotive type boilers came back into fashion and weights increased until Sentinel perfected its designs in the early 1920s and the lighter vertical boiler made its come back. The undertype could be a difficult wagon to design and maintain but it had one great point in its favour; if the failings in boiler design were cured, it's compact design took up very little load space.

Stephens with his advocacy of a modern and cost effective approach to rural transport would have been very aware of all these developments and must have wished to try them. We can be fairly sure that he was actively involved in the design of the new railcar and took a particularly proprietorial attitude to it when it appeared. The firm he found to build the carriage portion was his current favourite R & Y Pickering of Wishaw near Glasgow who were predominantly wagon and carriage builders with no knowledge or experience of steam machinery. The new railcar's mechanism seems to have been purchased separately from Messrs Hutchinson and Company some months before the railcar was delivered. Messrs Hutchinson and Co were not a lorry or crane manufacturer although there was a Hutchison and Company, Boilermakers, 25 Mair Street, Glasgow in the 1905 Glasgow trade directory. Glasgow University, which holds Pickering's archive and in particular their specification book, can find no trace of the order or specification of this railcar. This is unusual for such a job. It is also frustrating to the historian because we have virtually no details of the mechanical components of the railmotor. Was it a modern unit or was it second-hand; was it a road type unit with good lubrication or was it adapted from a steam crane or a marine ancillary engine. We only have the bare details. It had a pair of 5½" (5" in K&ESR records) cylinders with ordinary (Stephenson) link motion, supplied with steam by a vertical multitubular boiler, and driving a layshaft connected by pitch chain to the nearest axle.

Later secondary sources claim a piston stroke of 9", a boiler 2' 10" diameter by 5' working to a relatively low pressure of 140lbs. This suggests a far from modern design by road standards but as a whole the rail motor was set up with considerable affinity to steam lorry style. The boiler was at the front with chain gearing to the front wheels and amidships it carried a small quantity of water (quoted later as 150 gallons, perhaps enough for ten miles) to counter balance the weight of the power unit. However there are doubts this was a satisfactory distribution of weight. Without a decent load in the passenger accommodation this distribution would have resulted in a very bouncy ride which would have got worse as the water was used up. An underslung lorry unit between the wheels would have vastly improved the weight distribution and consequent ride. Stephens was never good at designing trackworthy vehicles.

The railcar body itself was a basic example of the Edwardian coachbuilder's art. A 17 foot wheelbase 4 wheeler, 30 foot over the buffers and with a body 27' 1" long, 9' wide and 10' 9" high it looked handsome but like the later petrol railmotors passenger comfort was minimal to non existent. Adjoining the engine room was, logically, a smoking compartment with 11 seats then a non-smoking compartment for 20 and after an intermediate vestibule open to the elements both sides, a guards compartment claimed to seat 6 and stand 4 with 12-14 milk churns and baggage. The guards compartment also contained basic driving controls with a form of steam shut off, a whistle cord and a gong to signal the driver. This all seems a little improbable in the space provided and if ever loaded like this on market days it would put modern tube travel in perspective.

The steam railmotor clearly lived up to its experimental label. High engine speeds stressed the crankshaft and two new ones were made in the first three years and new connecting rods were needed in 1909. From the start the Hutchinson boiler was shown as inadequate and after only two years it was replaced in July 1907 by a new one from Messrs White Bros, Stratford. The London trade directory for 1907 lists a Messrs White Brothers , Engineers and Machinery Merchants, Princes Wharf, High Street, Stratford, East London but no further details are known. It seems likely that this boiler was second-hand.

The boiler change and associated work seems to have changed the appearance of the vehicle in several ways. The chimney was shortened and a large safety valve appeared on the roof to join the already prominent hooter. This hooter incidentally appears to be all but identical with that fitted by Stephens in about 1912 to *Gazelle* which she still carries. The rail motor also appears to have a single acetylene or carbide lamp in mid cabin with some sort of associated container on the front of the guards end which she kept for a year or so when Stephens was experimenting with such things. The new boiler was also almost certainly the cause of a piece of work which Rolvenden probably carried out and should have been, and probably was, ashamed of. Two ugly doors were inserted in the driver's end next to the boiler with strap hinges of such crudity that later commentators, with some justice, compared them with garden shed doors. However practical this might have been its appearance was the cause of some unjustified ridicule of the whole rail motor concept. The boiler also required a new feed pipe to be somewhat crudely plumbed in from the water tank. On a brighter note she probably also changed her identity at this time from her original designation of coach No. 16 to the more dignified engine No. 6. This increase in status seems to have been achieved simply by repainting the middle body panels from ivory to brown and painting on it K&ESR No. 6. This gave a less flamboyant but no doubt more practical finish. Interestingly the internal vestibule was not repainted but kept its middle panel painted ivory until the end.

Mechanically the railmotor might have settled down to service but conventional wisdom supported by the lack of photographic or written evidence suggests she never entered revenue earning service. However, in spite of this, public timetables for the period 1908-1914 show a potential diagram around sundry Tenterden - Robertsbridge Junction short workings, and the castle side siding at Bodiam was installed in 1910 and specifically authorised for railcar use. Further a photograph of the railmotor with its second boiler taken in the 1908-1911 period shows it displaying a Robertsbridge Junction destination board. Routine repairs, such as re-tubing, commensurate with regular use are given in the Rolling stock register for 1909, 1910, 1911 and 1913. If she did see regular service then she was at least as successful both mechanically and as a traffic machine as the contemporary railcars of the larger railways. Substantial body repairs were evidently called for and probably carried out in June 1913. These involved the replacement of cracked side panels near the boiler and replacement and alteration of the beading on the guards end panels. It seems likely also that the guards end was substantially altered at this time with the old three window layout replaced by a more practical two window arrangement. At this overhaul too she probably lost her smart ivory and brown livery to adopt the then usual overall brown. Despite all this work the experiment was coming to an end. The railmotor seems to have come to the end of its operational life sometime in 1912, following failure in service at Wittersham Road. It was certainly recorded as non-operational in 1915. Nelson Wood, a long-time K&ESR employee and petrol railmotor driver reported to researchers in the 1970s that her end had come directly as a result of failure to generate sufficient steam to surmount that enemy of all under powered trains, Tenterden bank. One wonders how many times this had occurred before and why this event should have finally brought its service to an end.

No. 6 did not "go gently into that good night". She was clearly a favourite child of Stephens and she was kept in good repair throughout the period of government control. She had become sufficiently well known in technical circles for Kyrle Willans, the originator of the use of Sentinel engine units into locomotives and railcars, to refer favourably to her conception and she survived in good order well into the era of these her moral successors and cousins. The heyday of these successful machines in the mid 1920s saw the Pickering carefully stored in Rolvenden sidings and when her panelling deteriorated she was extensively repaired. Her old single long side panel on her most photographed left side was replaced with two new ones, complete with matching beading, and two other panels here were replaced. Did the Colonel have plans to replace the Achilles heel of old fashioned and worn steam plant with more up to date units like the Sentinel which by then were reliable, relatively cheap and probably available second hand off steam lorries. We know from photographs that the latest Sentinel locomotive was tested on the Shropshire and Montgomeryshire in 1927. Did this raise, even for a while, his interest sufficiently to get repairs done with the available scarce funds? Did the availability of the third petrol railcar, the Shefflex Set, bought in 1929 blunt or finish off any interest? We do not know.

With the Colonel's death in 1931 maintenance ceased and the Railmotor visibly dissolved at various Rolvenden locations over the next ten years, finally being broken up about 1941. According to W H Austen jnr her frame lives on as the steelwork in the base of the Rolvenden water tank. But as with so much about this elusive vehicle we may never know the real truth.

10.1   *The Pickering car was photographed at the factory before delivery. It was numbered 16 in the carriage fleet.*

10.2   *The car was renumbered 6 in the locomotive fleet and is seen with whistle and safety valve protruding.*

10.3   Extensive repanelling had been undertaken by the late 1920s and there were thereafter two panels below the windows, instead of one. The garden shed doors did not enhance it.

10.4   This fascinating vehicle was retained as long as possible. It was recorded at Rolvenden on 21st May 1939, in the company of the remains of the "Ilfracombe Goods" Rother. (S.W.Baker)

Chapter 11

A Bad Day at Biddenden

by Stephen Garrett (1987)

When the Kent & East Sussex extension from Tenterden to Headcorn was authorised by the Rother Valley Light Railway Extensions Order 1902, the line was permitted to choose whether to erect gates at its level crossings or not. Stephens chose not to do so and relied instead on erecting warning notices on the roads concerned together with a requirement that trains should slow down and whistle twice before crossing. This system was inspected and approved by Major Pringle for the Board of Trade before the extension was allowed to open. Not only did it avoid the expense of erecting gates but also that of replacing them after trains had inadvertently run through-a circumstance occurring four times between 1905 and 1914 on the gated section of the K&ESR! The system also avoided any need to employ gatekeepers or to stop trains while the train crew opened and closed gates.

Unfortunately this also carried with it a higher degree of risk and on 22nd April 1914 the inevitable collision occurred. The accident and its consequences are recorded in a bulky Board of Trade file now in the keeping of the Public Record Office under the reference MT6/2398/2. The file opens with a number of different reports on the accident including the following by Charles Palmer, the Station Agent at Biddenden:

I beg to report that the 9.11 am train here this morning collided with a Motor Car on the Level Crossing at Biddenden Station. The Motor when I first saw it, was travelling at a fast speed, and on the Engine Driver whistling again just by the signal, the car seemed to swerve across the road towards our fence, and then come gradually to a standstill, with the two front wheels over one of our metals, and the Driver looking Halden way. The car seemed to be still about a second before the engine buffer hit the bonnet, turning the car round and hitting the body up against the fence, which fell to pieces, and appeared to pitch 3 men out - one man was dragged about 20 yards by the Motor which was caught on the guard which is fixed to the front of the Engine.

I rendered every assistance and procured a Doctor at once from the Village, who said he must have assistance, also a car, so I telephoned to Tenterden Agent to fetch Dr. Skinner and a motor from Simminson's to take the injured to Maidstone Hospital.

The car belonged to Marchant & Tubb, Outfitters, Maidstone. The occupants were - Geo. Bowles, Driver, Lewis Matson, Herbert John Bowers and Clarence H Cole.

The injuries were as follows :

Geo. Bowles-Fractured skull and was delirious. Lewis Matson-Scalp wound and back injured. Herbert John Bowers-Face and knee slightly injured (Allowed to go home from Hospital).

Clarence R Cole-Nose scratched and hand (This man did not go to Maidstone Hospital).

The Driver of our train was Brazier, Guard, J Stanford, Engine No. 4

I have names of witnesses-Mr. Tuscon, Bishopsdale Farm, Biddenden; Gun, Guy House, Biddenden; Capt. Hall, Birchley, Biddenden; Pinnock, Wagstaffe, Biddenden; H Seagrave, National Sanatorium, Benenden.

I also beg to state I judged the speed of our train at 3 to 5 miles per hour when the accident happened. (Signed) C Palmer)

Other reports on the accident add that the fireman was William Meggett and that the train, hauled by 0-8-0T *Hecate*, consisted of ex-LSWR carriages 1, 2 and 19. The train drew to a halt in 38 feet and the speed of the car was estimated by one witness as 40mph. Several witnesses reported the car driver as looking in the direction of Biddenden Station, the opposite direction to that of the approaching train. On a subsequent inspection of the site Major Pringle was satisfied that it was in much the same condition as when he had reported it as safe for the line to open. He suggested that larger warning notices should now be erected and that some shrubs and trees obscuring the view of the crossing should be levelled. Stephens undertook to erect new signs but had some difficulty in removing the shrubs and trees as they were not on railway property. Eventually their owner was persuaded to remove the shrubs "but he did not feel disposed to cut any trees."

With the Board of Trade happy that the KESR had fulfilled its obligations under the 1902 Order, the whole incident might have ended there and then had not Mr Bowers, one of the occupants of the car, decided to take the KESR to court. The basis of his claim was that the Railway had been negligent in failing to provide gates at the level crossing, negligent in failing to provide a watchman at the crossing and negligent in failing to give sufficient warning of the approach of the train. The case was heard before a jury at the Cranbrook County Court in September 1914. In vain did the KESR argue that since the Board of Trade did not consider gates necessary then the Railway had done all it needed to do to maintain a proper standard of care. The jury were not only persuaded that the car was only travelling at 10mph but also that the Railway should have provided both gates and a watchman and had failed to give adequate warning of the approaching train. On the latter point it is not clear whether jury felt that the warning was given but insufficent or that the train had in fact not whistled as required. The amount of damages awarded against the company is not known.

The KESR was naturally very concerned at losing the case and gave notice of appeal. They were not the only ones to be worried. The Light Railway Commission realised that the whole basis on which light railways operated was at stake. In October they communicated this concern to the Board of Trade making the point that, "It will be seen that if due compliance with, and the statutory authority of, the Order are no defence against charges of negligence, the steps taken under the Light Railway Acts in the direction of economical methods of working are made of no effect; and it results that the governing conditions may be those to be laid down in a County Court rather than those fixed by the Board of Trade under the authority of Statute." In addition to seeking the observations of the Board on this issue in general the Commission also suggested that the Board might be disposed to assist the Railway in conducting its appeal.

The Board did not assist the Railway with its appeal. Reading between the lines the Board seems to have been afraid that such a step would unleash a torrent of requests for their assistance. They were, however, able to justify their inaction on this occasion with the excuse that the Railway had not actually asked for its help. Unfortunately, the appeal, heard by the King's Bench Division in January 1915 served only to strengthen the original decision. Not only did the judges see no reason to overturn the jury's verdict but they clearly emphasised that compliance with a LRO order was no substitute for stringent safety precautions. Mr Justice Ridley put it quite unambiguously: "The same principles applied to a light railway as to any other railway-the company must do everything necessary to show the exercise of reasonable care in the conduct and management of its business." No further appeal was to be allowed against this decision.

At this point one of the other occupants of the car, Lewis Matson, initiated an action for negligence against the Railway. Citing the absence of gates, watchman or adequate warning he claimed the cost of a new suit and £20 medical fees. This time Stephens seems to have unsuccessfully sought the assistance of the Board of Trade as the file contains this uncharacteristically modest letter from Stephens enquiring, "Why it was not thought considered advisable that the Company should have the benefit of the assistance of the Board of Trade herein? It is regretted if any action of the Company caused the Board of Trade to take an unfavourable view of this case."

To be fair the Board was not entirely ignoring the situation. To avoid such problems in future LRO they had devised a new form of wording based on the Order for the Milford & St Bride's Bay Light Railway: "The Company shall not be required to erect gates at any level crossing but they shall erect gates at any level crossing at which the Board of Trade require the Company so to erect and maintain gates." Whether the jurors of Cranbrook would have accepted this as sufficient excuse for not erecting gates must remain open to doubt.

Matson's case was not, however, heard at Cranbrook County Court but at the Kent Assizes before Mr Justice Darling in June 1915. The result was such an overwhelming victory for the Railway that Stephens had a transcript of the judge's summing up printed and distributed it to railway companies throughout the land. The following extract gives the flavour of the judge's views:

"Here the Board of Trade has taken this matter in hand; but the plaintiff says: "It is negligence if you do not put gates, and you must put them." Suppose they are put. If they are put at every crossing, it might very well be that the line could not pay at all; and then what is the use of it to the people who construct it? People will not run these trains as philanthropists. If you make the line so expensive that it will not pay, the line will become derelict, and the farmer will not he able to get his goods to the market; and all those services which the line performs will not be performed."

A naturally jubilant Stephens could not resist a gentle rebuke to the Board of Trade. Heading his letter "Strictly Unofficial" he sent them a copy of the transcript with the added comment: "We were successful off our own bat. I think, with assistance, we should have probably secured the "execution" of the plaintiff!"

Matson did not appeal against the decision and no further case was brought against the Railway in respect of the accident. The threat that had been posed to the legal status of light railways passed but not without some lingering doubts at the Board of Trade. The file concludes: "In view of the conflicting decisions it seems doubtful whether Mr Stephens is justified in saying that this matter is now closed."

11.1   This is the view towards Headcorn from Biddenden level crossing in 1931.

11.2   Hecate was a substantial locomotive and was an unfair match for a car. After nationalisation, it was put to work at Clapham Junction carriage sidings for several years.

ROBERTSBRIDGE JUNCTION and HEADCORN JUNCTION.
Kent and East Sussex.
Eng., Gen. Man., and Loco. Supt., H. F. Stephens, Tonbridge, Kent.

	Down.	Week Days.											Sundays.		
Miles from Robertsbridge		mrn	mrn	mrn	aft	aft	aft	aft		aft			mrn	mrn	aft
	262 London (Charing Cross)...dep.	....	9 5	2 25		4 50	4 50			7 30		....		9 45	....	7 15
	262 „ (Cannon Street) „	5 24	....	9 45	2 03		5 05	0		7 40		....		9 51		7 24
	262 „ (London Bridge) „	5 30	....	9 48	1 s27		5 27			7 43		....		9 51		7 24
	263 Hastings	8 58	56	12 0	3 50		6 7	6 7		9 0		....		9 20		8 20
	Robertsbridge Junction......dep.	8 35	9 28	12 35	4 30		6 c51	6 41		9 35		....		11 14		9 35
	Junction Road, for Hawkhurst	....	Sig.	Sig.	Sig.							....		Sig.		
4	Bodiam, for Staplecross	8 43	9 38	12 45	4 40		6 c50	6 50		9 45		....		11 23		9 45
7	Northiam, for Beckley and Sand	8 52	9 48	12 55	4 50			6 59		9 55		....		11 32		9 55
10	Wittersham Road........[hurst	8 59	9 55	1 24	4 57		7 5			10 3		....		11 39		10 2
13	Rolvenden	9 8		1 10	5 5							....		7 52	a	a
15	Tenterden Town	9 13	10 8	1 16	5 25		7 16	8 10		10 16		....		7 57	11 45	6 52 1015
16	Tenterden St. Michaels	Sig.		Sig.	Sig.		a	Sig.				....		Sig.	a	Sig.
18	High Halden Road	9 21		1 24	5 33			8 18				....		8 5	7 0	
20	Biddenden	9 29		1 30	5 41		7 32	8 26				....		8 13	12 57	8
21	Frittenden Road	Sig.		Sig.	Sig.			a				....		Sig.		Sig.
24	Headcorn Junction 246, 250 arr.	9 38		1 40	6 5		7 50	8 36				....		8 25		7 30
67½	250 London (London Bridge) arr.	1122		3 13	8 18		1132		1132			....		1025		9 9
68½	250 „ (Cannon Street) „	1126		3 18	8 22		1137		1137			....		1031		9 9
63½	250 „ (Charing Cross) „	1138		8 32								....		1043		9 19

	Up.	Week Days.										Sundays.		
Miles from Headcorn		mrn	mrn	mrn	aft	non	aft	aft	aft	aft		aft	mrn	aft
	246 London (Charing Cross)...dep.	....		....	12 0			4 27	4 27			7 5		....	
	246 „ (Cannon Street) „	....	7 40	....	12 3			4 40	4 40			7 17		....	
	246 „ (London Bridge) „	....	7 50	....	12 16			4 43	4 43			7 20		....	
	Headcorn Junction........dep.	....	10 0		2 0			6 30	6 30			9 15		8 40	7 32
	Frittenden Road	....	Sig.		Sig.			Sig.				Sig.		Sig.	Sig.
4	Biddenden	....	1012		2 15			6 40				9 25		8 50	7 42
6	High Halden Road	....	1020		2 24			6 48				9 33		8 57	7 50
8	Tenterden St. Michaels	....	Sig.		Sig.			Sig.				Sig.		Sig.	Sig.
	Tenterden Town	7 30	8 13	1030	1135	2 35	2 34	3	55 27			9 41		9 5	8 0
11	Rolvenden	7 35	8 18		1140	2 40		3 10	5 32			7 12		9 12	8 5
14	Wittersham Road......[hurst	7 42	8 26		1148	2 48		3 18	5 40			7 20		9 20	8 14
17	Northiam, for Beckley and Sand	7 49	8 33		1152	2 55		3 25	5 49			7 27		9 27	8 22
20	Bodiam, for Staplecross	7 58	8 42			2 59		3 35	5 59			7 36		9 37	8 32
	Junction Road, for Hawkhurst	Sig.			Sig.	Sig.		Sig.				Sig.		Sig.	
24	Robertsbridge Junc. 262, 263 arr.	8 7	8 55		12 13	3 15		4 56	9			7 46		9 47	8 46
36½	263 Hastings	....	....	arr.	8 46	1059		12 53	4 2		4 42	6 35		9 4	8 21	11 01013
71½	263 London (London Bridge) „	....	....		2 25	6 36		6 36	8 42			10 0		10 0		11 22 1039
72½	263 „ (Cannon Street) „	....	....		2 30	6 41		6 41	8 47							
73½	263 „ (Charing Cross) „	....	....		9 56	1026		2 42	....		....	8 57		10 7		11 32 1050

a Stop to set down.   c Runs to Headcorn Junction on informing the Guard   g Runs to Robertsbridge Junction on informing the Guard at Headcorn Junction.   h Stops to set down.   o Leaves Charing Cross 1 15, and Cannon Street 1 24 aft. on Saturdays.   s Saturdays only.

Bradshaw 1915

Chapter 12

Trials with Railmotors K&ESR

by Brian Janes (2003)

The Austen papers gifted to the Colonel Stephens Railway Archive on the K&ESR continue to yield much of interest.

Two large sheets of lined paper, completed in pencil in W H Austen's handwriting, shed considerable light on the initial performance and duties of Stephens' first Ford Petrol Railmotor. No delivery date for this pioneering set has been fully established, but the sheets commence on Thursday 15 February 1923 and it is highly probable that this was the first day of normal service.

The sheets detail the daily mileage and petrol and lubricating oil consumption for the next few months closing on June 9th, listing in passing service failures (although unfortunately not specifying the reasons) and the trains on which those failures occurred. From this some interesting deductions are possible.

The railmotors appear to have been used during the trial period to directly replace steam services. They worked the 7.06 am train from Tenterden Town to Robertsbridge Junction returning to Headcorn at 8.18. On leaving Headcorn at 9.51 they reached Tenterden at 10.23, travelling on to Robertsbridge at 10.40 with arrival there at 11.22. Departing at 11.40 to Tenterden, on arrival at 12.25 they were relieved by a steam train for the reminder of the Headcorn run. This was the end of their Saturday turn. On weekdays they left at 3.50 for a Headcorn trip arriving back at Tenterden at 5.05. The daily weekday mileage given for this was 93 miles 14 chains which will have included an empty stock run from Rolvenden to Tenterden and return each day. Saturday workings omitted the Headcorn run so totalled 74 miles 6 chains (no Sunday trains ran).

The first failures occurred on 26th and 27th February 1923 when the motors could only complete the first round trip to Robertsbridge on both days. Two weeks later on 14th March a more serious in service failure occurred when the set failed and was unable to do the last Headcorn run. It was out of service for two days, then failed again the next day at Rolvenden on the first trip before it could complete the run up the bank to Tenterden. It did not work at all the next day (the 19th) and on the 21st did not start to run till the afternoon. Caution and perhaps traffic levels then dictated that it should not run over Easter (28th March to 6 April) as no entries were made. Although the railmotors then resumed their normal roster, petrol consumption had been rising during the latter part of May and continued to rise reaching some 50% above previous levels. Enough was enough and they were taken out of service for a week commencing 21 April.

There might have been a myriad of reasons for individual failures but the problems of March and April seem to have been due to the carbonising of the engines. An analysis of the lubricating oil was sought from David Kirkaldy & Sons, Testing and Experimenting Works, 99 Southwark Street, London and a report dated 28th May 1923 written in elegant longhand is also in the Austen papers. It states:

"This sample is a light mineral oil of good quality though the flash point is somewhat low. It is of too low a viscosity for general use in petrol engines... and would only be suitable for those employing a splash system of lubrication. The addition of about 5% of non-drying fixed oil such as lard is desirable, tending to reduce the liability to carbonise in the cylinder."

From the suggested use of lard it will be seen that the days of mineral oil additives had not yet arrived. A de-coke* and change of oil seems to have done the trick. The set returned to service with one round trip on 30th April and settled down in regular service with petrol and oil consumption reduced for the rest of the trials, the records for which terminated on June 9th.

The railmotors having proved themselves they were then used to establish a new service pattern that was shown in Bradshaw for July 1923. The set was used to supplement the existing somewhat minimalist steam services established during World War 1. In this it now followed the classic pattern of railmotor use by increasing service frequencies in an attempt to counter competition from road transport. In the July timetable the railmotors were shown as working the 9.20am train from Tenterden Town to Robertsbridge Junction returning to Headcorn at 10.20. On leaving Headcorn at 11.55 they reached Tenterden at 12.35p.m and travelled on to Robertsbridge at 1.20 with arrival at 2.10; returning at 2.25 (2.45 on Saturdays) to Tenterden. On weekdays they then substituted, as they had during the trials, for a previously steam service which left at 3.50 for a Headcorn return trip arriving back at 5.05. This finished their weekday service but on Saturday and Wednesday they finished with an evening round trip to Headcorn

This augmented service was a bold and much needed marketing effort. Bus competition had been serious enough to warrant mention in annual reports as early as 1913. In that year 105,000 passengers were carried, by 1919 the figure had dropped to 85,000 and to 68,000 in 1922. With the coming of the railmotors the 1923 total train mileage leapt by nearly 25% to 84000 miles, marginally surpassing pre-war levels. The railmotors accounted for all of this and more. These high total mileages were maintained until in 1932 the railway went into receivership and services were cut to the bone. Initially, therefore, the railmotors were not used simply to cut overall running costs but to control increased costs in the expectation of increased receipts. For the struggling Headcorn section however, some savings were urgent and the motors continued to be used to replace obviously unremunerative steam runs.

When the second railmotor set came into use in 1924, cost savings became increasingly attractive and the railmotors slowly took over more steam mileage, generally around a third of all mileage at a little short of 30,000 miles each year. Indeed during 1926 with a prolonged coal strike and the General Strike the railmotors accounted for well over half of all services. With the arrival of the new Shefflex railmotors in 1929 mileage rose again by about one third although this did not last as the pioneering set was finally withdrawn soon after.

Despite initial success the railmotors had not been able to staunch the haemorrhage of passengers. Holding steady briefly in 1923 passenger numbers continued to decline and although they recovered slightly in the later 20s they had by then reduced to half the 1919 levels. With the railway passing into receivership in 1932, the end of the experiment was in sight. Annual passenger numbers fell precipitately to 20,000. As passengers had deserted to the more comfortable and frequent buses and steam was needed to move the goods, railmotor mileage never again exceeded 14,000 a year and both sets fell out of use in 1937/38.

*For those of the younger generation who did not experience the joys of pre-1960s motoring this is the physical de-carbonising of the inside of the cylinders of petrol engines.

However back in 1923, Stephens had good cause to be pleased with the railmotors and the results of the initial trials. Capital costs were low; reliability and high daily mileages seemed possible and indeed so proved. Average petrol consumption was a very good, 15 miles to the gallon, particularly when it is considered that the second unit was always being hauled. Nor in all probability was it realised at that stage that the type of gearbox fitted to these cars was never completely in neutral and was causing extra wear and drag when hauled. This deficiency might incidentally account for the relatively early demise of the pioneering unit. Subsequent railmotors were fitted with the Supraphord transmission that eliminated this problem. Other costs would also have been favourable; one member of the crew was saved, the driver probably received less than an engineman and overtime was no doubt cut on the loco side. Economies could be made and the service supplemented, and if comfort was cut for the passengers then they were certainly no worse off than using the contemporary competing road bus services (although rapid road vehicle development soon changed this dramatically).

Spare one final thought for the workman who no doubt laboured up the hill from Rolvenden to the garage to fetch up to ten one-gallon cans of petrol each working day. No bulk supplies were available then. Running railways was a tough business even when the internal combustion engine arrived.

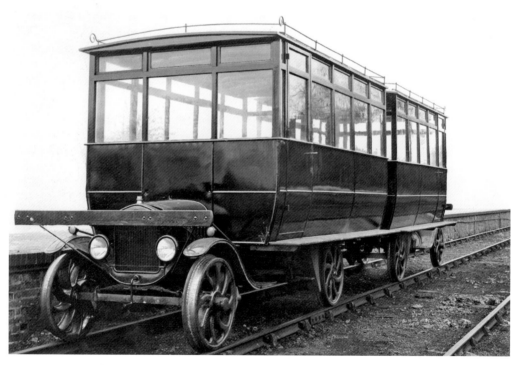

12.1   An official photograph features the Ford Set No. 2 at Tenterden soon after its completion in 1924.

12.2   No. 2 Set was posed at Tenterden in traffic in 1924.

12.3   Fairly work-weary, No. 2 was recorded amongst the loco ash at Rolvenden.

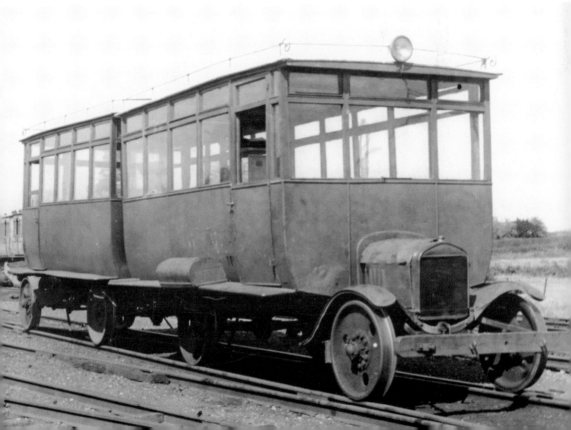

Chapter 13

Driving Railmotors on the K&ESR

By Monty Baker (1995)

What it was like to drive the famous Back to Back Railmotors as recounted by a former K&ESR employee.

The Ford Railcars had a completely different method of driving than the Shefflex cars, the latter having a conventional gearbox, with clutch, and a foot accelerator.

On the Fords the steering column was retained, minus the steering wheel, and shaft, leaving the hand operated advance and retard lever on the left, with the hand throttle lever on the right.

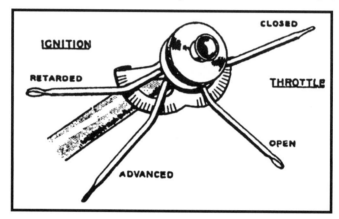

In the summer starting the Ford was not too bad, but in winter it was horrific. There was no such thing as anti-freeze, so radiators were emptied at night, and refilled with some warm water from a loco in steam in the Shed in the morning, plus a handful of horse dung to seal the many leaks in the radiators.

The engine was 4 cyl. Bore 3¾" Stroke 4" capacity 2892cc. There was no oil pump, but the sump was the flywheel casing. As the flywheel revolved it splashed oil around the bearings, some being deposited into a small funnel on a forward sloping pipe that conveyed oil to the timing gears at the front of the engine.

Ford recommended an oil consumption of one gallon of engine oil to 500 miles, so the levels had to be constantly checked, especially at the start of the day. There was no dipstick, so the driver crawled underneath to check the two taps on the flywheel casing, a Max level, and Min level. As the oil filler was at the front of the engine it entailed more crawling to check when oil started dripping from the Max tap, then close it. Imagine that consumption and checking it that way on a car today.

Next job in the preparation programme was to top up the sand buckets, one each side of the drivers seat. A 1" bore iron pipe went through the floor by each sand bucket, down to the rail near the rear driving wheels. Each pipe was topped with a funnel, and each bucket contained a tin, or a chipped enamel mug with which the driver tried to pour an equal amount of sand down each pipe, whilst controlling the hand throttle with the inside knee of his right leg.

It was a difficult job to get from Rolvenden, up the bank to Tenterden on a frosty morning or if the rail was at all damp. Remembering that only one pair of the eight wheels was powered; on many occasions slipping was so bad that the journey to Tenterden was abandoned, and after a phone call to George Dobell to notify him, and check he had no passengers waiting, the first journey of the day to Robertsbridge would start from Rolvenden.

The manner in which the gearbox and clutch of the Ford Model T was operated (for its day) was exceedingly ingenious and simple. The three foot pedals, all the same size, and from left to right were; Clutch, Reverse, Footbrake.

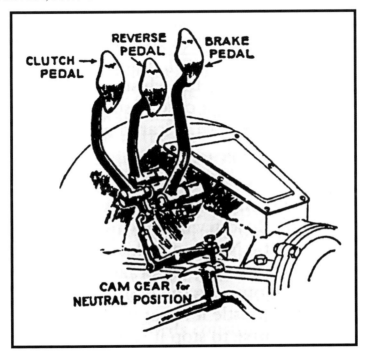

To introduce low gear the clutch pedal was pushed forward as far as it would go. It then tightened the contracting band on the low gear drum by means of cams, and brought this gear into operation for the purpose of climbing a steep hill, or moving away from a standstill.

To introduce the high gear the clutch pedal was allowed to come back towards the driver under the influence of the clutch spring. In this position the low gear brake band was released, and at the same time the clutch discs were bought closely into contact with one another and consequently furnished the drive. Midway between the low gear position and that in which top gear was engaged there was an intermediate point, at which the low gear was disengaged and the clutch was also out of action.

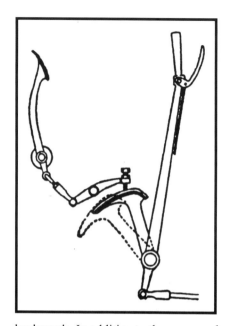

This was neutral, and in order to make it possible for this pedal position to be retained without requiring the driver to keep his foot down, a very clever interconnection was made with the handbrake lever, whereby the latter, on being pulled back, thus holding the vehicle stationary, inserted a small cam shaped arrangement under the clutch operating mechanism. As you can see the handbrake was used for much more than holding the railcars stationary. The central pedal controlled the reverse gear which was brought into action exactly similarly to the low forward gear. It will be obvious from the explanation that has already been given that when either of these gears was in engagement the top gear clutch must be completely out of action.

Therefore, before depressing the reverse pedal, the driver must see that his handbrake lever is in such a position that the discs are disengaged. Pressing down the reverse pedal would then permit the car to travel backwards. In addition to the gears as described so far, the second railcar set was fitted with the Supaphord Patented Auxiliary Gear Box, which gave an extra two gears forward, and reverse. With very few cars on the roads, there were not many people with driving experience about, and the steam drivers, fitters and firemen, who had to drive the railcars when they were introduced, had no experience of the internal combustion engine, or infernal as it was more commonly known at that time.

With no self starters, one very quickly learned that having mastered starting the thing, one did not stall it, as this meant setting up all the controls again and leaping off the platform into the four foot, ducking under the buffer beam, cranking it up, and climbing up on the platform again. This was often repeated several times, with various alterations of ignition, and hand throttle positions, before it restarted.

Horse manure was a vital part of the emergency equipment carried at all times, this also included the spanner which tightened the band drives on the gearbox. The terrific vibration on the radiators caused them to leak a lot, and whilst ample provision was made for carrying a good supply of petrol, it was vital to carry an even greater supply of water. A return journey to Headcorn from Rolvenden on a hot summer's day was not unlike crossing the Sahara desert. Towing the parcels truck meant low gear all the way up the bank to Tenterden with a change of feet pressing on the clutch pedal occasionally to prevent your legs going dead. After boiling most of the way up the bank the radiator needed topping up for a repeat performance up St Michaels bank, with luck making High Halden before topping up again. Frittenden bank was the only obstacle coming back, albeit a tough one, with sometimes a fill up at the summit before proceeding on to Biddenden. Perhaps some readers have seen photos of Nelson Wood carrying a can, maybe it was a petrol can, but it was an old one used for carrying water and was always kept in sight. In addition to the foot band brake, which was mainly used for stopping at stations, there was a wheel handbrake which applied a pair of cast iron shoes to the front pair of wheels.

This was used when descending banks to save wear on the band brake. In emergency, such as suddenly being confronted by half a dozen big steers that had broken through the fence on to the track, the right hand rapidly wound the wheelbrake on, the left hand pulled the handbrake on, and the right foot pushed the footbrake on, after of course remembering to slam the hand throttle shut first.

A unique warning system that was used to warn traffic that the railcar was approaching a level crossing, was a tubular whistle which was hinged to the end of the exhaust pipe, and normally held away from the pipe by a spring. A length of wire connected the whistle to a handle by the driver's seat. What an ingenious idea you may say; it was, if you were going, for example, uphill towards the Cranbrook Road Crossing (ungated in those days), in low gear and nearly full throttle, the whistle produced a sound resembling a cage of startled budgerigars. In fact it scared all birds away for miles around. It does not take a lot of working out what happened on the downhill crossing of Cranbrook Road trying to whistle with the throttle shut - Nothing! This was overcome by partially applying the brake, going into neutral and opening the hand throttle, pulling the whistle lever at the same time. Ready of course to stop if you saw any traffic coming. Many first time passengers suffered severe trauma after hearing the chirruping banshee opening up beneath their feet.

Based on the standard 1st & 3rd Class railway rating, the Ford Railcars came about 7th Class. The seats were made up of narrow wooden slats, covered initially by strips of thin carpet tied to the seat with tapes. This did help to cut down the impression of the slats on one's posterior a little. Unfortunately once the tapes had worn out, and they kept falling on the floor, other uses, such as doormats, were found for them. Passengers who were brave enough to tolerate the cold (there was no heating on the Fords), usually carried an extra item of clothing to fold up as a cushion to prevent being branded on the rump. It was known for one driver to conjure up a mat with no tapes, that he had hidden under his own seat, for an elderly lady passenger, or a particularly pretty young one.

There were no demisters or windscreen wipers on the Fords, and it was very difficult for the driver on a very frosty first trip to see just where he was, it was a case of hoping that the hole he scraped through the ice on the windscreen at one station would last long enough to see to the next station. The backrests on the passenger seats consisted of a 4" wide strip of wood attached to an iron frame, hinged to the base of the seat, enabling it to be moved according to your preference for a forward or rearward facing seat. This did seem an unnecessary luxury, remembering that the Colonel had been in at the design stage. He must have realised it himself later when watching passengers alighting from the Fords at the end of their terrible journey. They just did not know whether they were coming or going!

Lighting was very frugal. Fords only used a 6v system until well after the war, and the interior of the cars was illuminated by two bare 3w. sidelight bulbs. Only one headlamp was used to save the batteries. Springing on the Fords consisted of one transverse spring across each axle. The chassis was attached at the centre of each spring, front and rear with stops on the rear axle only to prevent excessive roll. This was very noticeable when stepping on to the running board at the front entrance door. A gusting side wind could cause severe nausea. Headwinds made timekeeping difficult, when blowing on the vast flat front of the body, but certainly helped make up time on the return trip.

What a contrast to the automobiles of today. Can you imagine any driver tolerating an oil consumption of 1 gallon of oil for 500 miles. Petrol was eventually delivered to Rolvenden in 50 gallon steel barrels at 1/- to 1/3 a gallon. In today's coinage 5p to 6p a gallon or approx. 1p per litre. The railcars were hated by the staff, but they still repaired them, then cannibalised them, till they just could not run any further than the Hay Road at Rolvenden. Now they are no more than memories.

13.1   On the K&ESR, the "Tin Lizzies" sometimes ran with ugly drooping bonnets.

13.2   On the S&MR, railcars were rarely seen running with a trailer. The sets there were known as "Tin Lizzies" as well.

13.3   The WSR cars were invariably used with a small wagon, for barrels, churns and boxes. A film records standing passengers travelling therein.

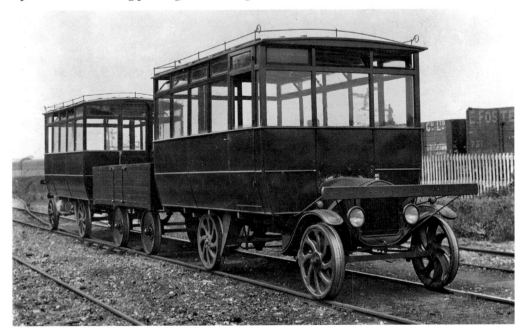

Chapter 14

Dangerous Practices on the Kent & East Sussex

by Stephen Garrett (1986)

The Public Records Office at Kew holds many documents relating, directly or indirectly, to the Kent & East Sussex Railway. Most of these have fairly prosaic titles like 'St Michaels Halt' or 'Cheap fares for Seamen' but file MT6.2254/1 rejoices in the intriguing title 'Dangerous Practices on the K&ESR'. The practice concerned was that of collecting fares and checking tickets by the conductor or guard who had to move along the train and from carriage to carriage on the outside. The file opens with a letter from Guy Ewing & Co of Tunbridge Wells to Major Pringle of the Board of Trade Inspectorate, dated 5 February 1903.

Dear Sir,

re Rother Valley Railway Robertsbridge to Tenterden

We heard yesterday when travelling on the line that you were down the day before to inspect the extension from the present station to one nearer the town. In passing from Robertsbridge up the line you can hardly have failed to notice what we regard as a most dangerous practice which would not be permitted on any other line under any circumstances. Not only is it unnerving to passengers to see a man walking along the footboard from carriage to carriage but we regard it as a highly dangerous practice and venture to think the Company should not be permitted to call upon their servant, the guard, to do so. Why cannot tickets be issued at the stations as on other lines or in the alternative have corridor carriages so that the man can walk along without risking his life on the footboard, particularly in wintry weather.

We beg to remain, Dear Sir
Yours obediently
Guy Ewing & Co

The file notes that a similar complaint had recently been received concerning the Southwold Railway and asks for a letter to be sent to the Rother Valley Railway requesting an explanation. The reference to the Southwold Railway is curious as this line had balcony carriages and gangways which made it very easy to move from one carriage to another. Stephens' reply on behalf of the Rother Valley is characteristic of his uncompromising approach:

Sir,

In reply to your letter R1625 of 13th inst. Eight of our nine carriages on this line are constructed internally on the corridor principle. No danger is feared from the guard following the universal continental practice of getting from one carriage to the other as the steps are adapted for this purpose.

The practice has been in use for nearly 3 years without accident or complaint and the traffic does not justify the employment of persons capable of issuing tickets at the various stopping places.

Your obedient servant
H F Stephens

In fact, Stephens was not entirely candid in this reply. It is true that six of the line's carriages, the original Hurst Nelson stock, had been built with internal gangways and it is possible that two of the second-hand ones subsequently acquired had been fitted with internal gangways by this date, but in 1903 the Company owned eleven coaches rather than nine. As for the 'adapted' steps, it is true that the footboards on the Hurst Nelsons projected some distance beyond the carriage ends but there is little evidence of any such work having been done on the second-hand stock. The Board of Trade certainly seem to have had their doubts about the matter because the file now calls for a sketch of the stock and an interview with Stephens. There are no minutes of this interview, but a summary is given of its conclusions:

* footboards to be extended as far as possible without fouling each other
* extra handrails to be provided
* end doors on carriages either to open inwards or to be hinged so that doors open away from end of carriage
* if new stock were to be acquired it should be of the end-corridor type.

In September 1903 Stephens wrote to say that all the carriages except for No. 11 had now been attended to and that in future tickets would be issued at the stations at Bodiam, Northiam, Tenterden Town and 'partially' at Rolvenden. Stephens may have been over-optimistic because he wrote again in December 1903 confirming that the necessary work was 'in hand' and enclosing a diagram 'of the carriage stock'. This is a curious affair showing a five carriage train. The vehicles can be identified as

* ex-Great Eastern 2-compartment brake No. 9 with no sign of an internal gangway or any other alteration except that one compartment seems to have lost half its seats.
* a Hurst Nelson third-class apparently as built.
* a Hurst Nelson first-class apparently as built.
* a five-compartment carriage with an internal gangway cut through the compartment partitions along one side and seating altered to suit (this is either ex-Cheshire Lines Committee No. 11 or ex-Great Eastern No. 13)
* a three-compartment Ex-G.ER brake No. 10 with the compartments and brake compartment joined by an internal gangway, but no apparent alteration to hinges or footboards.

What is not clear from the diagram is whether it purported to describe all the passenger stock on the line. What it did show all too clearly was that there might be a gap of at least 3' 3" between the footboards of some carriages which would be even greater on the outside of a curve in the line. Even more curious is the fact that shortly after the diagram was drawn up all the Hurst Nelsons were sent away to be converted into three bogie coaches.

This fact and a diagram of the conversions forms the substance of a letter from Stephens to the Board of Trade in June 1904. He adds that "arrangements have been made to book passengers at all stations except Robertsbridge and Junction Road thus very materially reducing the necessity of the guard moving from car to car" and that "the guard is not to enter or leave the cars other than those on the corridor system while the train is in motion". Needless to say, the Board of Trade's requirement that new stock be fitted with end corridors was ignored as it was also ignored in the case of three new bogie carriages obtained from Pickerings shortly afterwards. Similarly there seems to have been no attempt to adapt or convert any of the second-hand stock which was subsequently acquired.

The Board of Trade seems to have been happy to let matters rest until rudely awakened by the following letter, dated 4 March 1911.

Dear Mr Buxton,

I would like to call your attention to what appears to be a peculiarly dangerous practice on the K&ESR Company which has a line extending from Robertsbridge to Headcorn. The Company has no booking office at Robertsbridge and the guard in consequence climbs from carriage to carriage while the train is in motion in order to collect fares and to give tickets. The rolling stock is very old and there appears to be no handrails to assist him in crossing from one compartment to another and the element of danger is, therefore, great especially in winter. I think it is a matter to which the attention of the Board of Trade should be called.

Yours very truly
Arthur Sherwell MP

Once again Stephens was requested for his observations on this matter as well as for information as to whether the line had acquired any new stock since 1904. With injured innocence Stephens replied that he had thought the Board to be satisfied with this method of operation and added that, 'There is no difficulty in reaching from one hand rail to the other on the train in question, this was carefully tried prior to the system being put into use and where necessary additional hand rails were fitted. As the Department are no doubt aware the system is quite common on the Continental Railways.' He admitted that additional carriages had been acquired, but these were mainly used on the Headcorn Extension.

The Board seem to have taken their cue from Stephens and replied to Sherwell that they were well aware of the practice in question but that it had been in use without incident for eleven years and must, therefore, be safe. They even pointed out that the practice was common on the Continent! Sherwell replied that he was still unhappy with the situation, but does not seem to have taken the matter further. About this time the bogie stock seems to have been laid aside and most of the 'adapted' stock disposed of to the East Kent Railway. However, the Board of Trade seems to have had no further interest in pursuing the matter because when Salehurst Parish Council wrote complaining of the practice of guards 'going from carriage to carriage on the outside' in January 1914 the Board dealt with the matter by acknowledging the Council's letter but taking no further steps as the Council had neither asked for action nor for a reply!

Thus guards continued their athletic practices on the Kent & East Sussex until 1944 when true corridor coaches made a belated appearance on the line. In the event, nobody was ever recorded as being injured by this 'dangerous practice' though whether this was due to luck or exceptionally fit guards we shall never know.

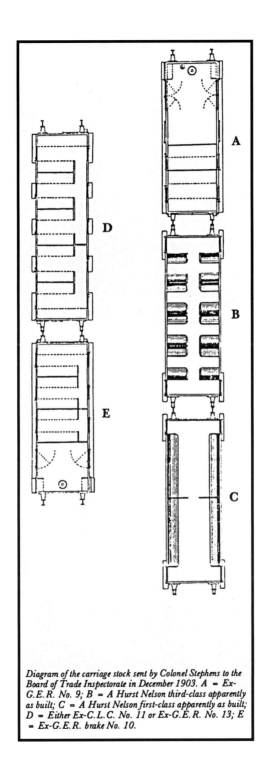

Diagram of the carriage stock sent by Colonel Stephens to the Board of Trade Inspectorate in December 1903. A = Ex-G.E.R. No. 9; B = A Hurst Nelson third-class apparently as built; C = A Hurst Nelson first-class apparently as built; D = Either Ex-C.L.C. No. 11 or Ex-G.E.R. No. 13; E = Ex-G.E.R. brake No. 10.

14.1   K&ESR No. 1. Note the grab handles at each corner of the body.

14.2   K&ESR No. 5. Note the top footboard extending outwards.

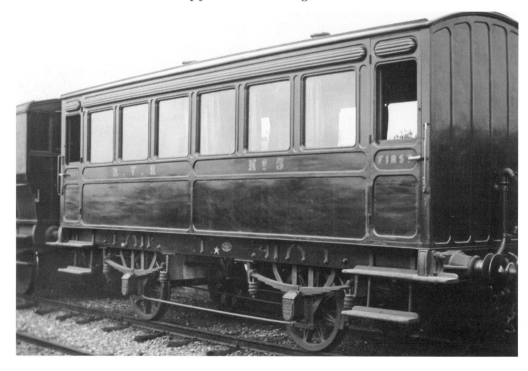

14.3   K&ESR No. 9. This view from about 1928 shows the continuous footboard.

14.4   K&ESR No. 11. Note that the door on the left is left hung.

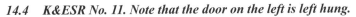

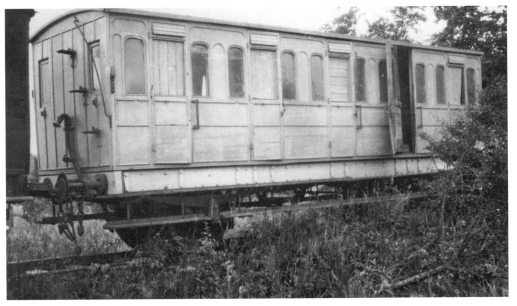

Chapter 15

Memories of the Selsey Tramway

by H C Casserley (1975)

My first acquaintance of the Colonel Stephens railways was with the Kent & East Sussex, now no less than half a century ago, on 29 August 1925 to be exact. I had never seen anything quite like it before, and even today that visit remains one of the most vivid recollections of a lifetime of exploration of the railways of Great Britain and Ireland. Anyway, it started off an enthusiasm which made excursions to other similar concerns essential, particularly those of the Colonel Stephens group, which proved to be among the most fascinating of all.

This gentleman was not only General Manager and general factotum of the K&ESR, East Kent, Selsey, WC&PR, and Shropshire & Montgomery, but as his headed notepaper, emanating from his address at Tonbridge, (of which I have still some specimens in the form of letters of authority to visit his various railways) indicated, he appeared to claim some sort of interest, probably as a consulting engineer, in several other lines. These included the Rye & Camber, Snailbeach District, Ashover, the Festiniog and Welsh Highland and even the recently constructed North Devon & Cornwall Junction, which was in effect a new branch of the Southern Railway.

I paid my first visit to the 'Selsey' on 16 July 1927, but initially this turned out to be something of a disappointment, as on my arrival at Chichester behind B2X class 4-4-0 No B205, I found in the adjacent 'Selsey' station not the vintage loco and ancient carriage I had hoped for, but a very disagreeable Ford railcar (this had also happened on the occasion of my first visit to the K&ESR, very off-putting, but compensated by the wonderful array of stuff which I found at Rolvenden).

On arrival at Selsey I also found that the shed there was large enough to accommodate all the five working engines, and the only one outside, which I found lying derelict, hidden in a yard at the back, was a withdrawn 0-4-2ST No 3 *Hesperus*, built by Neilson & Co in 1871, which Colonel Stephens, as was his customary practice, had obtained second-hand (or rather third in this case) in 1912 from the Plymouth Devonport & South Western Junction Railway. It worked on the Selsey until 1924, and was still in the yard at the time of my second visit, late in 1928, but was broken up about 1930.

However on that first occasion there was an engine which had been at work that day, and which still had a little steam left in her. This was No 1 *Selsey*, a 2-4-2T, rather an odd type for this sort of railway, which had come new from Peckett to the railway when it was first opened in 1897.

This was very rare with Colonel Stephens railways; most of his engines were obtained in whatever bargain basement he could locate which had anything for sale which might be useful, generally from the main line railways, usually the LSWR, LB&SCR, or SE&CR.

Fortunately there was a co-operative driver (or possibly fireman) still around, who with a little monetary inducement agreed to get up enough steam to pull all of the engines out of the shed for photography. These. were, in order, *Selsey*, No 5 *Ringing Rock* (Manning Wardle 1883), obtained from McAlpine in 1917, No 2 *Sidlesham*, a veteran of 1861, built by Manning

Wardle, and obtained in 1907 from Hawthorn Leslie, who had somehow acquired the engine and rebuilt it, and No 3 (formerly 4) *Chichester*, built by Hudswell Clarke in 1903, and used in 1924 in connection with the construction of Wembley Exhibition, afterwards acquired by Colonel Stephens.

The reason for renumbering when *Chichester* took No 3 from *Hesperus* was to avoid confusion with the fifth engine, a Manning Wardle 0-6-OST of 1866, which had been transferred in 1924 from another Colonel Stephens line, the Shropshire & Montgomery, where it had been known as No 4 *Morous*. It still retained its S&M identity on the Selsey until it was scrapped, along with the other surviving engines, when the line was closed in January 1935. *Sidlesham* and *Chichester* had by then already gone, in 1932.

In November 1928 I had to go to hospital for an operation, as a result of which I went to the Isle of Wight for a period of convalescence. Being midwinter it was hardly the time for recuperating on the beach in the sunshine, so after a few days travelling around on the island's railways I began to make a few excursions to the mainland, and one turned up hopefully at Chichester, this time to be rewarded by the sight of *Selsey* with a couple of coaches and a van. A very pleasant amble over the flat countryside of the Selsey promontory made a very satisfactory day's excursion.

I never saw the line working again, but paid a final visit by car on 17 March 1935, soon after its closure, at which time everything was still more or less intact. *Ringing Rock* was standing in the yard at Chichester, *Selsey* and *Morous* in the shed at Selsey, whilst outside were a couple of quite recently acquired coaches from the Southern Railway, old LC&DR six wheelers, still with their SR numbers, 1636 and 3639, but bearing the legend "West Sussex Railway", the later title which the railway had adopted. It had been incorporated as the "Hundred of Manhood & Selsey Tramways", usually known colloquially as the "Selsey" or "Selsey Tramway".

The number of surviving enthusiasts who remember this little railway, of a kind now extinct apart from preservation projects, is inevitably declining over the years, and I count it as my good fortune to be one of those who are still around.

Chapter 16
Colonel Stephens in the Isle of Wight
by Stephen Garrett (1985)

Holman Fred Stephens was never a man to hide his light under a bushel. It is all the more surprising then that his various published curricula vitae omit any reference to his connection with the Isle of Wight Central Railway.

Although no part of the Isle of Wight Central was authorised sufficiently late to be classified as a light railway under the Light Railways Act 1896, it shared many of the characteristics of such a line. Its track was somewhat more substantial than that to be found on the Kent & East Sussex, but the trains that travelled over it comprised a very comparable mixture of antiques and second-hand bargains, mostly financed by hire purchase.

Stephens' first recorded contact with the Isle of Wight Central was in 1904. The line had been contemplating the purchase of a steam railmotor and had received a letter from Stephens in January "as to steam motor carriages". The Secretary was instructed by the Board "to ask Mr Stephens for the results of his experiments." As the Kent & East Sussex did not possess a steam railmotor in January 1904, this was perhaps a reference to the use of a Kitson steam railmotor on the Sheppey Light Railway by the South Eastern & Chatham Railway. Stephens had presumably maintained some sort of interest in this line after its construction by him.

The Isle of Wight Central's interest in railmotors became more active with the formation in November 1904 of a potential rival in the form of the Isle of Wight Express Motor Syndicate. Mr Conacher, the line's manager, requested and secured his Board's permission to obtain tenders "for a car to run on our rails." In December he reported that Messrs R Y Pickering had offered to build "a car similar to one supplied to the Kent & East Sussex" for £400. Mr Conacher was instructed to see the car and report back, but would have faced some difficulty as the Pickering car was not officially recorded as delivered to the Kent & East Sussex until March 1905. The Isle of Wight Central Board of Directors Books minute a meeting in February 1905 and record that Conacher had not yet been able to see the Kent & East Sussex railmotor.

In the event alternative tenders were invited in May 1905 for either one or three railmotors from Hurst Nelson, Birmingham Carriage & Wagon Co, Metropolitan Railway Carriage & Wagon Co and Kitsons. In October it was agreed to accept Hurst Nelson's tender for £1450 for just a single railmotor, the Motor Syndicate presumably not having proved as great a rival as had at first been feared. No more is heard of Stephens for some time after this though there occurred a very 'Stephensesque' episode in 1907. Pleased with the performance of the Hurst Nelson railmotor, the Isle of Wight Central resolved to obtain a second one. Staggered by a quotation of £2040, the Board sought to economise by seeking tenders for the carriage portion only and attaching this to a diminutive Black Hawthorn 0-4-2ST of 1870 vintage that they already had in stock. Unfortunately the lowest quotation for the carriage portion on its own was £1125. Undaunted, the Board purchased a second-hand clerestory bogie carriage from the Midland Railway which, including a forward driving compartment and controls, only set them back £250.

Stephens' return to the Isle of Wight Central scene came in 1911. There seems to have been something of a palace revolution on the line and a new board of directors, financed by a loan from the Capital & Counties Bank, had employed a new manager, Mr Willmot, to reorganise the running and operation of the Railway. Further, the Board resolved on 26th April "that Mr H F Stephens be appointed Engineer to the Company for 12 months to supervise the Permanent Way and Locomotive Departments at a salary of £100 and out-of-pocket expenses."

Apart from the resignation in June of Mr Guest, the existing Locomotive Superintendent, the first signs of Stephens' tenure did not appear until July when the Directors approved a wide range of capital expenditure on new sidings, gas lighting for the carriage stock, an influx of second-hand rolling stock and other improvements. Stephens was also present as a shareholder at the Half Yearly meeting held on 11th August.

In September a further range of capital items was approved. Not only did this include provision of a waiting shed at Havenstreet Station, now the headquarters of the Isle of Wight Steam Railway, but it also included two items particularly characteristic of Stephens. The first of these was the provision of 'extra umbrella tanks' at Newport. One of these survives today at Havenstreet and is very similar to, if not identical with, the water towers erected by Stephens at Tenterden, Shrewsbury and Kinnerley. The Shrewsbury example, of course, now serves at Wittersham Road. The second item was the acquisition of a travelling crane - few Stephens' lines were without one. Like the Kent & East Sussex's second crane this was a six-wheeled example from the Midland Railway complete with match wagon, though the crane was only of five tons capacity compared with the ten ton example on the Kent & East Sussex. Remarkably this crane survived subsequent ownership by the Southern Railway and British Railways and now forms part of the stock of the Isle of Wight Steam Railway.

Unfortunately, Stephens' connection with the Isle of Wight Central came to an end shortly afterwards. The Board's Minutes for 24th October record: "With Ref. to Board Minute of the 26th April last it was reported that Mr Stephens found the weekly visit which was required occupied too much of his time and retired from the 30th September last which was noted." This is not entirely surprising as 1911 saw Stephens continuing the management of the Kent & East Sussex and the Selsey Tramway, taking over the management of the Weston Clevedon & Portishead, re-opening the main line of the Shropshire & Montgomeryshire with the rebuilding of Criggion Branch yet to be completed, and commencing the construction of the East Kent while planning and applying for extensions to that line.

No detailed records appear to exist of Stephens' work on the Isle of Wight Central though correspondence may survive in Midland Railway records. Perhaps Stephens felt that his period with the Isle of Wight Central was too brief to warrant recording for posterity but it is ironic that in the water tower and travelling crane there is a more tangible record of his connection with this line than survives of many of the other lines for which he worked longer and harder.

*16.1   Newport's water tower was for long a feature of the west end of the station. It is seen in
1935 with class O2 0-4-4T no. W29 Alverstone on the right. (S.W.Baker)*

Chapter 17

Passengers to Pontyberem BP&GVR

by Tom Burnham (1995)

Although the group of light railways managed from his Tonbridge office are what one usually thinks of as the "Colonel Stephens Railways", they were by no means the only lines with which H F Stephens was involved. Particularly in the earlier part of his career, he was in demand as a consultant to advise on railway works, particularly when an application for a Light Railway Order was involved. One line employing his services in this way was the Burry Port & Gwendraeth Valley Railway, a mineral railway in South Wales which decided to start a passenger service.

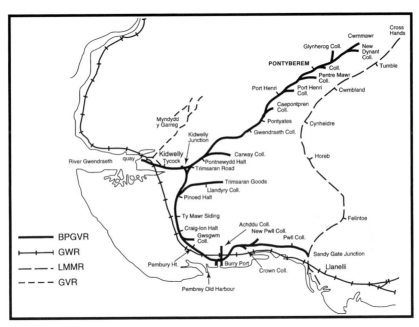

In order to understand Stephens' involvement with the BP&GVR, it is necessary to know something of its earlier history. Connecting the anthracite mines of the valley of the Gwendraeth Mawr in south east Carmarthenshire with the harbour at Burry Port near Pembrey, the "main line" of 13 miles from Burry Port to Cwmmawr was opened in 1869, in part using the alignment of a former canal - which resulted in problems in later years because of the substandard dimensions of the old canal bridges and the steep gradients where the canal barges had been raised by inclines. As one might expect, flooding has also been a recurrent problem. A branch to Kidwelly was opened in 1873, connecting with the Gwendraeth Valleys Railway (an independent concern, associated with the Kidwelly Tinplate Works) and with the Great Western (which had been converted to standard gauge in the previous year). A final extension took place in 1891, when tramroads between Pembrey and Llanelli were converted to provide a link between the BP&GVR at Burry Port and the Llanelli & Mynydd Mawr Railway at Sandy Gate Junction. The total route mileage was then some 21 miles, including minor branches to collieries.

The railway pursued an unprofitable existence during the latter half of the 19th century, spending the years from 1881 to 1898 in the hands of a receiver. Coal traffic was worked by an assortment of locomotives, including two double-boilered Fairlie engines, 0-4-4-0 *Mountaineer* and a 0-6-6-0 *Victoria*. From 1899, however, the BP&GVR shared in the prosperity of the South Wales coal industry and in 1900 was able to pay the first dividend on its ordinary shares, of 5%. This was raised to 6% in 1905 and to 10% in 1906 at which level it remained for the rest of the company's independent existence. From 1899 to the Grouping, the BP&GVR's affairs were in the capable hands of Mr Arthur Morgan, General Manager, assisted as the Engineer and Locomotive Superintendent first by Mr Robert Carr and then, from about 1907, by Mr John Eager. Considerable improvements to the track were made, and the collection of miscellaneous locomotives were replaced between 1900 and 1907 by seven 0-6-0ST engines, two from Chapman & Furneaux and the rest from Avonside. One of the Avonside engines, No.2 *Pontyberem* of 1900, was sold in 1914 and has, remarkably, survived to the present day to be preserved by the Great Western Society at Didcot. Incidentally, one of the old locomotives, a Manning Wardle 0-6-0ST of 1881, *Cwm Mawr*, went to Avonside in part exchange for a new locomotive of the same name and was resold by Avonside to the Weston Clevedon & Portishead Railway, where it became No. 3, *Weston*.

The line had no powers to carry other than coal and goods traffic, but towards the end of the 19th century the colliery companies requested the railway to carry miners to and from the pits. It was agreed in 1899 that each colliery should pay £2 10s a week for a special train leaving Pontyberem every day at 4.45pm (with, presumably, a corresponding working up the valley in the morning) and calling at each colliery. The carriages seem to have been owned by the collieries rather than the railway, although the latter did consider buying one in 1904 for the princely sum of £20 - which may indicate the general standard of accommodation. On Thursdays, one of the colliery coaches was run to carry the pitmen's wives to market, and passengers seem also to have been accommodated in the brake vans of coal trains, a charge of sixpence being levied for carrying some small item of luggage, in lieu of a passenger fare.

Further unofficial carriage of passengers occurred in connection with the "Mabon's Monday" holidays. These holidays were named after the bardic title of William Abraham, a Liberal MP and the first president of the South Wales Miners' Federation, who had been instrumental in negotiating the closure of the pits on the first Monday of each month - largely as a device for restricting production of coal. The miners used the day to attend union meetings while their families visited the seaside, and it was customary to run free trains to carry them. These trains consisted of open colliery wagons, cleaned and provided with wooden benches by the men, with ladders to enable the passengers to climb in and out.

Such proceedings were unlikely to meet with the approval of the Board of'Trade, and the company was severely criticised by the Inspecting Officer, Colonel Yorke, following a collision between a colliers' train and a light engine near Burry Port in August 1903, when one person was killed. Despite this, and despite a series of petitions and resolutions from the communities of the Valley, calling for a passenger service, the directors were very doubtful where the potential traffic would justify the cost of conversion. Eventually, in 1908 the secretary, Mr Seaton Taylor, met officials of the Board of Trade and the Light Railway Commissioners to find what would be involved in working parts of the line as a light railway, under the Light Railways Act of 1896. When he reported the results of the interview to the April meeting of the directors, it was decided that "with a view to ascertaining the probable cost, an Engineer of experience in similar applications should be consulted". One of the directors, the Hon Sidney Peel, agreed to make enquiries, and as a result, Holman F Stephens was asked to inspect the line, to report on what was needed to introduce a passenger service from Burry Port to Pontyberem, to estimate the probable cost. His report was ready in June, and Stephens attended the Board meeting in July to discuss it. Matters proceeded apace, and by the end of the year an application for a Light Railway Order had been deposited and Stephens had agreed to send a representative to carry out a detailed survey and prepare plans of the new works, which encompassed not only the main line from Burry Port to Pontyberem but also most of the Kidwelly branch.

Only two objections to the proposed Order were received by the Light Railway Commissioners. These were from the Llanelli Urban District Council, which requested that passenger services should be extended to the line from Burry Port to Sandy Gate Junction and Llanelli, and from 103 residents of the Pontyberem district, who signed a petition asking for the service to be extended beyond Pontyberem to Cwmmawr. The Commissioners considered that the BP&GVR could hardly be required to extend its proposals, and as no other objections had been received, they recommended approval of the application without a local public inquiry being held.

Meanwhile, tenders were accepted for signals to be supplied by Tyer & Co and electric staff equipment by the Railway Signal Co. Stephens was not responsible for the provision of rolling stock for passenger trains, which was arranged by Morgan and Eager, and on their advice, the Board agreed to start the passenger service with a new locomotive, a Hudswell, Clarke 0-6-0 side tank costing £1,670 (it was delivered as No. 8, *Pioneer*) and ten second-hand carriages (in need of repair) from the Metropolitan Railway for £600. The carriages were all straight-sided, 8-wheeled, 8 compartment thirds, made redundant by electrification. They were lighted with acetylene gas, using individual gas generators on each carriage, and as this system was similar to that adopted on the Kent & East Sussex and the Shropshire & Montgomeryshire, it is likely that Stephens gave some unrecorded advice. Last but not least, the Board approved Stephens' proposed fee of £400 plus expenses (his eventual account was for £464-0-1d).

In the hope of keeping the expenses to a minimum, Stephens wrote on 19 March 1909 to a Mr Stokes of the GWR at Paddington:

"I am engaged in the reconstruction of this line which has a junction with you at Burry Port. May I ask you if I can be favoured with an occasional pass between London and Burry Port pending the reconstruction?" The request was somewhat brusquely declined.

Nonetheless, work proceeded during the first half of 1909. The station buildings at Burry Port, Pontyates and Pontyberem, modest corrugated iron structures typical of Stephens' railways, were built by Powell & Co; a dispute with the Great Western over the ownership of part of the site of the BP&GVR's Burry Port terminus delayed construction of that Station (it was eventually resolved, some months after the new station opened, by an exchange of land). Tyer's bill was rather higher than originally expected, as additional signals were provided on the Kidwelly branch. Stephens sent down a Mr Burfoot to do the signal wiring, but he seems to have fallen foul of the BP&GVR management for reasons now unknown.

The Light Railway Order was confirmed by the Board of Trade on 30 June 1909, and the opening was fixed for the Bank Holiday Monday, 2 August. The BP&GVR Board decided to dispense with ceremony, but to allow Mr Morgan to spend £5 on entertaining the press to luncheon (not a large sum even in those days) and to give the employees an extra day's pay. None the less, many local people crowded the trains for their first official ride on the railway. A photograph shows Stephens standing proudly beside the first passenger train from Burry Port.

Four down and three up passenger trains were offered between Burry Port and Pontyberem on weekdays only, with an extra train each way on Saturdays. These trains were third class only and used four of the ex-Metropolitan Railway carriages (Nos. 1 to 4), while the remaining six carriages were used for workmen's trains, which in addition to serving collieries on the main line also ran over the Kidwelly branches as far as Ty Coch Halt. The new service proved a success, with over 10,000 passengers having been carried by the end of August. The Directors were sufficiently confident to approve the purchase of another new locomotive (No.9) from Hudswell, Clarke (despite No.8's propensity to run hot), and to seek further second-hand carriages. A modest improvement in passenger amenities was made, with expenditure of some £52 on lavatories approved in December 1909 and two old colliery coaches being bought at £5 apiece to be used as shelters. Ponthenry also seems to have acquired a station building at about this period; built in brick it was otherwise similar in size and style to the earlier corrugated iron examples.

Mr Morgan also arranged for the printing of a poster advertising the trains, whose spirited design included a map of the railway and its connecting lines, surrounded by vignettes of the docks and outer harbour at Burry Port, the stations at Burry Port, Pontyates and Pontyberem, the company's offices, and two Welsh dragons. This expenditure was offset to some extent by the receipt of £45 per annum for advertising on the stations and in the carriages.

Despite the petition which has been submitted even before passenger services had opened to Pontyberem, asking for an extension of the Light Railway Order to Cwmmawr, it took the Directors some time to decide whether to go ahead. The main reason for this was that the gradient of the old mineral line was as steep as 1 in 14 or 15 where the original canal had used a cable worked incline, and the tracks would clearly require expensive rebuilding to allow passenger trains to run. However, in the first half of 1910, it was decided to purchase the land for a realignment so that the gradients could be eased little by little. Stephens was again called upon to advise on the requirements for a Light Railway Order for the Cwmmawr extension, although not for extensions to Kidwelly and Sandy Gate, which had also been requested. His first report was submitted in September 1910, a preliminary report with plans and sections in February 1911, and detailed estimates and plans in March 1911. Incidentally, a fee of 150 guineas plus out-of-pocket expenses was agreed for Stephens' work on the Cwmmawr extension.

The Light Railway Order for the extension was confirmed on 4 October 1911. By this date, the purchase of land for the realignment of the track and for the terminus at Cwmmawr had been completed, and on Stephens' advice the contract for the additional signalling work had again been awarded to Tyer & Co. Progress with the regrading work was, however, slower than hoped, although more men were to be taken on in the spring to supplement the 25 being employed on the project over the winter of 1911-12. In the hope of reducing costs, the directors asked Stephens whether the Board of Trade was likely to sanction a gradient steeper than 1 in 40. The answer was evidently negative, as 1,000 yards at a gradient of 1 in 40 was eventually achieved. Other works required for the extension included the provision of a single platform and the usual corrugated iron booking office cum waiting room at the terminus at Cwmmawr, while at

Pontyberem a second platform was added to make it a passing place.

The extension was inspected for the Board of Trade on 14 January 1913 by Colonel C Drewitt, who pronounced himself entirely satisfied. It was opened on Wednesday 29 January, the Llanelli & County Guardian reporting that "the first train left Burry Port at 9.45, to which was attached the Company's Saloon, with the General Manager (Mr Arthur Morgan), the Engineer (Mr. J Eager) and others. The station at Cwmmawr was decorated for the occasion, and the train entered with grand salute of detonators. A large number of people witnessed the arrival, and many patrons availed themselves of travelling on the first day of the opening. Great credit is due to Mr Morgan, the general manager, and Mr J Eager, the engineer, for this improvement." No doubt the local paper considered it more politic to award the credit for this achievement to a Burry Port man than to an English Consultant, but it is to be hoped that Stephens had at least been invited to join the official party in the saloon. This was, incidentally, an ex-Lambourn Valley Railway four-wheeled vehicle with open balconies, which the BP&GVR seems to have used only for officers. Three sister vehicles were sold by the Lambourn Valley Railway to the Selsey Tramway.

Passenger traffic was buoyant during and immediately after the Great War, and further carriages (second-hand from London & South Western and North London Railways) and locomotives were acquired to handle it. However, in 1921 it was badly affected by a national coal strike which lasted the three months and gave a foretaste of the more serious problems which were to follow in the 1920s and 1930s.

Year	Third Class	Workmen	Total
1910	110,447	255,672	366,119
1915	158,024	271,644	429,668
1919	187,377	355,944	543,321
1920	190,972	347,808	538,780
1921	116,970	312,332	429,302

On 1 July 1922, the BP&GVR became part of the Great Western Railway, as a subsidiary company in terms of the 1921 Railways Act.

The collection of second-hand carriages was in poor condition, especially the stock used for workmen's trains which had broken windows and even missing doors. It was soon withdrawn and replaced by standard low-roofed GWR four-wheeled carriages dating from the 1890s, those used for miners' trains being painted plain brown and having only wooden seats. An interesting coincidence was that some of these carriages had been built for London suburban services and so had round-topped doors like those of the Metropolitan stock they had superseded. By the 1930s the GWR's supply of old four-wheelers was running low and the company had no bogie stock suitable for the line, as the maximum height allowed was only 11 ft 6in, compared with 13ft 6in on most of the rest of the GWR system. Swindon Works therefore built a batch of bogie stock specially for the line in 1939. This composed six brake thirds and one third, with low arc roofs but otherwise similar to the steel-panelled suburban stock being built at the period. The best of the four-wheelers continued in use, running with the bogie stock until passenger services ceased.

The total number of passengers had fallen to 83,965 in 1938 and to only 35,645 (mainly miners) in 1950, and so it is not surprising that British Railways decided to withdraw passenger services on 21 September 1953. What is perhaps more surprising is that much of the system remains in use for coal traffic to the present day.

17.1 *Burry Port station was recorded soon after its opening to passenger traffic in 1909. The track was very much older.*

Chapter 18

Gazelle

by Stephen Garrett (1997)

There can probably be no more appropriate locomotive for display in a Colonel Stephens Railway Museum than *Gazelle* - undoubtedly one of the most bizarre locomotives to have operated on Stephens' lines, but equally an excellent demonstration of Stephens' ability to put almost anything to a practical use.

Gazelle's origins were decidedly impractical. Designed and built in 1893 by Alfred Dodman & Company a general engineering firm and builder of traction engines, this locomotive was intended for the private use of William Burkitt, a seed and corn merchant of King's Lynn who also held a directors seat on the King's Lynn Docks & Railways Company. As a result of his railway interests Burkitt obtained running powers for *Gazelle* over the tracks of the Great Eastern Railway and the Midland & Great Northern Joint Railway. Only one of *Gazelle's* expeditions appears to have been recorded in detail. This was a trip from King's Lynn to Chesterfield, a distance of 105 miles, on 27th July 1897. The outward journey began at 06.10 with arrival at Chesterfield at 11.20 with an average speed of 24 mph if fifty minutes of delays are allowed. The return journey left at 15.00 and reached King's Lynn at 20.25.

Anyone contemplating a journey of 210 miles with more than ten hours to be spent on board would probably not have chosen to have travelled in *Gazelle*. It was a 2-2-2WT with a four seater passenger compartment at the back where one would have expected to find the coal bunker. Neither the cab nor the passenger compartment had any form of shelter and its dimensions were truly Lilliputian:

Driving Wheels	3' 9" diameter
Leading & Trailing Wheels	2' 3" diameter
Total Wheelbase	10' 6"
Cylinders	4"x 9"
Boiler centre line above rail	3' 11"
Height to top of chimney	7' 9"
Length over buffers	17' 2"
Weight	5 tons 6 cwt

One of the factors contributing to the delays on the Chesterfield expedition was the extra time taken changing tablets from the low level of *Gazelle's* footplate. Given that the journey was undertaken in gale conditions it is small wonder that we cannot find any trace of regular journeys of this type being undertaken. The only concession to Mr Burkitt's comfort would have been the employment of wooden centred Mansell wheels on all three axles which would have served to reduce the noise at least.

There is a possibility that *Gazelle* was the second of two identical locomotives as there are records of another locomotive being supplied to the West Norfolk Farmers' Manure & Chemical Co-Operative Company and subsequently being shipped to Australia.

Although Dodman is known to have repaired locomotives for the Co-Operative it is unlikely that a locomotive of *Gazelle's* design would have been of any use to an industrial concern and it is generally assumed that this locomotive was *Gazelle* itself carrying out some sort of running in trials. However, if there was a second locomotive it makes it rather difficult for the K&ESR to claim 'smallest locomotive' status!

There is some confusion as to *Gazelle's* career in the years following 1897, but it is known to have come into the hands of the dealer T W Ward by January 1910 and was bought by Holman Stephens in February 1911 for the Shropshire & Montgomeryshire Railway. *Gazelle* may seem to have been a strange choice but it should be remembered that Stephens was reconstructing a railway that had been out of use for twenty years but on which the track was substantially intact. Whilst it would have been folly to employ a fullsized locomotive on the line it would have been possible for *Gazelle* to venture out on tours of inspection along the line in advance of the serious track replacement. It is not clear whether *Gazelle* actually carried out any such expeditions as Stephens promptly despatched it to W G Bagnall at Stafford for rebuilding as an 0-4-2WT, the driving wheels being replaced by new wheels to the same dimensions as the leading wheels to which they were then coupled. *Gazelle* returned to the Shropshire & Montgomeryshire in July 1911 by which time the main line from Shrewsbury to Llanymynech had reopened.

The reopening of the branch line from Kinnerley to Criggion to passenger traffic in August 1912 brought an opportunity for *Gazelle* to play a new role. Traffic on the branch was rarely substantial and Stephens felt that *Gazelle* could provide an adequate service when loadings were particularly light. The vicar of Criggion, Reverend R Brock, thought otherwise as his letter of complaint of 23rd November 1912 to the Board of Trade shows: *"I booked today my fare by the 3.57 train from Abbey Gate station to Criggion on the Shropshire & Montgomeryshire Rly. I rode to Kinnerley junction by a properly equipped train. Proceeding to the branch to Criggion I was put with another man and two women into the back part of an engine with only a screen between us and the fire - no roof and the sparks and smuts falling over us - one spark nearly got into my eye - with danger of being blinded - my clothes too injured by the same. I wish to know whether passengers can thus be treated and deceived - for the last time I came about a fortnight ago I was conveyed in a carriage as I have hitherto been. I have had occasion to use the Rly for my wife and daughter and friends from London and of course I cannot subject them to such risk and barbarous treatment. If they cannot or will not serve proper accommodations through the journey, they should not be allowed to advertise it - there were carriages at the station (Kinnerley) and as an engine ran - a carriage could and should have been on the back."*

Stephens replied to the Board of Trade explaining the situation; *"I reply to your communication of 30th November and find that it is usual, owing to the slight traffic on the branch in question, to utilise the services of the inspection engine for the afternoon train as the occasion arises, wind screens are provided and in view of the smallness of the traffic it is considered that the action is justifiable."* The Board of Trade did not agree and replied that .... *"it is considered that a proper carriage for the conveyance of passengers should be run on the train in question."* Stephens was not to be dissuaded so easily but as a compromise *Gazelle* returned to W G Bagnall for the fitting of a cab and the enclosing of the passenger 'compartment'. Neither fitting was a thing of beauty. The cab was distinctly utilitarian with a shallow curved roof and bereft of all ornamentation apart from a pair of round spectacle glasses at the front and a spindly whistle protruding from the roof. The passenger cabin had all the welcome appearance of a portable prison cell. It too was fitted with round spectacle glasses at the front and two small square windows at the rear. The original waist high rear doorway (entrance and exit via the trackbed) was retained but the rest of the doorway remained open to the elements - very bracing when running backwards. Baggage could be carried on the roof which was surrounded by an incongruously ornamental set of luggage rails. None of this did anything for *Gazelle's* appearance since the passenger cabin was a foot or more lower than the driver's cab and the roof was curved at a much sharper radius.

There appear to have been no more letters of complaint from the vicar and it may well be that *Gazelle* was only pressed into passenger service when absolutely necessary. In 1915 or 1916 a more acceptable solution to the problem of lightly loaded passenger services on the Criggion Branch was found in the purchase and adaptation of a horse tram. This is reputed to have come from the LCC and was originally a doubledeck vehicle. The top deck, stairs and end platforms were removed and running gear was provided for operation on railway track. In this form it made an ideal light trailer for *Gazelle* which is unlikely to have been capable of hauling a conventional carriage. Although the tramcar was fitted with brakes these were operated by means of large handwheels protruding from either end of the tramcar body and it is likely that these were only used to keep the vehicle from running away when parked on its own. Entrance was by means of end doors and steps were provided between the buffers to assist access from the trackbed.

The idea of using a tramcar in this way was almost certainly borrowed from the narrow gauge Torrington & Marland Railway which had adapted two such cars in 1909. Stephens travelled on this line in August 1909 in connection with his application for the North Devon & Cornwall Junction Light Railway Order in November of that year.

Gazelle and the tramcar continued to operate the Criggion Branch passenger service until the late 1920s. By October 1928 a service was only operated on Saturdays and by October 1932 this was only running as far as Melverley because of subsidence to the piers of Melverley viaduct. By now *Gazelle* and the tramcar were out of use and it is likely that services were provided by the line's Ford petrol railmotor set between trips on the 'main line'. By May 1932 *Gazelle* had been partially stripped down in Kinnerley yard but it was unclear to visitors whether it was ever to be put together again. In 1936 W H Austen decided, to reinstate it as an inspection engine. A complete overhaul then took place and in June 1937 it emerged from the Kinnerley repair shop in olive green paintwork complete with polished dome and nameplates. To accompany it, the old Selsey Wolseley Siddeley railmotor body was fitted to the underframe previously used by the tramcar to form a new inspection saloon. *Gazelle* thus survived to serve the armed forces when they took over the Shropshire & Montgomeryshire in 1941. Painted light green with black framing and red motion *Gazelle* was particularly useful for running early morning patrols along the line to confirm that points were correctly set and to detect possible acts of sabotage. This role was eventually taken over by one of the Army's Wickham petrol trolleys and *Gazelle* was taken out of service in 1945.

While *Gazelle* was stored at Kinnerley, one of the Dean Goods locomotives ran into it and damaged the cab but otherwise the Army seemed to have taken care of what had become something of a mascot for their operations here. In May 1950 the remaining Shropshire & Montgomeryshire rolling stock was transferred to the Western Region of British Railways. Nearly everything was immediately condemned but *Gazelle* was saved from the cutter's torch and placed on permanent loan to the War Department. In June 1950 *Gazelle* was despatched to the Longmoor Military Railway where a thorough cosmetic restoration was carried out before being placed on display by the parade ground. After closure of the Longmoor Military railway in 1970, *Gazelle* was displayed at the National Railway Museum in York before going on to the Museum of Army Transport at Beverley.

With the closure of the last-named in 1997, *Gazelle* was able to snap up the last remaining square feet of display space in the Colonel Stephens Railway Museum at Tenterden on the K&ESR. Little trace remains of its passenger compartment and the elements have obviously taken their toll over the years but *Gazelle* is substantially intact and quite obviously a locomotive that has worked for its living despite its miniature size - it really has to be seen to be believed.

18.1   *Gazelle is seen on the S&MR in September 1921 attached to a former LCC horse tramcar. On the left of the loco is the passenger compartment, access to which could be between the buffers.*

Chapter 19

W H Austen - In the Shadow of the Colonel

by Philip Shaw (1994)

Colonel Stephens is well known to many readers and there have been numerous articles written about him, and his railways. This has been possible because knowledge has been enlarged considerably by the collection of papers and artefacts from the Salford Terrace offices amassed by his assistant and successor, William Henry Austen, and fortunately retained by Austen's son - William Holman Austen - until comparatively recent times when the material was placed in the archives of the Kent & East Sussex Railway.

Overshadowed by the charisma of the mighty Colonel, little has been written about Austen himself. When he succeeded to the top job in 1931, Austen was, by all accounts, a hard working and versatile manager, but he undoubtedly lacked the pragmatism and innovation of Stephens and never attracted the awe and affection of his staff for which the Colonel is remembered. Stephens' relationship with Austen was certainly one of mutual respect, paternalistic, perhaps bordering on friendship; gifts were exchanged between the two men and Stephens acted as Godfather to Austen's only son who also bore his name. But Stephens never socialised with Austen in the way that he did with, say, Gilbert Szlumper of the Southern Railway and other influential members of his London clubs, probably because of Austen's humble origins. Communications between the two men were more akin to master and servant over a period of forty years, evidenced by surviving correspondence. In connection with a visit to his parents at their riverside home in Hammersmith in August 1895, Stephens wrote, with reference to Austen, "Can you let my man have the servant's room?", and on Boat Race day in March 1897, "May I bring my man with me? He has never seen the race and would appreciate it I think." However, by the 1920s attitudes had softened and Stephens wrote. "Dear W H A" in memos, when Austen was away on site visits. Both Stephens and Austen amassed superb pass collections issued to them by the pre-grouping railway companies, but whereas Colonel Stephens was always issued with first class passes, "Inspector" or Mr Austen usually had to be content with third class travel. Austen did, however, receive some first class passes from the minor railway companies in the 1930s and a first class "All stations" pass for British Railways in 1948.

Stephens did not have a hierarchy of titles at Salford Terrace, the business was much too personal for that, but he referred to Austen verbally as his "outdoor assistant". In practice, this meant acting as resident engineer in the days of building new lines and general trouble-shooter in the latter years of management by memo and make do and mend, although it was usually Stephens who signed the memos. Stephens' "indoor assistant" was Arthur Iggulden, who joined the Salford Terrace staff straight from school in 1914. He proved to have a shrewd financial brain and remarkably retentive memory, and in due course was given responsibility for accounts, secretarial and audit matters. Iggulden also had the foresight to preserve a number of documents of immense historical value - notably the Stephens' family correspondence, which is now in the railway archive.

After Stephens' untimely death in 1931, without any nominated successor, it was Austen who obtained control and even purchased the Salford Terrace premises personally in order in ensure continuity. Iggulden stayed, but there was no love lost between the two men. Stephens had no surviving family and in his will his fortune was shared equally between Austen, Iggulden and two other Salford Terrace employees, George and Fred Willard.

Against the background of the mounting recession in the early 1930s, Austen dropped all ideas of expansion. This was in stark contrast to the late 1920s, when Stephens was still forging ahead with plans for new lines; these included extensions to the East Kent in furtherance of the development of Richborough as a major commercial port; also a completely new electric light railway, the Southern Heights, designed to serve new suburban housing estates then under development near Croydon. Neither of these schemes came to anything, and after Stephens' protracted illnesses, culminating in his death, Austen finally bowed to the inevitable and abandoned them.

The offices finally closed on 7th June 1948, after the Kent & East Sussex, the East Kent and the Shropshire & Montgomeryshire railways were nationalised and much of the general consultancy practice lost. Austen, then aged 70, retired; his son, who had also worked at Salford Terrace for over 15 years, had made little impact there; other senior members of the staff were also approaching the end of their working days and although some of them went on to pastures new in the nationalised system, it was the end of an era for light railways and Austen knew just that.

William Henry Austen was born at Snodland in Kent on 8th May 1878. The eldest of five children, his father (also William Henry) was a labourer at the nearby Aylesford Paper Mill. The family was poor and with so many mouths to feed, young William was sent to live at Cranbrook with his grandmother, Sarah, of whom he was very fond. Sarah had been married to Thomas Austen, a Master at Cranbrook School, and after his death in 1884, took in lodgers at her home, 29 High Street.

When William left school in 1891 at the age of 13, he was given an apprenticeship with Messrs Joseph T Firbank, the London railway contractors, who were then engaged on the construction of the Cranbrook & Paddock Wood Railway. It is almost certain that whilst engaged on this project he first came in contact with Stephens, who at the age of 22 and having completed his apprenticeship at the work shops of the Metropolitan Railway at Neasden, was working on the Cranbrook line as Resident Engineer under the overall supervision of consultant engineer to the project, E P Seaton, and lodging in the hamlet of Hartley. The line opened to Hope Mill (Goudhurst) in October 1892 and to Hawkhurst the following year.

By 1894, work with the contractors had come to an end, including the customary one year maintenance period after the opening of the line, and Stephens was looking for pastures new and for an assistant for his future consulting practice. After undertaking a small project for the Cranbrook Waterworks Company, Stephens then obtained a brief to design and supervise the construction of the Rye & Camber Tramway - a diminutive line which was built and equipped entirely for the sum of around £2000. Austen joined him, where he was "put in charge of the locomotive workshops" and to all intents and purposes was employed by Stephens as his assistant from this time although he never achieved any formal qualifications. The two moved on to the Selsey Tramway project in 1897 and then to Stephens' first major scheme, the Rother Valley Railway in 1898. During this time Austen, probably continued to live with his grandmother until her death in 1896. Stephens, who was by then lodging in Priory Road, Tonbridge, opened the famous light railway offices at 23 Salford Terrace in 1900, and Austen, who married in the same year, moved to 13 Douglas Road - conveniently near by. Austen and his wife Fanny had two children, William Holman ("Holly") born in 1902 and a daughter Ena.

During the next 30 years Austen assisted Stephens with all his schemes, being involved with general drawing office work, parliamentary plans, as well as the more practical aspects of railway construction and management. When Fanny died in 1922, her sister and her husband, Vincent Beretta, moved from Brighton to Douglas Road, where they set up a joint household with the Austens, moving later to a larger house in the same road.

Holly, who had been educated at the Judd School in Tonbridge and the Crystal Palace School of Engineering, where he failed to score academically, went to work for the Southern Railway in 1924. He was dismissed in 1929 and after three years of unemployment, his father gave him a job as his assistant at Salford Terrace in 1932. By then, Stephens had died and in order to accommodate Holly, Austen was obliged to dismiss James Ashworth, the senior draughtsman, a move which caused a great deal of resentment amongst the other staff, coming so soon after Stephens' death. Despite being a practical and in many ways a talented man, Holly did not respond well to discipline and never fulfilled the high hopes of his father. but he remained at Salford Terrace until the office closed in 1948. Holly married in 1936, but the couple were childless and the Austen dynasty was destined to come to an end with his death in 1981.

The year 1930 was a watershed in the history of the Stephens' lines. Stephens, who had enjoyed excellent health for all of his working life, suffered a stroke at the end of January. At first, he continued to attend the light railway offices, despite a pronounced limp, some paralysis and impairment of speech. The staff closed ranks and for a while little seemed to change; the prolific flow of memos to the men in the field with instructions and complaints continued, but with Stephens' signature in the form of a rubber stamp and a "per pro" squiggle underneath. Anyone who wished to speak to the Great Man was told that he was not well enough to be consulted.

Stephens' last attendance at a Kent & East Sussex Board meeting was on 7th May 1930; on 7th November Austen was appointed acting Manager, Engineer and Locomotive Superintendent. Likewise, on the East Kent, Stephens' last attendance was on 16th January 1930 and after that date Austen attended Board meetings as acting Assistant General Manager. On the Shropshire & Montgomeryshire, James Ramsey, who had been a Director since 1929, was elected temporary Managing Director in October 1930, based at Shrewsbury, but much of the office administration continued from Tonbridge.

Stephens' condition continued to deteriorate and early in 1931 he spent several weeks in a London nursing home, after which he went to convalesce at The Castle Hotel, Hastings. There he was visited frequently by members of the staff including Austen, who was sometimes accompanied by his nephew, little Peter Beretta.

Meanwhile, the tensions in the office continued to rise. At the suggestion of Sir Percival Horton-Smith Hartley MD, Stephens' physician, Iggulden obtained Power of Attorney on 17th January 1931 to deal with his personal affairs, a move which infuriated Austen who saw it as an attempt to obtain control. Two days later, Stephens' will was drawn up at a meeting where he could only signify his intentions by a nod or shake of the head. The document was initialled H F S in a shaky hand, leaving his estate in four equal parts to Austen, Iggulden and two other members of the staff, Alfred and George Willard - there being no surviving relatives.

Stephens died at the Lord Warden Hotel, Dover, on Friday 23rd October 1931 - by then he had become almost completely incapacitated. Austen was beset with grief and physically cried for days afterwards - things would never be the same again at Salford Terrace.

After Stephens' death, Austen moved to ensure the continuity of the railways, notably by purchasing number 23 Salford Terrace and giving the existing tenants the right to occupy the premises indefinitely. His key operational appointment was as Managing Director of the Kent & East Sussex Light Railway Company in November 1931, becoming Receiver and Manager on 22nd April 1932, at the behest of the Southern Railway, the principal debenture holder. He became General Manager of the East Kent on 21 January 1932. Both he and Iggulden were appointed Directors of the Shropshire Railways Company on 24 May 1932 and in October of that year Austen was appointed to the Board of the Shropshire & Montgomeryshire Light Railway Company. Both the Weston Clevedon & Portishead and the West Sussex lines were already in receivership and Austen was appointed General Manager & Engineer for the former and Engineer & Locomotive Superintendent of the latter.

He also became Consultant Engineer to the Ashover and Rye & Camber lines, in succession to Stephens, and a Director of the North Devon & Cornwall junction - a nominally independent line for which he had been Resident Engineer during the construction period, but worked by the Southern Railway since its inception in 1925. Austen was also a Director of a curious outpost of the empire, the Snailbeach District Railways, which Stephens had acquired in 1923, although the day to day management was under the control of James Ramsey, from the nearby Shropshire & Montgomeryshire.

Austen's involvement with the Festiniog and Welsh Highland Railways was no less stormy than that experienced by his predecessor. Stephens had been Chairman and Managing Director since 1925 and his bombastic style of management was not popular with the Celtic workforce. On Stephens death, Austen became Engineer and Locomotive Superintendent, but he was not offered a Board appointment and the Tonbridge influence gradually diminished. In September 1936, the Festiniog Chairman, Evan R Davies, wrote to Austen indicating that the Company had decided to reduce permanent way staff and dispense with the services of a boilermaker. To Stephens, this might have been music to the ears, but for Austen it was the last straw and he tendered his resignation. His final words were "My 40 odd years of railway experience does not either appear to be appreciated or considered, as long as the wheels turn today that is all that matters, no consideration for tomorrow".

Following nationalisation in 1948, Austen, then aged 70, was retained for two years as an advisor to the Southern Region of the Railway Executive. In early 1950, he made a nostalgic last trip on the Kent & East Sussex and said goodbye to all those who knew him. In his retirement, he had time for foreign travel notably to South Africa and Rhodesia, and also to indulge in his main hobbies of fishing and shooting - dividing his time equally between Dornoch in Scotland where he had a house and Tonbridge. He remarried in 1936 and he and his new wife Elizabeth and his daughter Ena moved from Douglas Road to a new house, number 26 Deakin Lees. There were no children of the second marriage. His son, Holly, married in 1936 and continued to work at Salford Terrace until closure, with the exception of a 6-month period in 1936 when he went to Llanberis as assistant to the Manager of the Snowdon Mountain Railway. Holly worked as an Engineer with Tonbridge Rural District Council until his retirement.

Austen died at home on 26th February 1956 in his 78th year. Looking back on his career, he certainly provided the continuity that was needed following Stephens' death, a task which he did more than adequately, despite having no formal qualifications and a very elementary education. The question of the longer term succession never really arose in Austen's mind as he had long maintained that the days of independent railways were over and that nationalisation would follow after the War.

Unlike Stephens, Austen had to contend with a growing interest in light railways from railway enthusiasts, which he found difficult to understand, but he usually co-operated with those who made written requests for visits

Austen's legacy is the huge amount of archive material that he put away, mainly for sentimental reasons rather than realising its value to future generations. This was passed on to Holly and is now in the Colonel Stephens Railway Museum, so that today's historians may know what it was like to build and run light railways in years gone by.

19.1   W.H.Austen was probably photographed in 1900 at the time of his wedding.

19.2   W.H.Austen is on the left of Camber in this photograph taken shortly after the opening of the Rye & Camber Tramway in 1895.

19.3   W.H.Austen was a key figure at Salford Terrace and was photographed towards the end of his career.

Chapter 20

Holman Stephens -The Military Man

by John Miller (1994)

The name of Colonel Stephens is widely known as the engineer and first general manager of the K&ESR and much has been written about his involvement with this and a number of other railways. However, surprisingly little has been published concerning his military career. Stephens was never a full-time Army officer, but a member of the "volunteer" forces (later the Territorial Force), and so was able to continue his railway work in parallel with his military duties.

The young Holman Stephens first showed an interest in the military whilst a schoolboy. Writing to his father from France in 1883 he demonstrated a keen eye for detail when commenting on the local French infantry (see letters to Dah and Mam in Chapter 2). When he returned to his studies at University College School, London, Stephens became secretary of his school cadet company. In 1888, at the age of 20, he was at summer camp at Aldershot when he wrote to his father, "I was on duty last night as Corporal of Piquet and nearly caught a tramp who was trying to sleep in an empty tent ... excuse my bad writing as this is written in a tent on a kit-bag."

Stephens continued his military interests whilst training with the Metropolitan Railway and during his first real job as resident engineer for the construction of the Cranbrook & Paddock Wood Railway. We know this because in 1915, he was recorded as having served for 28 years, ie from 1887, however, we have no record of his assignments, ranks or base up to 1896.

Stephens' first commission, as a second-lieutenant with the 1st Sussex (Volunteer) Royal Engineers based at 40 Junction Road, Eastbourne, is dated 2nd May 1896. The following year, on 8th December 1897, he was promoted to Lieutenant and on 3rd December 1898 to Captain, still at Eastbourne. He was by now 30 years of age.

During the Boer War (1899-1902), Stephens recruited 600 men to serve with the Royal Engineers in South Africa, and it is in the role of recruiting officer that he seems to have had particular success.

Although previously promoted to captain with the 1st Sussex (Volunteer) RE, Stephens received a fresh commission as a captain on 8 February 1905, this time with the 2nd Cinque Ports, Royal Garrison Artillery (Volunteers) also based at Junction Road, Eastbourne. He was to retain this post until 1 February 1907.

On 1 April 1908, the old volunteer companies (which had acted as a sort of citizens' militia since the Napoleonic invasion threats of the early nineteenth century), were superseded by the Territorial Force, forerunner of the Territorial Army. The Royal Engineers (Volunteers) were reformed into the Kent (Fortress) Royal Engineers with five companies, although at first these existed on paper only. Stephens was appointed Commanding Officer with the rank of major (not gazetted as a substantive rank until 29 May 1911) and by November 1908 had moved his headquarters to the Drill Hall, Chatham. He was given a regular officer, Captain V Thompson, as his Adjutant. The first task was to convert the "paper" companies into operational units. The companies were based on towns throughout Kent as follows:

Tonbridge	lst Kent (Fortress) Works Company
Ashford	2nd Kent (Fortress) Works Company
Southborough	3rd Kent (Fortress) Works Company
Gillingham	4th Electric Light Company
Gravesend	5th Electric Light Company

There was also a separate Sussex (Fortress) Works Company based at Seaford.

On 29 January 1913, Stephens was given command of the Cadet Battalion of the Kent (Fortress) RE, again with the rank of major and in addition to his other duties.

It should be remembered that throughout this time, Stephens was also running his railway empire from the Tonbridge offices. It is said he officially attended his Army duties once every fortnight though it may well have been more often. At some time before the First World War, Stephens' headquarters were moved to Pier Road, Gillingham, and at about the same time, though not a driver himself, he bought a 1912 Brasier car, for which he had an Army driver. On Saturday 2nd October 1915, the car was being driven to a garage in London by two sappers, when it was involved in a collision with a taxi-cab in Piccadilly. Sapper W Brown, Stephens' driver, who lived at Robertsbridge was unhurt, but the passenger was thrown out and needed stitches for a head injury. Although the Brasier was described as "smashed up", it was repaired and in later years was stored in the railway stables at Tenterden until at least the late 1930s. Its ultimate fate is unknown.

Following a fortnight's exercise at Chattenden Camp near Chatham in July 1914, the companies returned home. But on 4 August, war with Germany was declared and the sappers were recalled back into uniform. Initially, the five Territorial Kent (Fortress) RE companies were employed manning the defences of the Thames and Medway estuaries - the "electric light" companies were in fact responsible for search-lights. Early in 1915, the companies were mobilised into operational Field Companies, their training completed, and plans were drawn up for the companies to proceed overseas, some to the Western Front in France, others to Gallipoli fighting the Turks in the Eastern Mediterranean. Stephens remained at Chatham recruiting 2nd and 3rd line companies as replacements for the Field units.

In September 1915, Stephens featured on the front cover of a magazine *"The Review"*, which had the sub-title *"The Organ (Unofficial) of the Kent Engineers - Works, Field and Lights Companies"*. The editorial stated that Stephens "has worked tirelessly for the good of the men, both in times of peace and war", and "he has accepted the Presidency of the Committee formed for providing comforts for the men sent Overseas". The hope was expressed that the magazine would benefit recruitment and "good fellowship". A later issue records that Stephens presented a football cup, described as a "magnificent trophy", to be played for by the various Kent RE units. It was known as the "Colonel Stephens Cup". When informed that a draw for the cup was to be arranged shortly, Stephens, deliberately misunderstanding, replied, "You're not going to play for it after all then - you're going to raffle it!" Recent attempts to trace the whereabouts of the cup have been unsuccessful. Publication of the *"The Review"* continued until at least 1917.

In October 1915, disaster struck the lst/3rd Kent Field Companies RE based on Tonbridge and Southborough. They left their depot at Gillingham on 11 October 1915, and sailed the following day from Devonport in the troopship *"Scotian"* for Gallipoli. In the Mediterranean, the troops transferred to a small ex-South Eastern & Chatham Railway ferry requisitioned as

HMS *"Hythe"* and normally used as an auxiliary minesweeper. On the night of 28th October, the *"Hythe"* was rammed by a much larger ex-ferry, HMS. *"Sarnia"* and within minutes the *"Hythe"* sank. In the darkness, one officer and 128 men were drowned. The proceedings of the subsequent Court of Enquiry have never been published.

The officer was Captain David Salomons, only son of and heir to Sir David Salomons, Bart, of Broomhill, Southborough. Holman Stephens knew Sir David for two reasons: Sir David had been the Honorary Colonel of the Kent (Fortress) Royal Engineers since its formation in 1908, but he had also been a director of the South Eastern Railway and SE&CR since 1895 and he later largely influenced the policy of suburban electrification on the Southern Railway.

Stephens had played a leading role in the recruitment of the men lost in the *"Hythe"* disaster and in his grief, Sir David (or so it is said), irrationally placed the responsibility on Stephens for the loss of his son. It is said that the two men never spoke socially to each other thereafter.

There is conflicting evidence as to when Stephens was promoted to the rank of Lieutenant-Colonel. Harry Furniss, the cartoonist, addressed him as Major Stephens in a letter of January 1915 but *"The Review"* in September refers to Lt. Colonel Stephens. Other Royal Engineers' records give 4 January 1916 as the date of his promotion while in 1976, the Army Records Centre reported that he was gazetted as Lt. Colonel on 26th August 1921. Whatever the truth, he had certainly been known as Colonel Stephens since 1915.

Increasingly, Stephens gave more time to his Army duties as the War became bogged down and losses of men mounted. The loyal staff at Salford Terrace, Tonbridge, had to shoulder the burden of running the railways with very limited contact with him. In fact, he was only available for railway duties from Saturday mornings, returning on Monday afternoons to Gillingham. Even so, the War Office put pressure on Stephens to give his attention full-time to the war effort and eventually issued an ultimatum to him: become full-time or retire. The conflict of interest was too great and Stephens decided to return to his railway interests. On 1 April 1916, he was transferred to the Territorial Force Reserve with the rank of Lt. Colonel. In March 1917, he was Mentioned in Dispatches for his sterling services. During the first years of the War he had recruited 220 officers and 2,400 men for service with the Kent (Fortress) Royal Engineers.

Although most of the Stephens' railways had seen increased traffic during the First World War and income was reasonably healthy, the staff at Salford Terrace no doubt viewed with some relief his return full-time to the business of running and promoting railways. To celebrate his return and to thank his employees at Tonbridge, Stephens organised a staff dinner at the Criterion Restaurant, London, on 4th February 1916.

Stephens' batman during the Great War had been Lance-Corporal Albert Osborne of Coronation Villas, Church Street, Robertsbridge. He followed Stephens into civilian life and was given a job, firstly as crossing keeper at Northbridge Street and later as an assistant in the Salford Terrace drawing office. Stephens enjoyed a reputation for looking after his men and all the reminiscences of those who served under him show that he was well liked and regarded as a gentleman officer of the "old school". In fact, Mr Pardoe, on the staff of the Shropshire & Montgomeryshire, recalled in an interview in 1958 that Stephens had sent him food parcels whilst he was on active service in France.

However, Stephens' Army life was not over - he merely returned to the role of a Reserve officer and soon had a new command. In April 1916, a local newspaper reported, "The new Weald of Kent Battalion of the Kent Fencibles is to be placed under the command of Major H F Stephens of Tonbridge, who commanded the Kent (Fortress) Royal Engineers, and was responsible for the smartness and numerical strength of that unit, both before and after mobilisation. Now that the VTCs are to be recognised as a fighting body by the War Office, considerable impetus will be given to the movement, and Major Stephens possesses all the qualities for making it go. The battalion will include companies or platoons from Ashford, Tenterden, Headcorn, Staplehurst, Marden, Goudhurst and Hawkhurst."

Quite what the "Fencibles" did has yet to be researched, and it is assumed that VTCs were "volunteer territorial companies", but Stephens evidently held this command for the next five years or so. The reference to "Major" Stephens is interesting. Although the RE records indicate Stephens returned to the reserve list with the rank of Lt. Colonel, it is assumed that this was an acting or temporary rank and that his substantive rank remained that of major until he was gazetted as Lt. Colonel in 1921.

In 1916, an uprising began in Ireland against British rule and many members of the Royal Irish Constabulary were killed in the subsequent fighting. Quite what connection Stephens had with Ireland is unclear, but he organised a fund to support the widows and orphans of the police. At the time of his death, this was described as "perhaps his greatest deed", though it is not known how the funds were raised.

By 1921, it appears the War Office required a technical officer as Commanding Officer of the Sussex (Fortress) RE Territorials based at Seaford and Stephens was appointed to yet another command.

Regimental Sergeant Major Jacomb was the permanent staff instructor at Seaford, and when interviewed in 1976, remembered Stephens as a rather eccentric and independent old style officer and a gentleman. Stephens would send a telegram asking to be met with a car at the local railway station - but he would refuse to take parade. Instead, he would watch through field-glasses from his hotel bedroom window as a junior officer took parade. He was very generous to his men, buying them drinks, and RSM Jacomb recalled Stephens cancelling weekend camp at very short notice and personally paying for all the wasted food rations and other provisions.

Stephens' time at Seaford was short-lived. There was a re-organisation of the Territorial Force Royal Engineers and in 1923, the Sussex (Fortress) company was disbanded and the establishment transferred to the Cinque Ports (Fortress) RE based at Dover. RSM Jacomb was transferred as permanent staff instructor at Dover, alongside Stephens as the new Commanding Officer.

At Dover, on his fortnightly visits, Stephens stayed at the Lord Warden Hotel where he was to die in 1931. His eccentric ways continued. Sergeant Carpenter had been a boy bugler serving with Stephens at Gillingham in 1916 and in 1923 was posted to Dover. Interviewed, again in 1976, he also remembered Stephens as a very generous man, paying for things for the men out of his own pocket. Stephens confided in Carpenter that he did so because he regarded the Army as his sole hobby. Stephens decided to form a string, pipe and brass band and bought all the instruments personally. (Later, when Stephens' lodgings in Tonbridge were being emptied following his death, one room was found to be full of musical instruments.) Stephens also supplied a rowing boat for the men's use around Dover harbour.

It has been impossible to establish the precise date at which Stephens gave up an active role in the Territorial Force Reserve, but it was probably 1924 or 1925. By that time, his existing railways were under increasing financial pressure and he may have been pre-occupied with new schemes such as the North Devon & Cornwall Junction Light, Ashover and Southern Heights. Stephens died on 23rd October 1931 and at his funeral service at Hammersmith on 31 October 1931, his fellow officers were well represented, including Lt. Col. A Ruston, Major A Cooksey, Capt C J Holcombe, and Capt C H Igglesden who had commanded the 2nd (Ashford) RE Works Company during the Great War - all original officers in the Kent (Fortress) Royal Engineers. A wreath was laid on behalf of the officers and men of the Fortress Companies. By a strange coincidence, Stephens was buried on his birthday. He would have been 63.

20.1 Second-Lieutenant Stephens is left in this 1896 photograph, whilst in the 1st Sussex (Volunteer) Royal Engineers.

20.2 Captain H.F.Stephens is second from the left in this picture from about 1907. He is with other members of the Sussex (Volunteers) RE at Eastbourne.

20.3 Lt-Col H.F.Stephens was photographed, probably for the last time, in uniform, in 1923.

Chapter 21

Colonel Stephens at Portmadoc

by Philip Shaw (1981)

In common with many other minor railways, the Festiniog emerged from the period of the Great War and government control in low ebb. Services had been curtailed due to coal shortages and much of the works had been given over to munitions between 1915 and 1918. By 1920, the rails were badly worn, sleepers defective and ballast poor; locomotive maintenance had been sorely neglected. Slate and goods traffic still accounted for over 54% of total receipts, but annual slate tonnage had declined from 83,000 in 1913 to 53,000. Nevertheless, operating inefficiencies were such that the amount of shunting required to deal with the lower level of business had increased by no less than 44%! Passenger numbers had dropped by 10% over the same period.

It was against this background of acute financial difficulty that in 1921 proposals were put forward by the North Wales Power and Electric Traction Company, led by its Managing Director, Henry Jack, for amalgamating the powers of the North Wales Narrow Gauge Railway and the adjacent Portmadoc, Beddgelert & South Snowdon Railway and transferring them to a new company, the Welsh Highland Railway and entering into a working agreement with the Festiniog. The Traction Company had owned the two first named lines since before the war and amalgamation had been suggested at an earlier date, but its recent acquisition of a controlling interest in the Festiniog had added a new dimension to the proposals.

The necessary light railway order was obtained on 30th March 1922 and McAlpine, the contractor, started work on building the link sections and reconstruction work that would bring the Welsh Highland into being. Finally, on 30th January 1923, the Festiniog obtained powers to make a connecting line to the Welsh Highland at Portmadoc and to work its existing line as a light railway. This was formally opened on 2nd June 1923 with a through train from Blaenau Festiniog to Dinas, a distance of some 36 miles.

It was at this point that Stephens arrived on the Festiniog scene. The exact nature of his introduction does not appear to have been recorded, but he had been active in the formation of Associated Railways - a body formed to further the interests of all minor lines in the immediate post war period. New management was needed to ensure that the enterprise got off the ground and on 1 April 1923, H F Stephens was appointed civil engineer and locomotive superintendent of both lines, operating from his offices at Tonbridge, whilst the secretariat and most of the senior general administration was transferred from Portmadoc to Jack's own offices at Dolgarrog. The existing General Manager, S C Tyrwhitt, remained at Portmadoc until September when he was due to retire anyway.

In addition to Tyrwhitt, management staff at Portmadoc included Robert Williams, the former Festiniog Locomotive Superintendent, who stayed on in a junior capacity; Robert Evans, general factotum cum accountant, who had joined the company as a booking clerk as far back as 1894 and H Nevitt, who reported on engineering matters on a part time basis, visiting the line about twice a week. Stephens had little regard for either Williams or Evans but of necessity most of the day to day correspondence was conducted through the latter, liaison with Dolgarrog being confined to important matters.

Despite tackling the job with his usual energy and enthusiasm, Stephens ran into difficulties from the start. Not being a director of either company, he lacked the authority to take policy decisions on matters which he considered necessary to ensure the viability of the undertaking; furthermore traffic did not develop as had been hoped.

When Tyrwhitt retired, he was replaced, on a temporary basis by John May, who was given the new title of Traffic Superintendent. After consultation with Jack, Stephens put forward a number of proposals for reducing costs such as abolishing porters and changes in signalling.

However, May was critical of some of the suggestions made and made it clear that he was unwilling to implement them. In the event, he left on 31 August 1924 to become Manager of the Ashover Light Railway, which was due to open at that time; it was probably coincidental that this line had also been engineered by Stephens. In May 1924, E H R Nicholls (an ex GWR man) joined the company as Managing Director, based at Portmadoc; probably with some degree of relief, Stephens gave three months notice of his intention to resign as engineer. Writing to Nicholls immediately after his appointment, Stephens commented "after 14 months experience, my great trouble is to get Williams out of the groove he has got into and to start anything fresh. Of course you will realise I have not had a free hand in these matters or in fact any matter, no doubt for very good reasons, bearing in mind the financial position of the Company". Nicholls, however, made very little impact at Portmadoc, despite being given full executive responsibility. It seems that the appointment was in a part-time capacity as he still remained an employee of the Great Western.

A Board minute of 5th September 1924 confirmed that "all officers of the company are under the control of and directly responsible to the Managing Director with powers of appointment and dismissal". Nicholls resigned and disappeared suddenly at the end of 1924 - in February 1925 Stephens was still unable to make contact with him. A further complication was that Jack had offered his resignation at the Festiniog AGM in the previous April to take effect from November 1924, following shareholder criticism which, in effect, blamed him for the poor trading of the combined ventures.

The way was now open for Stephens to assume full executive control; he joined the Festiniog board on 20th November 1924 and was appointed Chairman & Managing Director of both companies with effect from 1 January 1925, at a salary of £400 per annum. He immediately set about implementing the cost cutting measures, including reducing station staff, which he had advocated earlier.

Stephens was not as popular with the staff at Portmadoc as he was with the shareholders; his military style of management involved making flying visits from Kent (or sending his assistant W H Austen) followed up by long lists of instructions, mainly to Evans, threatening dire consequences for anyone who did not comply. He had little affinity or patience with the Cymric race, "the FR people are quite different to our people" he wrote to Austen in 1926, "they can't help it, it's their nature, we have got to put up with it whilst we have the job". As year followed year, correspondence with Portmadoc, usually vitriolic, but often scintillating, became increasingly prolific. "You had better tell Morris Jones (fitter at Boston Lodge) that it is nearly time to get the Baldwin tractor to work or else send in his resignation" he wrote to Evans . . . "I confess I am tired of Morris Jones and his delays and troubles and as Nevitt seems disinclined to move and incur the men's displeasure I suppose I shall soon have to move. The book says, when a man gets very old, a man gets indecisive. I suppose we are suffering from this in direction of output."

Between 1925 and 1928 Stephens conducted a lengthy dialogue with Evans on the subject of carriage cleaning. Fortunately the letters, together with copies of Evans' replies have survived and they illustrate, if nothing else, the problems of communication over long distances, when the use of the telephone was an expensive luxury.

10.8.25 Why are the windows of the 1st class compartment allowed to be open during heavy rain; letting the windows down for air does not mean letting them down for rain to beat in ... You seem to have some perfectly stupid people to deal with or people who are not properly looked after.

Your first train for passengers purposes is 8.00am. Surely you can get a woman to come on at about 5.30 am to 6.00 am for a few days to have two hours scrubbing ... Now will you take this as a direct order to get this work done and let us have no more trouble.

26.8.26 re your letter of 25 inst, the carriage cleaning is being done by coalman T Morgan and the porter at Portmadoc. All the carriages were scrubbed out in May this year, do you wish for them to be scrubbed out again?

27.8.26 Yes, I want the carriages scrubbed out again; surely my letter of the 25th inst. stated this. "'Why give me the trouble of writing another letter.

8.8.27 Have you a woman carriage cleaner? if so what does she do?

10.8.27 We have no woman carriage cleaner on either the FR or WHR

12.8.27 Why have you no woman carriage cleaner? Can you get one? Can you use the Perfectol carriage cleaner?

15.8.27 The only time we had a woman carriage cleaner was when on your instructions the carriages were washed inside. We can use the Perfectol carriage cleaner.

(The guard remarks on his journal for 8.00am on Saturday, "passengers refusing to go into 3rd class compartments, too dirty, had to put them in 1st class)

16.8.27 Take on a woman carriage cleaner temporarily on the best terms that you can arrange.

19.8.27 I am unable to get a woman carriage cleaner ... there is a young man about here, a sailor by trade, and he is unable to get work, who I could put on to clean the carriages.

20.8.27 You had better take on the young sailor you mention on half time to start off with. You should pay him at the rate of 40/- per week so that he will draw £1 per week as he is on half time.

13.12.27 How are you off for Perfectol for carriage cleaning please?

15.12. 27 We have a supply of Perfectol. I am sorry that when this is used it takes the paint off the carriages, especially the yellow paint.

28.12.27 If the Perfectol is used properly it will not fetch the paint off. It shows you are using it too strong.

20.1.28 Letter from a Capt L Davies to Colonel Stephens "I herewith return free pass which you granted me last year and I beg to acknowledge pass for this year ... I used it once last year ... I should mention that after leaving the carriage I looked more like a sweep than a first class passenger".

The correspondence continued in similar vein for the rest of the year, with apparently no answer to the problem. There was, however, a softer side to Stephens nature, a genuine concern and respect for those employees who had worked loyally and hard. "I understand that one of the drivers is ill, very ill," he wrote to Evans. "Can you send him some fruit or soup, or something from me."

Stephens remained Chairman and Managing Director of the Festiniog until his death on 23rd October 1931 and Receiver and Manager of the Welsh Highland, to which he had been appointed in 1927. However, after February 1930 his involvement in a practical sense was minimal, following a series of strokes, which eventually completely incapacitated him. It is recorded that he did visit the line in April 1931, during a period when he made a partial recovery.

Stephens did much to try and encourage new traffic to the lines; bus services had commenced between Bleanau and Portmadoc in February 1923, but tourism was growing in the area. The "Five Valleys" circular tour was introduced in conjunction with the LMS, enabling passengers to travel over the Conway Valley line to Blaenau, thence over the Festiniog & Welsh Highland to Portmadoc and Dinas, returning to their original point of departure via the LMS, Caernarvon and Bangor. Sadly, poor timekeeping often resulted in lost connections - disastrous for such a marathon trip. Nevertheless, publicity was good, albeit perhaps a trifle eccentric. "Visit the wonderland of Wales in comfort" - said the handbills "Travel across country in safety away from the dusty and crowded roads, seeing beautiful scenery not visible from the highways on home-made steel instead of on imported rubber, by home produced coal instead of by imported oil and Support the local lines". Stephens' attitude to the technical press was less euphoric; when J F Gairns, the then Editor of the *Railway Magazine* applied to Evans for a pass "to renew my acquaintance with these lines", the matter was referred to Stephens, who replied, "I do not propose to issue passes to this gentleman ... I should discourage any time being spent showing him round . . . between ourselves the *Railway Magazine* and the *Railway Gazette* are no good whatever to the small companies. If they were daily newspapers, of course, one's attitude would be different."

On the freight side, attempts were made to revive coal traffic from Whitehaven to Portmadoc, which had existed prior to the War and Stephens was prepared to finance personally a collier, similar to the one that he had in use on the Weston Clevedon & Portishead Railway. However, the quarries, tired of delays and inefficiencies, were all trying to lessen their dependence on the railway and showed little interest. The combination of poor coal, an apathetic workforce and inadequate money to maintain the locomotives and permanent way, all combined to produce impossibly unreliable services. Experiments were tried with internal combustion engines and a Simplex petrol tractor was purchased for shunting purposes in July 1923, to be followed by others, including a Baldwin and an Austro-Daimler from the contractors of the North Devon & Cornwall Junction Light Railway. Problems with fitting continuous brakes delayed attempts to use these on passenger services on the Welsh Highland in winter, hauling a single coach.

Festiniog passenger numbers peaked at 199,304 in 1925 and thereafter went into steady decline; slate traffic held up well, until the depression of 1930, when it suffered a major drop. Stephens wrote to Evans in March 1929 on the subject of Festiniog Railway finances; "The Company takes about £14,000 per annum, which is, roughly speaking, £270 per week. The wages cheque each week comes to about £150, which leaves a balance of, say, £120 per week or £480 per month, but we never have £480 per month to pay accounts, etc. Can you offer any explanation? As a rule, when you take about double your weekly wage bill on these small lines you can get along fairly comfortably, but we are certainly far from being comfortable". Evans explanation, if there was one, has not survived.

After Stephens' death, W H Austen took over as Engineer and Locomotive Superintendent, but the influence that he exerted was considerably less than his predecessor. Evan R Davis became Chairman and Managing Director, although Evans continued as the man on the spot. In September 1936, Evans wrote to Austen indicating that the Company had decided to reduce further the permanent way staff and dispense with the services of the boilermaker. Austen considered that this was reducing maintenance to an unacceptably low level and tendered his resignation. His final words were - "My 40 odd years of railway experience does not either appear to be appreciated or considered and as long as the wheels turn round today that is all that matters, no consideration for tomorrow." It was the end of an era, but even then the links with Tonbridge were not finally severed. Arthur Iggulden continued to act as Audit Accountant from Salford Terrace until the outbreak of War.

Looking back on Stephens' period of office, it is easy to be cynical; what were his achievements? - The railways entered the 1930s in an even more precarious state than when he took over in 1923. The Welsh Highland was in receivership and traffic generally was on a downward trend. Yet the problems he faced from every angle were probably insuperable and he did provide the continuity of management that the Companies so desperately needed at the time of Jack's and Nicholls's resignations, despite being 300 miles away. What is certain, is however, that Stephens left his own highly individual work on that 150 years of history; a colourful era which did little to cement Anglo-Welsh relations, but which will never be forgotten!

21.1 Fairlie 0-4-4-0T Merddin Emrys stands at Blaenau Ffestiniog attached to one of the original four-wheeled coaches. The terminus of the GWR branch is beyond the left border of the picture.

21.2   Minffordd was the location for this photograph of Fairlie no. 8 James Spooner on 5th April 1926. It was withdrawn in 1933. (K.Nunn/LCGB)

21.3   This postcard view of Palmerston after arrival at Portmadoc Harbour was posted by Arthur Iggleden on 30th August 1935, during a visit as audit accountant.

Photo: H. G. W. Household

21.4   Seen at the same location in 1925 is the WHR's Russell, after its cab had been reduced in height in an attempt to make it fit for the FR's loading gauge.

21.5   Standing at the WHR station at Beddgelert is a FR train hauled by Little Giant. Both coaches still exist. The railways had different braking systems; the vehicle on the left is fitted with hoses for both.

21.6 A memorable feature of the FR in the 1930s was the station mistress at Tan-y-Bwlch. Mrs Bessie Jones has the single line staff in one hand and postcards in the other.

21.7 The October 1923 timetable shows the early service on the combined FR/WHR. Stephens bought some cheap Belgian coal, which made timekeeping impossible particularly in view of the poor condition of the locomotives.

DINAS JUNCTION, PORTMADOC, and BLAENAU FESTINIOG.—Welsh Highland and Festiniog.

Miles.	Week Days only.		mrn	mrn	mrn	mrn	aft	aft	aft	aft	aft
	Dinas Junction	dep.	....	....	7 22	9 50	1 5	...	5 25	8 0	....
2	**Tryfan Junction**		....	....	7 34	10 3	1 18	....	5 38	8 13	....
3¾	**Waenfawr**		....	....	7 46	10 15	1 39	....	5 50	8 25	....
4¾	**Bettws Garmon**		....	....	7A51	10A20	1A44	....	5A55	8A30	....
5¾	**Salem**		....	....	A	A	A	....	A	A	....
7¼	**Quellyn Lake**		....	....	8 8	10 37	2 1	...	6 12	8 47	....
9¼	**South Snowdon** †	arr.	....	....	8 17	10 46	2 10	...	6 22	8 57	
		dep.	....	....	8 19	10 59	2 14	....	6 42	9 2	
10¾	**Pitt's Head**		....	....	A	A	A	....	A	A	Saturdays only.
11¾	**Hafod Ruffydd**		....	....	A	A	A	....	A	A	
13¼	**Beddgelert**	arr.	....	....	8 44	11 24	2 40	....	7 7	9 30	
		dep.	....	....	8 47	12 18	3 0	....	7 10	9 38	
15¼	**Nantmor, for Aberglaslyn**		....	....	8 59	12 30	3 12	....	7 22	9 50	
16¼	**Hafod-y-Llyn**		....	....	A	A	A	....	A	A	
17¼	**Hafod Garregog**		....	....	A	A	A	....	A	A	
18¼	**Ynysfor, for Llanfrothen**		....	....	9A15	12A46	3A28	....	7A38	10A6	
19¼	**Pont Croesor, for Prenteg**		....	....	9A21	12A52	3A34	....	7A44	10A12	
21¼	**Portmadoc (New)** * **140**	arr.	....	....	9 31	1 3	3 45	....	7 55	10 23	
		dep.	5 15	8 15	11 10	2 0	4 10	6 0	....	....	9 0
24	**Minffordd 140**		5 25	8 28	11 25	2 15	4 23	6 12	....		9 15
25¼	**Penrhyndeudraeth 141**		5 31	8 33	11 30	2 21	4 29	6 18	....	Sats. only.	9 21
29¼	**Tan-y-Bwlch, for Maentwrog**		5 53	8 55	11 51	2 42	4 56	6 39	....		9 45
31¼	**Dduallt**		A	A	A	A	A	A	....		....
33¼	**Tan-y-Grisiau**		6 14	9 15	12 11	3 2	5 16	6 58	....		10 5
34¼	**Blaenau Festiniog 144, 401**	L. M. S. arr.	6 20	9 20	12 17	3 8	5 22	7 3	....		1011
		G. W. "	6 22	9 22	12 19	3 10	5 24	7 5	....		1013

Miles.	Week Days only.		mrn	mrn	aft	aft	aft	aft	aft
	Blaenau Festiniog	G. W. dep.	6 50	9 30	1236	3 30	4 25	7 10	
		L. M. S. "	6 53	9 32	1238	3 33	4 28	7 13	
1½	Tan-y-Grisiau		6 58	9 37	1243	3 38	4 33	7 18	Sats. only.
3½	Dduallt		A	....	A	A	A	A	
5½	Tan-y-Bwlch, for Maentwrog		7 18	9 54	1 3	3 57	4 54	7 39	
9½	Penrhyndeudraeth **141**		7 38	10 12	1 21	4 15	5 13	7 58	
10½	Minffordd **140**		7 45	10 19	1 29	4 24	5 20	8 6	
13½	Portmadoc (New) * **140**	arr.	7 55	10 30	1 40	4 35	5 30	8 15	
		dep.	9 35	11 25	2 10	5 15	Except Saturdays.	....	8 35
15½	Pont Croesor, for Prenteg		9A46	11A36	2A21	5A26		....	8A46
16½	Ynysfor, for Llanfrothen		9A52	11A42	2A27	5A32		....	8A52
17½	Hafod Garregog		A	A	A	A		....	A
18½	Hafod-y-Llyn		A	A	A	A		....	A
19¾	Nantmor, for Aberglaslyn		10 8	11 58	2 43	5 48		....	9 8
21½	**Beddgelert**	arr.	10 20	12 10	2 55	6 0		....	9 20
		dep.	10 24	12 25	3 5	6 5		....	9 39
23½	Hafod Ruffydd		A	A	A	A		....	A
24½	Pitt's Head		A	A	A	A		....	A
25½	**South Snowdon** †	arr.	10 54	12 55	3 35	6 35		....	10 9
		dep.	10 56	1 0	3 40	6 39	....	....	10 13
27½	Quellyn Lake		11 8	1 13	3 53	6 52	....	....	10 26
29½	Salem		A	A	A	A	....	....	A
30½	Bettws Garmon		11A19	1A26	4A6	7A3	....	....	10A39
31	Waenfawr		11 27	1 35	4 16	7 12	....	....	10 49
32½	Tryfan Junction		11 38	1 46	4 27	7 23	....	....	11 0
34½	**Dinas Junction 407**	arr.	11 47	1 55	4 36	7 32	....	....	11 10

NOTES.

A Stop when required.

* Station for Borthygest; ½ mile to the G. W. Station.

† About 3 miles to the Summit of Snowdon.

Chapter 22

Maritime Venture at WC&PR.

by Geoff Wheat (1996)

Many people have been fascinated over the years by the history of Lt.-Col. Stephens' empire, and interest is further aroused by the discovery of the book *Last of the Sailing Coasters*, by Edmund Eglinton. Therein is included one of the best descriptions of coastal barge operations in connection with Stephens working to his River Yeo Wharf at Wick St. Lawrence. Consequently much effort has been made to unearth as much as possible about this aspect of his empire and the results of that research is the subject of this chapter.

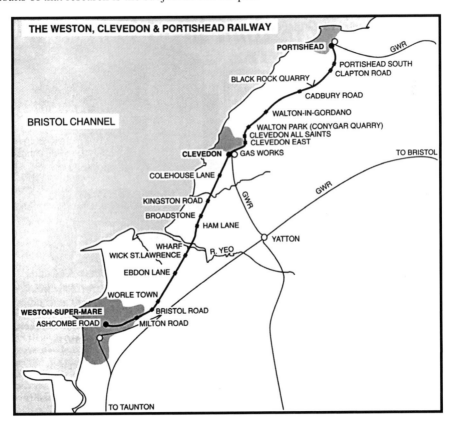

Apparently the Colonel had persuaded C E Heath of the Excess Insurance Co (principal creditor of the railway) that considerable traffic, and thus income, would be generated by the construction of a ship to rail interchange on the railway. In 1913, a spur line was built at Wick St. Lawrence from the 'main line' to the bank of the Congresbury Yeo, and the following year this, and the appropriate land, were transferred to C E Heath, to enable him to construct a wharf. The concrete wharf and the timber trestle jetty leading to it were shown on a map dated 1915, but they were not completed until after the First World War. The wharf, jetty, and the land for the siding, were leased back to the railway Company at £150 per annum.

The concrete wharf was 80ft. long, the wooden approach trestle 190ft. long. Ample concrete and timber piles protected the structure from shipping damage, and supported its weight in the estuarial mud. A mobile pile driver was used for repairs (even in 1993 six unused concrete piles about 20ft. long with iron caps lay in the undergrowth). The track on the wharf was laid on sleepers set in a continuous mound of loose concrete under each rail, rising to the outer end.

In 1919 a local boatman was engaged to clear debris from the river bed, to prepare for the expected ships, and in 1921 the first Muir-Hill Shunting Tractor was purchased for the jetty. About the same time a 10cwt steam crane was installed there, but it was not until 1922 that a suitable craft, the ketch *Sarah*, was located. This was purchased by Heath, and reconstructed with a Bergius petrol engine to assist the sails, and the coamings were raised to carry extra coal.

Apparently the *Sarah* made several journeys with coal to Ireland before bringing South Welsh coal to Yeo Wharf in about July 1924. By the second visit on 9 August 1924, word had got round and virtually the entire village watched her arrival on the tide.

Subsequent shipments were about every two or three months, from Lydney, Newport, Barry, or Penarth, and was normally locomotive coal. Occasionally the Clevedon Gas Works took a cargo, although normally their coal came via the GWR connection at Portishead. The ships involved worked to many Bristol Channel ports and beaches, and to Ireland, but the revenue was poor. It is said that on occasion barge captains loaded coal in South Wales for Wick, but returned with their cargoes when it was obvious they were not going to be paid 'up front' for their efforts.

There are no records or memories of any commodity other than coal being imported or exported over the wharf, although records for the railway describe 40 wagonloads of turf, cut from the saltings near Ham Lane Sidings, being moved. As this was for a bowling green in the Isle of Wight, it is quite possible that it left by coastal ship from the Yeo Wharf.

The railway could now incorporate in its promotional literature the words 'Seaborne Traffic Can Now be Dealt With at Wick St.Lawrence' However, the wharf was singularly unsuccessful in attracting the revenue which was its raison d'etre. By far the majority of the coal handled was for the Company's own use. The light railway only served three towns, and coal could already be taken to each place in small vessels, landing on the beach if necessary. The small coastal sailing craft industry was already dying and rarely economic. Apparently, although Col. Stephens had persuaded Heath that the purchase of *Sarah* would show a saving in coal costs after paying for the upkeep of the ship, it was subsequently shown that he had not provided for insurance. This was a great problem with small craft, and was usually brought down to an acceptable level through mutual insurance associations based on a port where every member knew and trusted each other. Heath was unable to enter into such an arrangement.

The first Muir-Hill shunter was damaged beyond repair after de-railing whilst being towed to Clevedon Works "within a year of entering service", which would make it 1925. Indeed the replacement Muir-Hill shunter, the garden shed on equal sized wheels, came in 1926. In 1927 an even smaller ship, the *Lily*, was purchased by the Colonel himself for the Yeo Wharf traffics, but was lost on 9 June 1929 at the mouth of the Usk. The crew were saved, and the report in the following day's *South Wales Argus* is so descriptive of conditions in the industry that it is worth quoting verbatim:

Boat Sinks Under Crew's Feet After 16 Hours at Pump

The small ketch Lily of Barnstaple, sank under the feet of her crew of two just outside the mouth of the River Usk on Sunday morning, after they had spent 16 hours on end at the pumps in a frantic effort to keep her afloat.

For a day and a night the Lily had been buffeted helplessly by the waves of the Channel. Waterlogged from only a short time after she left Newport on Friday evening, she was unmanageable for the whole of the time afterwards, and in her perilous drift up and down Channel at the mercy of the tide, she was carried down to Barry Roads, only just missing the Flat Holm, and back again to the lightship.

At the lightship, the Lily providentially encountered the Newport pilot cutter Nancy, and was taken in tow, but after half an hour's running she lurched, turned turtle, and sank under her exhausted crew's feet. They swam to the cutter, and were taken back to Newport.

The Lily, a 60 ton ketch (23 ton register) was owned by the Weston & Clevedon Light Railway Co, and it left the river on Friday evening carrying a cargo of about 30 tons of coal, bound for Yeo on the Somerset coast.

...but we had only gone a short way when we discovered a leak.

Very soon we had to start the pump, and then we realised that we had a very bad leak.

...we found that she was carrying so much water that she would not answer the helm, and we could not steer her.

...but then the flood tide came, and we were swept again. All the time decks were awash, and we had to keep at the pump.

...Here the strain of the night proved too much for the master, and he collapsed on the hatches.

"Then" said Mr. Hunter. (the mate), "she began suddenly to fill more quickly, and we saw that it was all over. I had just dived overboard, followed by Tom, (the master), when she shot up in the air, turned turtle, and went down to the bottom."

...thanks to the prompt action of Rev. Fogarty, a taxi was waiting to rush them to the (Seaman's) Mission. When the Rev. Fogarty took charge of the crew, he found them almost collapsed with exhaustion. Their food locker had been swamped on Saturday morning, and from then they had no food nor drink.

From 5.30 pm on Saturday till 9.30 am on Sunday... continuous turns at the draw bucket and pump the master's hands were bruised and bleeding... (at the hostel) he could not even sign his name.

The sandbanks and rocks of the Bristol Channel were a continuous problem, and Eglinton recalls, in his book, the *Lily* being aground on a new sandbank adjacent to Lydney Pier. Because of the delay to the locomotive coal, this was reported to Head Office where somebody, possibly the Colonel, wrote to the master of the ship that he had: "never heard such rubbish! Was he expected to believe that the bottom of the sea had changed a few yards from the pier and so prevented the *Lily* From entering the dock? Such excuses were unconvincing. It was bad navigation. Nothing else and you are discharged sir, discharged forthwith!!" The Clevedon Manager was as upset as the crew; he had to find a competent replacement immediately. The crew solved the problem. Relying on the fact that Head Office would not know the name of the mate, it being normal practice for the master to employ and pay his own choice of mate, the mate's name was forwarded to Head Office as the new master. Aboard ship nothing changed!

The *Sarah* herself was sold in 1931, but may well have continued to visit the wharf, as she was still a coal hulk when lost in the estuary in 1947. A regular visitor in later years was the *Edith*, although her owners had no apparent railway connection. She was the subject of a series of photographs taken at the wharf in 1937.

In 1931 the steam crane was retired to the goods siding at Wick Station, and thereafter the ship's derrick was used for discharging the coal, using a kibble or large tippable bucket.

From Eglinton's book it is possible to envisage the procedure for getting a loaded ship to the wharf. After loading on the Welsh Coast, the ship would sail to Woodspring Bay on a falling tide, and anchor in the shelter of St. Thomas' Head. On the arrival of flood tide, the ship would creep to the mouth of the Yeo and sail gently up, if there was any wind, or drop stern-first up the river with the current, if there was none. The anchor would hang over the bows as a brake in the latter case, and there would be plenty of time for the craft to nudge up until there was sufficient water to moor alongside the wharf. As the tide ebbed, the ship would sit on the mud. On the first trip, the Bergius engine was used to motor up to the wharf, but it was rarely used after that, and was eventually described as being rusted up.

Train drivers would be looking out for the arrival, as they crossed the adjacent bridge over the Yeo, and would report the news at Weston or Clevedon. Empty wagons would be taken to Wick St. Lawrence, and propelled onto the jetty four at a time by the Muir-Hill shunter. Weight restrictions prevented any steam locomotive, or more than four wagons, from passing onto the jetty. Even on the siding leading to the jetty, a timber bridge over a rhyne collapsed in 1934 under the locomotive *Hesperus*, leading to reports of "The Wreck of the Hesperus!" The wagons would be loaded from a bucket filled in the ship's hold by shovelling, and hoisted up by the steam crane or ship's derrick. A man was engaged to knock out the catch of the bucket as it swung over the wagon, so as to tip out the coal. The four loaded wagons would be drawn clear of the jetty, and replaced by four empties from the loop siding, by the Muir-Hill.

Two rakes of four loaded wagons would be made up into an eight wagon train, and drawn back off the spur by a steam locomotive. The wagons would then be propelled to Clevedon by the locomotive, with the guard riding astride the coal of the first wagon. Sometimes this propelling locomotive would already be at the head of a freight or passenger train. The train would be propelled straight into the facing sidings at Clevedon loco sheds or the gasworks unless, as sometimes happened, the gasworks coal had first to be weighed on the WC&P weighbridge at Portishead.

An earlier wharf had bean projected on the opposite bank of the Yeo, in connection with the export of coal found near Clapton Court (The Cadbury Light Railway), but this had not materialised.

The railway served two stone quarries, which provided much of the railway's revenue, and it is likely that the Colonel envisaged stone exports over Wick Wharf. Pennant-stone was quarried at Conygar Quarry, near Walton Park Station, and limestone at Black Rock Quarry, with transhipment from narrow-gauge between Cadbury Road and Clapton Road Halts. In the late 1930s, negotiations for a major expansion of quarrying in the area led to raised hopes, but the decision to concentrate on road haulage sounded the death-knell for the railway. By this time one would expect small steam or motor coasters to participate in such traffics, but there are no records of such visits.

In 1940 the railway closed, the tracks and the Muir-Hill shunter being scrapped. The concrete wharf remains, however, gradually collapsing into the estuarial mud.

APPENDIX: The Craft.

SARAH: Official No. 68208, registered at Newport, after 1905 at Bridgwater.
Built at Framilode, Glos., 1873, by Ben. Gardner.
Registered Dimensions:
    78.5ft. length
    17.4ft. beam
    7.6ft. depth in the hold.
Transome sterned.
Net Register Tonnage 42.7
Owned by C. E. Heath & Co. Ltd., on behalf of the railway, 1922-1931.
A 1916 Bergius petrol engine fitted 1923, but little used.
Sold for conversion to dumb coal hulk 1931.
Lost off Lydney 1947.

LILY: Official No. 108020, registered at Falmouth, after 1916 at Barnstaple.
Built at Penryn, Cornwall, 1897, by Rapsons.
Registered dimensions:
    56.0ft. length
    16.0ft. beam
    5.7ft. depth of sides
Approx. capacity 32½ tons cargo.
Net Register Tonnage 25.25 (reduced to 23 tons after Bergius engine fitted 1927)
Gross Register Tonnage 60 tons.
Owned by Lt.-Col. Holman F. Stephens 1927-1929

EDITH: Official No. 111392, registered at Bridgwater.
Built at Chepstow, 1901, by William Hurd.
Registered dimensions:
    74.6ft. length
    17.1ft. beam
    5.7ft. depth of sides.
Elliptical Stern.
Net Register Tonnage 44.
Owned by Renwick, Wilton & Co ., Torquay (Coal Merchants) 1927- ?
Bergius petrol engine (2-cyl., 30 h.p.) fitted 1927.
Second engine, making the ship twin-screwed, added 1932.
Broken up 1960.

NOTE: All three ships ketch rigged, i.e. main mast and sail assisted by smaller mast and sail just forward of the steering position. The EDITH later altered to sloop rig by the removal of the aft mast.

22.1 *A photograph from about 1927 shows Lily on the mud at low tide at Wick Wharf and one of the tipping buckets near the wagon on the right.*

22.2 *The second Muir Hill tractor was recorded on Wick Wharf in around 1927. It was a desolate location.*

Chapter 23

Edge Hill Light Railway Runaway

by Tom Burnham (1998)

Of the railways with which Colonel Stephens was associated, the Edge Hill Light Railway must have been the most ill-fated. Never officially opened, it had an economic role for less than three years, and an accident during its construction cost the life of Stephens's successor as its engineer, a man described as "probably the last of the old school of railway promoters". The EHLR was essentially a branch of the Stratford-upon-Avon & Midland Junction Railway, the 'Shakespeare Route', which extended from the London & North Western Railway at Blisworth via Towcester, Fenny Compton and Stratford-upon-Avon to the Midland Railway at Broom Junction near Alcester. Branches linked Towcester with the Midland at Ravenstone Wood Junction, Olney, and with the L&NWR at Cockley Brake Junction, Banbury, and there were also connections with the Great Central Railway at Woodford and the Great Western Railway at Stratford. The SMJR had been rescued from bankruptcy and near dereliction in 1909 under the chairmanship of Harry Willmott, who had previously served as general manager of the Lancashire, Derbyshire & East Coast Railway for the whole of its brief independent life.

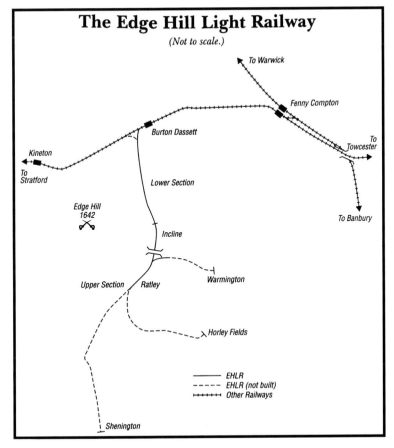

The Edge Hill Light Railway
(Not to scale.)

131

The East & West Junction Railway (predecessor of the SMJR) tapped the Northamptonshire Sand ironstone field between Blisworth and Towcester, and the Banbury ironstone field at Byfield, and its promoters had looked forward to carrying the ore to the ironworks of South Wales and the Midlands. However, the traffic did not develop to the hoped-for extent. Several mines were started, but their production was small and erratic, as the South Wales ironmasters in particular found that it was usually more economic to bring higher grade ore from Spain and the north of England by sea.

During the Great War, action by enemy submarines against coastal shipping revived interest in iron ore that could be transported by land. The Home Ore Department of the Ministry of Munitions was established to encourage the development of such resources, including deposits of ironstone that were known to exist in the vicinity of Edge Hill (the site of a battle in the Civil War). In March 1917 Harry Willmott was interviewed on the subject by the *Birmingham Gazette*, suggesting that the proposed quarries could be worked by prisoners of war, and on 26 April he visited Edge Hill accompanied by the deputy chairman and engineer of the SMJR (Sidney Herbert and Russell Willmott) to assess the prospects for a branch line from the SMJR, running southwards from the goods siding at Burton Dassett. This had been used to rail small quantities of ironstone carried by an aerial ropeway from nearby quarries.

The Ministry of Munitions was unwilling, and the SMJR unable, to finance the building of the branch railway, and so it was carried forward as a separate company under the title of the Edge Hill District Minerals Light Railway, sponsored by the directors of two related Black Country iron companies, T & I Bradley Ltd. of Bilston and T & I Bradley & Son of Darlaston. Harry Willmott became chairman of the light railway company and Arthur E Diggins of the SMJR was its secretary and later traffic manager. The promoters acquired mineral rights over 600 acres around Edge Hill and appointed Holman F Stephens, who had lately reduced his military commitments, as engineer. Stephens' office in Tonbridge proceeded to draw up plans for a total of 11¼ miles of railway, including a triangular junction with the SMJR at Burton Dassett and three branches serving different parts of the ore field. In August 1917 an application for a Light Railway Order was submitted. Stephens gave evidence at a public enquiry by the Light Railway Commissioners, held at Banbury town hall on 8 and 16 November 1917. In view of objections from landowners and the local authorities, the proposals were scaled down to a total of 5¾ miles, and it was agreed to construct bridges instead of a number of level crossings. The SMJR would have running powers from Burton Dassett to the foot of a cable-worked incline (just over two miles) and passengers might be carried over this portion. A high-level line from the summit of the incline to the quarries would be for mineral traffic only. The maximum permitted speed was 12mph on both parts of the line. The Light Railway Order was finally approved on 17 July 1918, and it was sealed by the Board of Trade on 20 January 1919. The railway's title had been shortened to Edge Hill Light Railway, although the revised scheme did not in fact reach Edge Hill itself. Once the Light Railway Order had been obtained, Colonel Stephens seems to have stood down as engineer in favour of Russell Willmott. Russell Willmott, Harry Willmott's son, was already secretary, general manager, engineer and locomotive superintendent of the Isle of Wight Central Railway (of which his father also happened to be chairman), as well as the part-time engineer and locomotive superintendent of the SMJR-a railway equivalent of Pooh Bah in W S Gilbert's *The Mikado!*

Construction of the Edge Hill Light Railway (which had by now become a subsidiary of the

Banbury Ironstone Co Ltd.) began shortly and, at the annual meeting of the SMJR in February 1920, Harry Willmott expressed the hope that it would be feeding traffic to the SMJR by the end of the year. This was not to be the case, however, and construction work was suspended for a while.

Two Brighton 'Terriers' were purchased to work the low-level line, No 1 (an AIX, LB&SCR No 673), which had been on loan to the Longmoor Military Railway in 1919 and No 2 (an unrebuilt A1 class, LB&SCR No 674) in 1920. The Edge Hill had no engine shed, and the spare 'Terrier' was kept at the SMJR's Stratford-upon-Avon locomotive shed, where any repairs that might be needed were also carried out. It seems that this arrangement was a 'gentlemen's agreement', no doubt facilitated by the fact that the two companies shared chief officers. As a quid pro quo, the SMJR is said to have used one of the 'Terriers' for its Stratford to Broom Junction trains at times when it was short of locomotives.

Tragedy struck the Willmott family in 1920, when on 25 June, Russell Willmott died at his home at Newport, Isle of Wight, after a long illness. He left a widow and three children. He was aged only forty and had seemed to be embarked on a promising career in railway engineering and management.

To replace Russell Willmott as engineer of the SMJR and EHLR, Harry Willmott brought in a civil engineer of his acquaintance, Edgar Ferguson, who although more or less retired could be persuaded to act on a consulting basis. Edgar Oswald Ferguson was born in Lewisham in 1846 and, while still a young man was appointed in 1869 as one of the Midland Railway's engineers for the difficult 17 mile section of the Settle & Carlisle railway from Settle Junction to Dent Head. In 1871 his responsibilities increased when the contractor for Ferguson's section was unable to complete the work, which therefore had to be finished by the railway company itself. After this, he acted as engineer for a number of railway projects in the Yorkshire Dales before joining the Manchester, Sheffield & Lincolnshire Railway where he was resident engineer for part of the company's Derbyshire Lines from Beighton to Annesley, including the Chesterfield tunnel.

About 1893 he left the MS&LR and set up as a consulting engineer with an office in Corporation Street, Chesterfield, becoming well known as a promoter of railways in the bustling coalfields of Derbyshire and South Yorkshire. Among the lines with which he was connected was the Sheffield District Railway, opened in 1900, which provided the Lancashire, Derbyshire & East Coast Railway with a route to the Midland Railway's Sheffield station. This brought him into close contact with the LD&ECR's general manager, Harry Willmott, whose headquarters were at Chesterfield Market Place station. Indeed, Edgar Ferguson had been one of the guests at the official luncheon to commemorate the opening of the LD&ECR in 1897.

Edgar Ferguson continued to be involved with railway developments in South Yorkshire, particularly in connection with the Sheepbridge Coal & Iron Co, which owned several of the newly built collieries in the district. He was also resident engineer for the Yorkshire Dales Railway from Skipton to Grassington, opened in 1902. He became interested in light railways, and was engineer of the Derwent Valley Light Railway (opened in 1911-12). He was engineer of the proposed Barnoldswick & Gisburn Light Railway (1904) and the twenty-four mile Longridge & Hellifield Light Railway, which had been proposed as late as 1918 to serve the new Fylde waterworks. Ferguson was well known to the lawyers of the Parliamentary bar, and by the time of his Edge Hill appointment had moved to London from Chesterfield (though he still kept up an office in the latter town), and was living with his wife and a grown-up daughter, Joan, in Holland Park.

It was said of Edgar Ferguson that few could tell so many stories or relate more of the inner workings of the early days of railways, and the Parliamentary fights on many of the great schemes, and that he was always ready with a joke and a smile, even in depressing times. He certainly succeeded in charming the author of an article about the Yorkshire Dales Railway in the *Railway Magazine* of 1902, who, having been supplied with "a great mass of statistics" by Mr Ferguson, concluded that "the rapidity with which the new line has been completed is only another proof of his ability and foresight". Under Edgar Ferguson's direction the construction of the Edge Hill Light Railway was resumed, and by June 1922 the incline was complete enough to enable a third locomotive to be carefully hoisted up to assist with building the upper part of the line. This locomotive was a typical Manning Wardle 0-4-0ST named *Sankey*, and one of its nameplates can be seen on display in the Colonel Stephens Railway Museum at Tenterden.

The cable-worked incline was the only such installation on the railways serving the ironstone industry of the Midlands. It raised the line from 400 to 700 feet above sea level and had a ruling gradient of 1 in 6. It was worked solely by gravity, with descending loaded trucks pulling up empties by means of a steel cable that passed round a horizontal steel brake wheel, 15 feet in diameter. The incline had a rather unusual layout. There was a single track on the lower portion, a short section of double track in the middle so that ascending and descending wagons could pass, and three rails (with a common centre rail) on the upper portion. At the summit, the three rails converged into a single track and then divided again into three. The three rails were crossed by the Camp Lane overbridge, which was the only shelter for *Sankey* as the upper part of the line had no engine shed. The brake wheel was located south of this bridge, but was controlled from a brakesman's hut north of the bridge, near the top of the incline. When the incline was completed, there was no communication between top and bottom, and the brakesman had to rely on flag signals and on his judgement of the speed of the cable.

On Tuesday 10 October 1922, the chief officers of the light railway arrived to inspect the incline, where a permanent brake wheel had just replaced the temporary one used during construction. Harry Willmott, Arthur Diggins and Edgar Ferguson, respectively chairman, general manager and engineer of both the EHLR and the SMJR, were standing by the top of the incline, just past the hump. John Brenchley, the ganger in charge, had had four trucks loaded with 9 tons of ironstone apiece the previous day, and now he worked the points for them to be shunted into place at the top of the incline and hooked on to the end of the cable. The same number of empty trucks were fastened to the bottom end of the cable, and the men took their positions - Robert Taylor in the brakehouse at the top of the incline, Cyril Woodfield at the runaway points at the bottom of the incline, and another pointsman at the incline top points. Brenchley checked the brakes on the loaded wagons, put one of them on, and started the set of wagons off down the hill, a little too fast for his liking. Taylor, the brakesman, could see no more than about eighty yards from his hut, and had to judge his braking according to the speed of the cable. He also thought it was going too fast, and screwed the brake on as quickly as he could. The brake was slow to act as the screw had a fine pitch, but at last it was on and clouds of smoke billowed from the brake wheel. However, instead of slowing down as they had done in tests the previous Friday, the loaded trucks got away again after a slight check, and gathered speed down the incline, pulling the empties up faster and faster.

Woodfield at the bottom of the incline saw what was happening when the loaded trucks were about half way down, and pulled the point lever to divert them into the sand drag at the end of the runaway siding. (E S Tonks suggests that they collided with one of the 'Terriers' but there is no mention of this in contemporary reports. It may have happened on a later occasion.)

Things did not go so well at the top of the incline. Brenchley shouted a warning to the three men standing by the top of the incline, who were busy watching the operation of the brake wheel. Arthur Diggins turned round, and was horrified to see that far from being brought to a standstill by the brake, the empty wagons were hurtling towards them over the hump, travelling at thirty to forty miles an hour. He shouted to the other two to stand clear. Harry Willmott hastily stepped out of the way, followed by Arthur Diggins. Edgar Ferguson started to follow, but as the oldest of the group at 76, he was not so quick on his feet, and as he stepped over the last rail the leading wagon struck him below the left shoulder, throwing him clear of the running line. He fell awkwardly, with his left leg under him, and lay unconscious beside the track.

As the noise died away, the men hurried to his aid. No doctor could be found to come quickly to the spot in that remote part of Ratley parish, so Arthur Diggins got a motor car and had Mr Ferguson taken straight to the Stratford-on-Avon hospital, a distance of some fifteen miles. Dr Earnshaw Hewer set the compound fracture and Joan Ferguson hurried to her father's bedside. He tried to explain to her how the accident had happened, but could not make himself clear. He died of shock and concussion at 11.45pm on Thursday 12 October.

At the inquest (from the report of which in the *Stratford-upon-Avon Herald* many details of the accident have been taken), the coroner recorded a verdict of death from shock and injuries as the result of an accident, and stated that there should be a better indication to the man applying the brake as to what he ought to do. A telephone was provided by the company for this purpose.

The Edge Hill Light Railway continued in use for little more than two years after the accident. At times as many as thirty five wagons a day of ironstone were despatched to the Midlands, but the ore was all consigned by the light railway company itself, excavated from cuttings along the upper part of the line. The EHLR was always shown in official returns as "under construction" and "not open to traffic", and seems never to have received a formal visit from an Inspecting Officer of Railways. The last load of ore was brought down on 27 January 1925, and the railway was "temporarily" closed in the face of falling demand (Bradley's Bilton iron works had in fact dosed in 1922). The track and rolling stock were not scrapped but left to rust where they stood - at first no doubt in the hope that activity would shortly be resumed. They became the object of much curiosity from railway enthusiasts in the 1930s and were photographed on several occasions (curiously enough, no surviving photographs of the line before closure are known). Between 1940 and 1943 much of the low-level part of the EHLR was covered for a new munitions depot, connected (as it still is) to the former SMJR line at Burton Dassett. The remaining EHLR rolling stock, including all the locomotives, which were by then in a very sorry state, was cut up for scrap in 1946, and the light railway company itself was wound up in 1957.

23.1 *A view towards the summit in 1935 includes Camp Lane bridge and the brakesmans cabin. The line had not been used for ten years. (Rail Archive Stephenson)*

23.2 *This view down the incline it is from the bottom of the three-rail section.*

Chapter 24

Colonel Stephens in West Somerset

by Tom Burnham (2004)

The West Somerset Mineral Railway is not regarded as a 'Colonel Stephens railway'. None the less, he was a director of the company for more than seven years, albeit during a period when the railway was closed, and indeed when its track had been lifted.

The history of the WSMR is detailed in the late Roger Sellick's definitive book on the subject. In brief, the line was authorised in 1855 and was opened from the Bristol Channel at Watchet Harbour to Gupworthy in stages from 1857 to 1858. It was a standard gauge line some 13 miles long, including a rope-worked 1-in-4 incline at Comberow. Its raison d'être was to carry iron ore from mines in the Brendon Hills to Watchet for shipment to South Wales, and its main promoters were partners in the Ebbw Vale Company, then one of the foremost firms in the iron and steel industry. The WSMR was leased by the Brendon Hills Iron Ore Co for 7 years from 29 September 1859, and then by the Ebbw Vale Company for 55¼ years from 24 June 1864. The Ebbw Vale Company was liquidated and reorganised as the Ebbw Vale Steel, Iron & Coal Co Ltd. in 1868, and this new company took a fresh lease of the railway for 51½ years from 25 March 1868 at the same rent and terms as before.

Following an inspection by Captain Tyler of the Board of Trade, a passenger service started in 1865 from Watchet to the foot of the incline at Comberow. Passengers could in fact continue in open wagons free of charge and at their own risk up the incline and on the upper level of the railway. However, passenger traffic was never very important, apart from chapel excursions.

The broad gauge West Somerset Railway (forerunner of the present preserved railway) was opened in 1862 from Watchet Junction (later Norton Fitzwarren) to Watchet, where there was a branch to the harbour, although not to the pier already served by the WSMR. A separate company extended from Watchet to Minehead in 1878. The branch was initially worked by the Bristol & Exeter Railway, and was eventually acquired by the Great Western and converted to standard gauge.

The Brendon Hills ore proved particularly suitable for the Bessemer steel process which transformed the iron and steel industry in the 1860s, and the mines and railway were modestly prosperous for some years. Ore production for the period 1858-1883 amounted to more than 723,000 tons, with the peak production of 46,000 tons in 1877. Up to 3,000 tons a month were shipped through Watchet Harbour, which could accommodate vessels of up to 500 tons. From about 1879, the South Wales steelmakers found that they could import Spanish iron ore more cheaply, and the Brendon Hills mines lost their market, finally closing in September 1883. Many of the miners moved away, and the township of Brendon Hill became largely derelict. From that date the train service was reduced to two mixed trains a day, run at a considerable loss. Most of the stock apart from one engine, a Sharp Stewart 0-6-0ST named *Pontypool*, two carriages and a few wagons were gradually returned to Ebbw Vale. In 1892, the Ebbw Vale company proposed that it should stop working the line and that the WSMR company should be wound up. The WSMR directors considered the proposed compensation inadequate, and rejected the proposal. The service was reduced to one train a day in January 1898, and then in November 1898 all rail traffic ceased, by an agreement under which the Ebbw Vale company continued to pay the minimum rent specified in the lease of £5,575 a year (which guaranteed a dividend of 5% on the ordinary shares) and to meet its other obligations (including a minimal level of maintenance) for the remaining term of the agreement. The 0-6-0ST *Pontypool* and a smaller Neilson 0-4-0ST shunter were removed to Ebbw Vale, but the other rolling stock was evidently not considered worth moving, and was left to decay at Watchet station, with windows and doors broken and the bodywork rapidly disintegrating. Watchet Harbour continued to be used for general coastal traffic, and indeed was rebuilt at a cost of £25,000 in 1904 after it was badly damaged by storms in December 1901 and in 1903.

Some attempts were made to revive the railway. The Somerset Mineral Syndicate was formed in 1907 to reopen the mines and railway, in the hope that an Osman briquetting kiln built at Washford would increase the value of the product and make the ore easier to ship. The Colton mine was reopened but the Syndicate's hopes proved unfounded and the railway was closed again in 1909. The Syndicate was wound up in 1910.

A R Angus Ltd., a company organised by an inventor from Sydney, Australia who had patented a system for automatic train control, leased a portion of the line at the Watchet end in 1911 for test work, which continued until early 1914. He later conducted trials in Sweden and Russia, and finally on the Dyke branch near Brighton, in 1920-21.

H L Hopwood, the author of numerous articles in the *Railway Magazine* in the early years of the 20th century, visited the WSMR in September 1913, and walked over the line from Washford to Comberow which he found "to be a most desolate spot, with little or no sign of population, and looking at the grass-grown incline, he could not help contrasting its then neglected condition with that of some years previously, when traffic had been in full swing". He then ascended the incline to Brendon Hill, which "proved a formidable climb, especially as a camera and tripod were carried, and walking was rendered additionally difficult by the neglected state of the permanent way". In general, "the whole equipment was in fair order", but "owing to the exposed situation of Brendon incline, this section had suffered to a greater degree".

As the WSMR was closed to traffic at the outbreak of the Great War, it did not come under the control of the Railway Executive. However, the Ministry of Munitions requisitioned the rails and other permanent way material under the Defence of the Realm Act in January 1917, and the Ebbw Vale company arranged for them to be lifted by a local contractor, Thomas Barton Peel. Part of the trackbed was then used by the Timber Supply Department of the Board of Trade for a narrow gauge tramway to carry timber from Watchet to sawmills at Washford from September 1918 to early 1920.

Three of the four directors of the WSMR in 1917 had connections with the Ebbw Vale Steel, Iron & Coal Co J H Robinson, the chairman of the WSMR and a former Ebbw Vale director, Edward Coulman, the Ebbw Vale solicitor, and John W Beynon (later Sir John Beynon), who was a director of the Ebbw Vale company and went on to become its chairman and managing director. They clearly saw no point in continuing to pay rent for a railway with no track and no serious prospect of ever reopening and called an extraordinary general meeting of the company for 22 November 1917 to consider a resolution from the directors to abandon the railway.

This development was not well received by those of the shareholders who were not interested in the Ebbw Vale company, and the opposition was organised by the fourth director of the WSMR, Frederick Pring Robjent (1859-1938), a Newport stockbroker, who suspected that the other directors had been holding meetings to which he had not been invited. He was supported particularly by the Sun Life Assurance Society, the Bristol Building Society and a Mr Darby (presumably a descendent of the celebrated ironmaster Abraham Darby IV who had been one of the founding partners in the Ebbw Vale ironworks in the 1850s and a WSMR director in the early days). The rebels called another extraordinary general meeting for the previous day, 21 November 1917, which was boycotted by the other three existing directors. The meeting voted to remove them from office, and elected three new directors in their place, in addition to Robjent who now became chairman. The new deputy chairman was Sidney Herbert, a London stockbroker who specialised in the finance of smaller railway companies. He had been responsible for the financial reorganisation of the Stratford-upon-Avon & Midland Junction Railway, and had orchestrated shareholder revolts which had resulted in changes of management of the Cambrian Railways and the Isle of Wight Central Railway. Robjent and Herbert were already chairman and deputy chairman respectively of the Mold & Denbigh Junction Railway. Also elected was Richard Davies, a partner in a Chesterfield, Derbyshire, firm of solicitors, Davies, Sanders and Swanwick. They had been much involved in railway promotion in the East Midlands, and another partner, Dixon Davies, had become a director of the Great Central Railway. Finally, Colonel Holman F Stephens was elected as the only member of the board with practical experience of railway construction and management. It is very likely that he was recommended by Sidney Herbert; Stephens had been brought in as part-time engineer of the Isle of Wight Central Railway for a period in 1911 by the new management which resulted from Sidney Herbert's manoeuvres and at the time in question was engineer to the Edge Hill Light Railway, of which company Sidney Herbert was also deputy chairman. Like the WSMR, the Edge Hill was built to serve ironstone deposits, and Stephens' presence on the board would no doubt have added credibility to proposals to rebuild and reopen the WSMR. As this never occurred, Stephens seems to have taken little part in the company's affairs beyond attending meetings and collecting his fees.

At the meeting on 22 November, the previous board's motion to abandon the railway was lost. The new board elected Harry Milner Willis, to make up the prescribed number of five directors. Willis acted as company secretary to a number of limited companies, including the Mold & Denbigh Junction Railway, of which Robjent and Herbert were directors. The board also appointed Davies, Sanders and Swanwick as their solicitors, as the company's previous solicitor, Edwin Hellard of Stogumber, Somerset, who had been the company secretary since 1877, had continued to act for the old board. The first of a number of lawsuits which were to occupy most of the company's remaining existence followed immediately, when J H Robinson and his colleagues claimed that the new directors had not been validly elected. Mr Justice Astbury found in favour of the new board on 7 December 1917, and Edwin Hellard returned to his position as secretary. Hellard acted jointly with Davies, Sanders and Swanwick as solicitors to the WSMR thereafter. Robjent took the lead in directing the company's affairs, and fortunately much of his correspondence with Edwin Hellard has survived in the Somerset Record Office.

General meetings of the WSMR, like those of many smaller railway companies in the pre-grouping era, were held at the Great Eastern Hotel, Liverpool Street, and the new directors usually held board meetings in London as well, often at Willis's offices in Walbrook. In addition to their fees, the directors received expenses of five guineas (£5.25) for attending meetings if they resided outside London, and two guineas (£2.10) if they were in the London area. This caused some consternation amongst the directors when the company was required to deduct income tax from expenses payments not covered by receipts! Like most of his fellow directors, Stephens was unable to provide the evidence which Edwin Hellard requested.

The capital of the WSMR consisted of

Class A 6% preference shares	£32,500
Class B ordinary shares	£42,500
Debenture stock	£30,000

J E G Lawrence (the business partner of the Ebbw Vale solicitor, Edward Coulman), now brought an action against the WSMR on behalf of himself and other holders of the debenture stock (who were mostly connected with the Ebbw Vale company). This action aimed to make the railway treat the rent received from the Ebbw Vale company as capital, and not use it to pay dividends on the ordinary shares, as the WSMR's existing assets were insufficient to cover the repayment of the debenture capital. The case was heard in June 1918 before Mr Justice Eve; who ruled that not only could the WSMR continue to distribute the rent as dividends (provided the interest on the debentures had been paid first), but that the debenture holders (who had no vote at general meetings) had no right to bring an action against the company, provided their payments were not in arrears. The case is still quoted in legal textbooks.

Meanwhile, the new directors had a number of other problems to deal with. T B Peel had largely finished lifting the track - he was dismissed by Robjent as "by profession a tailor"; before the war he had worked in his father's tailor's shop in Watchet, but had now set up in business on his own account as a "commission shipping agent". However, in January 1918 the Ministry of Munitions stopped further shipments of material (perhaps they had realised what a poor state it was in), and the remainder was left dumped at Watchet and Washford. Protracted negotiations with the Ministry ensued and eventually resulted in payment for the material that they had actually taken. As late as March 1918, T B Peel was found to be breaking up a wagon in the yard at Watchet on questionable authority; he defended himself by pointing out that it was fit only for scrap.

The railway was under the superintendence of Norman L Hole, who had a workforce of three labourers plus another man to look after the line above the Comberow incline. Norman Hole had been employed by the Ebbw Vale company, who had insisted on approving every item of maintenance work. In practice, this had been limited to work needed for legal obligations and public safety to bridges, fences and retaining walls, and repairs to tenanted property. The track and railway buildings had been allowed to decay more or less unhindered. Mr Hole was now employed directly by the WSMR and expenditure was approved by Robjent, although costs were controlled as tightly as ever.

One of the last acts of the old board had been to commission an Exeter surveyor, T H Andrews, to draw up plans of the line, and his report was duly submitted in March 1918. The new directors were, however, interested in the cost of putting the railway "into good repair and proper working order and conditions for the purpose of using it under modern conditions for the conveyance of traffic" - either as a practical policy or to support them in negotiations with the Ebbw Vale company. They appointed Robert Elliott-Cooper (1845-1942; later Sir Robert), an eminent consulting engineer and a past president of the Institution of Civil Engineers, who came down to inspect the line in April 1918 and reported the following month. Negotiations with the Ministry of Munitions eventually led to the WSMR being paid £12,505 for the material which had already been despatched. The rest of the material at Watchet and Washford included 50 tons of flat-bottomed rail, 15 tons of bullhead rail, seven push trolleys, two pump trolleys and one motor for a trolley (out of repair). It was all advertised for sale in October 1919. Several prominent dealers declined to tender, including the Bute Works Supply Co who commented that one of their staff had called at Watchet while in the area the previous year, but had not seen anything the company would be interested in. The successful bidder was Thos. W Ward, who did not bother to make an inspection as their long and wide experience of permanent way materials allowed them to make a fair estimate of value. They were wrong where the WSMR was concerned; when the sleepers they had bought at a good price reached their works, they were found to be barely fit for firewood and not worth the cost of carriage.

In February 1919 the WSMR deposited a Parliamentary Bill which sought relief for the company from circumstances arising from the Great War. In particular, it proposed that for the purposes of the working agreement with the Ebbw Vale company, all the works necessary for putting the railway in good repair should be deemed to have been completed before 29 September 1919, the end date of the agreement between the companies, notwithstanding that the works were actually carried out after then, "provided that such works shall be executed within two years from that day". As the Financial Times pointed out, the object of the Bill was "to enable the railway company to repair the railway at the expense of the Ebbw Vale Steel, Iron and Coal Company".

If this move was intended to put pressure on the Ebbw Vale company to reach an agreement it seems to have succeeded, as later that month the parties agreed to appoint Sir Lynden Macassey (1876-1963) as arbitrator. The four-day hearing took place in March. A legal point was referred to the High Court, and following an unfavourable decision, the arbitration went against the WSMR.

At this point the fate of the railway was decided, whether or not it was realised at the time. Robjent wrote to Edwin Hellard on 19 March 1920, "I understand the Mining proposition is at present under consideration by large Steel Manufacturers, and I am still hoping something may result, but of course the present position of the Railway as a dismantled concern, is a very different proposition to a line which we had hoped the Court would have held the E V were bound to put into good running order, and I suppose unless we can get the Steel people to entertain the Mining proposition fairly quickly, the best course in everyone's interest will be to get an abandonment order as soon as possible, but there are, as you know, difficulties in the way of getting even that done".

While the legal processes were grinding slowly on, the directors followed up a suggestion by Sir Robert Elliott-Cooper that the Great Western Railway might be interested in acquiring part of the trackbed of the WSMR to give them access to the other side of Watchet Harbour and to the paper mill at Wansborough. Even after some initial confusion had been resolved, when the GWR thought they were being invited to take over the whole of the WSMR, the offer was declined. The GWR Engineer's Office commented that a proposal for a siding connection to Wansborough paper mill had been put forward in 1913, but fell through as the paper company were not prepared to pay the tolls proposed.

The WSMR had appealed against the decision of the High Court, and on 6 July 1920 the Court of Appeal (Lord Justices Atkin and Younger) found for the WSMR and remitted the award to the arbitrator. Sir Lynden Macassey awarded the WSMR the cost of repairs to bridges and buildings actually made up to 25 September 1919 (about £9800) and an additional item of £20,647, subject to some further legal points raised by the Ebbw Vale company. The parties returned to the courts, and in March 1922 Mr Justice Rowlatt ruled in favour of the WSMR, in particular deciding that the railway company could have put the line in order before 25 September 1919, if the Ebbw Vale company had not repudiated liability.

The Ebbw Vale company appealed yet again, but on 5 July 1922, shortly before the case came for hearing, an agreement was reached between the parties that the Ebbw Vale company would pay the WSMR £14,500 in settlement of all claims whatsoever. The amount of the settlement was not published at the time. The directors were now able to report to the shareholders that "the litigation between the companies is, therefore, at an end", and the half-yearly meeting of the WSMR on 4 October 1922 was followed by an extraordinary meeting at which a resolution to apply for abandonment of the undertaking was passed.

A Bill was accordingly drafted and considered at the next half-yearly meeting on 28 March 1923, and the West Somerset Mineral Railway (Abandonment) Act received the Royal Assent on 2 August 1923.

1924 saw the retirement of Edwin Hellard as company secretary after some 46 years in the post; H G Derwent Moger of Stogumber solicitors Charmer and Charmer was Acting Secretary for the remainder of the company's existence.

All the company's fixed assets apart from land and buildings had already been sold, and the latter went at an auction sale at the West Somerset Hotel in Watchet on Friday 8 August 1924. The West Somerset Free Press reported that great interest was taken in the disposal, the large billiard-room at the hotel being crowded with residents from all parts of the district once served by the long disused line, as also others interested in the company. The auctioneer was Mr Stanley Hosegood (of Risdon, Gerrard and Hosegood) and those present included F P Robjent (but apparently none of the other directors), H A Sanders (of Davies, Sanders and Swanwick), H G Derwent Moger, P Duddridge (Edwin Hellard's chief clerk) and Norman Hole (the superintendent) A total of £3,019 was realised, several hundred pounds more than the reserve prices. A number of the company's tenants took the opportunity to purchase the freehold of their cottages. There were also a couple of sales to directors - Mineral Cottage in the parish of St Decumans was bought by Sidney Herbert, and a piece of land at Watchet by H A Sanders, F P Robjent, Sidney Herbert and his brother Alfred Herbert jointly.

The last general meeting was on 7 July 1925, when the final accounts showed that the debenture holders had received 70% of the value of their holdings, but holders of the ordinary and preference shares got nothing. On the same day, the directors met for the last time and resolved that the company be wound up.

Writing in 1921, H L Hopwood wondered whether the removal of the track would be "the final chapter in the history of the West Somerset Mineral Railway. Such, however, would appear to be the case, for in view of the present day high cost of labour and materials and the thinly populated district served, it seems hopeless to expect that the railway will ever be re-opened". In hindsight it is clear that lifting the track certainly began the final chapter, even if there were some twists and turns before the story reached its end. The Brendon Hill mines never reopened and the WSMR never became one of Colonel Stephens' railways. Nor did F P Robjent's rebellion do more for the ordinary and preference shareholders than pay their dividends a few years longer. More compensation was undoubtedly extracted from the Ministry of Munitions and the Ebbw Vale company (which was in poor financial health itself) but only at the cost of substantial expense on litigation. As a postscript, although it is nearly ninety years since the metals of the West Somerset Mineral Railway were raised, public interest in the 'old mineral line' and in the much longer history of iron ore mining in the Brendon Hills has not diminished. In 1999 the Exmoor National Park Authority purchased the incline and winding house, and since then work has been done to remove undergrowth and to conserve historical features. In April 2004, a group headed by the Exmoor Society received a grant from the Heritage Lottery Fund to enable a full project design to be drawn up for the WSMR and its associated industrial past, including iron mining sites and the communities that worked there. This will lead to the conservation of these places and will help people learn more about them through high quality interpretation and better public access.

24.1   After the line reopened, a public excursion was operated on 4th July 1907, but no regular service was provided. Only one locomotive was purchased and this was a cheap and unsuitable 4-4-0T from the Metropolitan Railway, numbered 37.

24.2   The Comberrow incline was ¾ mile long. No. 37 and the disused station are seen at the bottom of it in 1908. In the early days, the incline had conveyed passengers at their own risk.

Chapter 25

The Weston Point Light Railway

By Tom Burnham (1998)

The Weston Point Light Railway is perhaps the least known of any engineered by Lieut. Col. H F Stephens, no doubt because of its industrial traffic and the fact that it never carried passengers. However, it is worthy of some attention, if only because it is still open for its entire length and is still carrying the traffic for which it was built.

Weston Point, near Runcorn in Cheshire, lies between the rivers Mersey and Weaver and has long been a centre for waterway communication. The Weaver was first made navigable in the 18th century to carry salt from the Cheshire mines and was improved during the latter half of the 19th century to accommodate coastal ships. Docks were laid out at Weston Point and were connected by the Runcorn & Weston Canal with Runcorn Docks, the western terminus of the pioneering Bridgewater Canal which carried coal from the South Lancashire coalfield. The Bridgewater was later acquired by the Manchester Ship Canal, opened in 1894, which also connected with Runcorn Docks. At Runcorn, the Crewe to Liverpool main line of the London & North Western Railway crossed the Mersey and (later) the Ship Canal by a large bridge, opened in June 1868, and a goods branch was built from near Runcorn station towards Runcorn Docks, where it made an end-on junction with the railways of the Bridgewater Trustees (later the Manchester Ship Canal Co).

The chemical industry at Weston Point began in 1882 when the Mersey Salt & Brine Co laid down the Marbury brine pipe, to carry brine pumped at Marston, near Northwich, to Weston

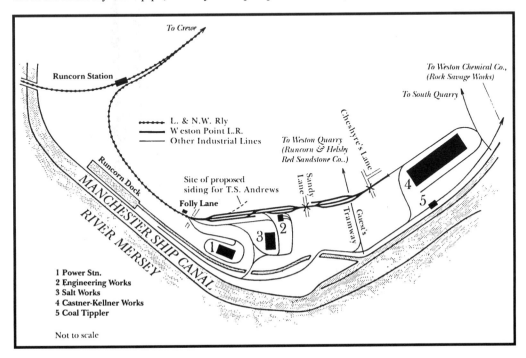

1 Power Stn.
2 Engineering Works
3 Salt Works
4 Castner-Kellner Works
5 Coal Tippler

Not to scale

Point where salt pans were installed to convert it to salt. This action aroused considerable opposition at the time, as it was felt that the prosperity generated by the salt industry should be retained in the area which had to suffer the subsidence it caused. In 1888, the Mersey Salt & Brine Co became part of the Salt Union, which continued to expand operations at Weston Point; during the period 1899-1910 an average of 66,400 tons a year of pure salt were despatched, 49,500 tons of it by rail. The works - which were built on land leased from the MSCC and served by its railway - were considerably enlarged in 1910 when a vacuum evaporation plant was installed.

In the 1890s, a new industry consuming brine came into existence. Soda had been made from brine and limestone by an inefficient and unsatisfactory process but in 1892 the chemist H Y Castner, in the course of unsuccessful attempts to refine metals, developed an electrolytic process to produce caustic soda and chlorine from brine. The Castner-Kellner Alkali Co Ltd. was incorporated in October 1895; erection of its Weston Point works began in 1896 and by 1897 the first 1000HP installation was set in operation, taking brine from the pipeline. The materials and equipment to build the works were all brought by road, but a rail connection was soon established by a siding from the MSCC railway, built partly by C-K and partly by the MSCC. C-K paid the MSCC £25 a year for the part it had built itself and a toll of 2¼d a ton on all its traffic passing over the MSCC line.

This arrangement was considered unsatisfactory as early as 1900, when the L&NWR offered to build a railway connection at its own expense, but it proved impossible to obtain the intervening land at a reasonable price. In 1902, when a corrugated iron shed for two engines was built at Weston Point, Mr Percy Allen of C-K wrote "I may say that there is a very strong desire among the inhabitants of Weston and Weston Point to have a direct railway connection to Runcorn Station, and I should think that at certain times of the year a considerable amount of traffic would arise from the forwarding of potatoes and general farm produce."

In 1906, C-K put forward to the owners of the two largest of the sandstone quarries in the ridge overlooking Weston Point, the Runcorn & Helsby Red Sandstone Co and Orme & Muntz, a plan for a siding from the Runcorn Dock branch to connect with the quarry tramways and give direct access to the C-K works from the L&NWR. C-K offered to pay the cost of construction, but the scheme again foundered on problems of obtaining land and wayleaves. Alkali production continued to expand. In 1909, in order to provide a use for surplus chlorine, the Weston Chemical Go. was established jointly by C-K and German interests to make chlorinated organic chemicals on a site to the south of the main C-K works. During the Great War, C-K's output trebled and new products included poison gas and hydrogen gas. In 1915 the Ministry of Munitions placed orders for as much liquid chlorine as could be produced, and the works also made phosgene and mustard gas. Up to 5 million cubic feet a month of hydrogen was supplied to the Admiralty for use in airships and there were frequent delays in loading and unloading cylinders due to severe congestion on the MSCC railway. The Admiralty complained and suggested a separate railway to the works. Colonel Stephens was brought up from Tonbridge in 1918 to draw up plans for the siding and C-K got as far as reaching an agreement with Lord Ellesmere, the most important landowner, for the railway to pass over his land and obtaining the consent of the local Quarter Sessions to divert various public roads. The work was not started immediately, perhaps because of the end of the War, and the land changed hands soon afterwards following Lord Ellesmere's death. However, although war production was being run down (the Chairman said in December 1918 "It's a comfort to have seen the last of mustard gas"), the output of the factory was still large and developments in the transport of bulk chemicals made a reliable rail connection still more important. Liquid chlorine was supplied in increasing quantities instead of bleaching powder to the textile and paper industries, and bulk caustic soda was shipped to the C-K sodium plant at Wallsend, near Newcastle.

Unfortunately, when a year later C-K attempted to revive the scheme, the new owner of Lord Ellesmere's land, Mr T S Andrews, proved much less accommodating. This resulted in a decision to construct the line under a Light Railway Order giving the promoters (the Castner-Kellner Alkali Co Ltd.) powers to purchase land compulsorily. Lieut. Col. H F Stephens was again the engineer, and the application was made in January 1920. It was intended to carry traffic not only for C-K and the associated Weston Chemical Co, but also for the quarries, and a workmen's passenger service to Runcorn was also envisaged, as the service of motor buses was considered inadequate. The line was about a mile long and would require two public roads to be diverted. A public inquiry was held on Tuesday 16 March 1920 at the Greenway Road School in Runcorn before the Light Railway Commissioners, H A Steward and A D Erskine. Counsel for C-K noted that the works received 159,000 tons a year by rail and dispatched 70,000 tons and that all this had to go via the MSCC sidings by a series of shunts. There were days and days when it was impossible to get the traffic away, particularly as the MSCC often used the empty wagons for its own traffic. About 1150 men were employed at the C-K works, many of whom had to walk from Runcorn. Mr. A T Smith, who had been the managing director of C-K since 1915, confirmed the poor service provided by the MSCC and reported that Mr. Latimer, of the MSCC, had said that "the trade from the works was not worth the change of a shilling, and that he would much rather be without it." Mr. Malcolm, who was the managing director of the Salt Union and engineer to the Mersey Power Co, which was about to build a large power station at the end of the Runcorn Dock branch, said that the proposed railway would relieve the L&NWR line and enable other traffic - including his own which was increasing every year - to be dealt with much faster. Support was also given by Runcorn RDC and UDC, the foremen at the C-K works, the Royal Air Force representative at the works and Mr. Savage, who was the general manager of the Weston Chemical Co

A letter from the Assistant General Manager of the L&NWR, Mr. Jepson, said that the railway supported the application and had agreed terms with C-K. He believed the Light Railway would reduce congestion and the L&NWR was prepared to equip the Runcorn Dock branch for passenger traffic if necessary.

Col. Stephens explained the location of the proposed line, which would present no engineering difficulties. The estimate (£49,842) allowed for about two miles of sidings and for passenger traffic.

The main objector was the Manchester Ship Canal Co, which claimed that the Light Railway would divert C-K traffic worth about £3000 a year from its railway; that there was no public demand for it; that the single line of the L&NWR Runcorn Dock branch was already fully occupied with MSCC traffic; and that the C-K works already had adequate railway facilities and could use the Weaver Navigation for water-borne traffic. In short "the proposal was solely an adventure of a limited company and was not in the public interest." The MSCC asked for a postponement of the inquiry, which was refused.

Other objectors included T S Andrews, who insisted on being given the same rights to connect sidings to the Light Railway as C-K had previously offered Lord Ellesmere, and Evans, Sons, Lescher & Webb Ltd. This company, tenants of Westfield Farm from Mr. Andrews, grew medicinal plants and feed for horses and were concerned at the loss of good agricultural land.

The Commissioners decided that the application should be granted as the existing facilties were "no longer adequate or suitable to meet either the needs of the industry which the Promoters carry on or the interests of the public in that industry" and protracted negotiations followed between C-K and the other parties involved, including Capt. Orred, a local landowner who had taken no part in the original inquiry. The Light Railway Commissioners held a meeting in London in July 1920 and the final details were agreed at meetings between Stephens and Mr. Andrews and MSCC representatives in September. Incidentally, Mr. Andrews's siding, which caused such problems, seems never to have been built. The Weston Point Light Railway Order was finally sealed on 2 December 1920.

The Light Railway as authorised was 7 furlongs 5 chains long from its junction with the Runcorn Dock Branch to a point near Bankes Lane. The maximum gradient was 1 in 80 and there were two public road level crossings, which needed gates only if required by the Ministry of Transport. The maximum axle load was up to 16 tons, depending on the weight of the rail used, and the overall speed limit was 25 mph. There were powers to lease the line to the L&NWR and clauses for the protection of the L&NWR, the MSCC, the Salt Union brine pipes and T S Andrews. The maximum fare for passengers was 2d, or 3d through to Runcorn station.

Provided with their Light Railway Order, C-K sought tenders for construction of the railway and in April 1921 agreed with Thomas Summerson & Sons Ltd. of Darlington to build the line at a cost of £22,836 11s 4d, excluding land and permanent way, telegraph, ballast and fencing materials. The embankments were to be built of waste dumped in spoil tips near Bankes Lane by the C-K aerial ropeway and a quantity of large clinker and broken concrete was also made available free of charge as bottom ballast. Lieut. Col. Stephens of Salford Terrace, Tonbridge, was named as C-K's Engineer for the purposes of the contract, although no doubt his responsibilities were usually exercised by a resident engineer. The first 60 chains from the junction with the L&NWR and the reception sidings were to be laid with standard L&NWR track and the remainder with 75 lb/yard flat bottomed rail with dog spikes. The railway was opened to traffic on 22 May 1922, considerably after the completion date of 31 October 1921 specified in the contract.

The line is still recognisable, although the flat bottomed rails soon started to be replaced by chaired track to support heavier wagons, the cattle grids at level crossings were replaced first by wooden and then by metal gates and the original post and wire fencing replaced by "unclimbable" metal fences.

The BR Runcorn Dock branch diverges from the Crewe-Liverpool main line just south of Runcorn station and runs behind the down platform before turning away to the west. Most of the branch is now double track (although it was single track when the WPLR was opened) and it is electrified with overhead wires at 25kV ac. A few chains from the end of the branch is the Folly Lane shunters' cabin, formerly a three-way junction with the WPLR to the left, the MSCC railway straight on and the siding to the Mersey Power Co on the right. The other two connections have now been lifted, with only a short stub of the MSCC line on which a BR diesel shunter stands between duties. The WPLR drops southwards at 1 in 80 over a bridge known locally as Swintons' Arches and widens into fans of BR and ICI reception sidings, known as Balloon A and Balloon B. The BR overhead electrification extends into the reception sidings, so this is the only line engineered by Col. Stephens equipped for electric traction. West of these sidings a branch to the salt works and the locomotive depot and engineering works connects. The WPLR reverts to single track for the Sandy Lane level crossing, south of which was a fan of five sidings (Balloon C), now reduced to two. A siding near the crossing, Watson's Dead End, removed in 1986, used to provide space for six to eight wagons for a local coal merchant, the nearest approach to the public goods and passenger services which were proposed before the line was built. A further gated level crossing, across Cheshyres Lane (still with an enamelled warning notice headed Weston Point Light Railway), brings the WPLR into a third fan of sidings alongside Bankes Lane, where the line authorised under the Light Railway Order connected with the existing factory rail system. In 1926, Castner-Kellner became part of the Imperial Chemical Industries combine and this led to a curious sequel to the Weston Point Light Railway story in the middle of the Second World War. ICI decided, notwithstanding what might have been thought more pressing matters, that the time was ripe finally to wind up the affairs of C-K, and wrote to the Ministry of Transport enquiring whether the powers granted to C-K by the Order of 1920 could be transferred to the ICI. Although the 1920 Order included a clause permitting the railway to be leased to the L&NWR, there was apparently no provision for transferring the powers, although as a civil servant minuted, "unfortunately there seem to be no note-books, etc. on light railways. I rather imagine the zeal for salvage has outrun discretion and any notes there may have been have gone for pulp." A polite reply to ICI was drafted, indicating that there would be no alternative to a new Light Railway Order but suggesting that further action should be deferred until a more auspicious time.

A draft Order was finally submitted in January 1948. Advertisements produced no objections and, following the precedent of the Kingsnorth Light Railway (Transfer) Order of 1929, it was decided not to hold a local public inquiry. The Weston Point Light Railway Transfer Order was made on 9 April 1948.

The 1950s were perhaps the high point of WPLR traffic, when everything needed for the massive complex of chemical works, including ammunition for the rifle club, arrived by rail and the day after a Bank Holiday could find wagons filling every available siding, making the shunter's task almost impossible. By this time, ICI was also providing shunting services for the MSCC which no longer kept a locomotive at Runcorn Docks - a curious reversal of the situation which caused the WPLR to be built. However, although the volume of traffic has fallen off considerably in recent years, the WPLR is still open for its entire length as authorised and is still an important part of the works transport system. The salt works provides 8 to 10 wagons a week, but most of the traffic consists of caustic soda and a certain amount of chlorine being despatched and fuel oil coming in. The locomotive fleet now consists of three Yorkshire Engine Co 0-6-0 diesel electric shunters, named *Richard Borrett* (2669/1958), *Danby Dale* (2714/1958), and *R A Lawday* (2878/1963), the latter recently rebuilt with new cab windows and doors and improved sound insulation.

25.1   The WPLR curves to the left of the class 08 diesel locomotive and continues straight on to the MSCCR in this 1987 view.

Chapter 26

The Snailbeach District Railways

by Stephen Garrett (1998)

Each of the railways engineered or operated by Colonel Stephens had its own character and its own eccentricities. The Snailbeach District Railways Company was no exception to this general rule though in three respects it had quite a lot in common with Stephens' much more ambitious client, the East Kent Light Railways. Both lines were primarily mineral railways, the official titles of both included 'Railways' in the plural rather than the more conventional 'Railway', and neither was ever placed in receivership. This last may, of course, be regarded as the ultimate eccentricity in a 'Colonel Stephens Railway'.

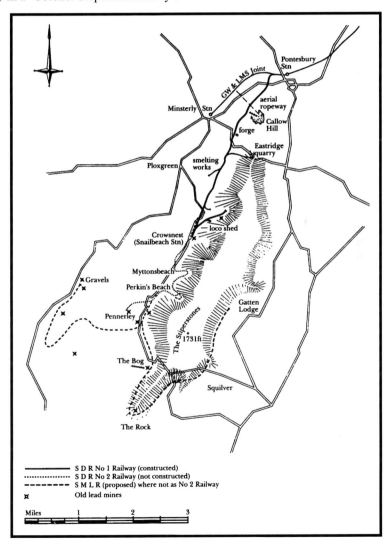

The Snailbeach was a 2' 4" gauge railway opened in 1877 to serve the lead mining district along the western flank of the Stiperstones range of hills in Shropshire. Authorised by an Act of Parliament in 1873 it was intended to consist of two railways. Railway No. 1 ran some three miles from sidings near Pontesbury on the GWR & LNWR joint Minsterley branch line to a terminus at Crowsnest. From Crowsnest a branch ran, initially on a gradient of 1 in 25, to the lead mine of the Snailbeach Mine Company. The railway's locomotive shed was built at the top of the 1 in 25 incline. Railway No. 2 would have been a continuation of Railway No. 1 just under two miles long to lead mines at Pennerley but was never built. The significant feature in the construction of the Snailbeach was that it had an uninterrupted downward gradient from Crowsnest to Pontesbury, even the roads it encountered crossed its course by bridges rather than level crossings. It was therefore ideally suited to gravity working. Although there do not appear to be any accounts of the working of the line in its early years, it is clear that the main function of the line's locomotives in later years, was to haul trains of empty wagons back up the line that had previously come down loaded, driven by the inexpensive power of gravity.

The Snailbeach prospered at first, regularly paying dividends of 3%, but the closure of one of the largest lead mining companies in 1884 more than halved the line's traffic. Further mine closures followed and from 1898 operating costs exceeded receipts. Rescue came with the opening of a granite quarry at Eastridge to which a branch from the Snailbeach was opened in 1905. This quarry belonged to the Ceiriog Granite Company, which was the major customer of the Glyn Valley Tramway. The Snailbeach Chairman, Henry Dennis, was also a very active director of the Glyn Valley and it is thought that it was due to his influence that the Ceiriog Granite Company opened its Eastridge Quarry. The 'Dennis Connection' went even further. By 1905 one of the Snailbeach's two locomotives was worn out and Dennis arranged for the loan of one of the Glyn Valley Beyer Peacock 0-4-2T locomotives, *Sir Theodore*, to help out on the Snailbeach. Unfortunately the Glyn Valley gauge was half an inch wider than that of the Snailbeach and *Sir Theodore* is alleged to have spent more time off the rails than on. The acquisition by the Snailbeach of a new Bagnall 0-6-0T in 1906 enabled *Sir Theodore* to be returned to the Glyn Valley and for the worn out Henry Hughes 0-4-2ST *Belmont* to be broken up. The Snailbeach's other locomotive at this time, an 0-6-0ST named *Fernhill*, is something of a mystery. All that seems to be known of it, apart from rumours of a photograph existing in the National Railway Museum collection, is that it was purchased from the dealers Lennox Lange in 1881 and was disposed of in 1912.

The opening of the Eastridge branch restored traffic to a healthy level with a record 38,000 tons being carried in 1909. However, by 1912 traffic had fallen to 8,800 tons. The coming of war in 1914 led traffic to revive and until 1919 respectable quantities of stone and increasing quantities of merchandise were carried. Both stone and merchandise traffic almost halved again in 1920. In 1921 only 4,800 tons were carried and in 1922 the line's sole surviving locomotive *Dennis* had to be taken out of traffic for major reconstruction. All traffic was now reliant on gravity and horse power. Only 3,177 tons were carried in 1922.

It was at this stage that Colonel Stephens and a group including H M Bates, J C White and Sir R F Bowmaker took an interest in the Snailbeach. The new Board of Directors took over in January 1923 and Stephens promptly set about reviving the line. Worn out sleepers were replaced with second hand standard gauge sleepers cut in half and much of the 'main' line was relaid with 45lb rail. The Eastridge branch was also taken up about this time, the Ceiriog Granite

Company having ceased business here.

Three second hand locomotives were acquired and converted to 2' 4" gauge. The first of these was a Kerr Stuart 'Skylark' Class 0-4-2T No.802 built in 1902 to 2' 6" gauge for Lovatt & Co of Hartington, Derbyshire. It had served a succession of owners until purchased by Stephens from the Ministry of Munitions Disposals Board at Neasden in London. It became Snailbeach No.2 and the dismantled *Dennis* was given No. 1. The other locomotives purchased were two of the familiar War Department surplus 60cm gauge Baldwin 4-6-0Ts also used by Stephens on the Ashover and Welsh Highland lines. The Snailbeach examples were Baldwin 44383 built in 1916, delivered to the Snailbeach still carrying WD. No. 538 and Baldwin 44572 built in 1917 and carrying WD No. 722. On the Snailbeach these locomotives were numbered 3 and 4 and could be told apart by No.4's retention of its water lifting equipment and protective hoods over its cab front spectacle plates.

It was not just the locomotives of the Snailbeach that had been worn out, but also its wagon fleet. The line had started out in 1877 with 29 coal wagons, 12 hoppers, 6 timber wagons and 6 goods wagons. An article in *Locomotive Magazine* in 1912 credited the Snailbeach with 50 wagons and one 'passenger vehicle' though the line's official return for the same year claimed 8 open wagons, 1 covered wagon, 41 mineral wagons and 7 timber trucks. There must have been a dramatic clearance of stock in 1913 as the figures for that year had dropped to 4 open wagons, 1 covered wagon, 17 mineral wagons and 4 timber trucks. Casualties continued so that by 1922 the stock had fallen to 8 mineral wagons and 4 timber trucks. Stephens augmented the wagon fleet by the purchase of surplus War Department vehicles. The return for 1924 gave 3 open wagons, 33 mineral wagons, 4 timber trucks and 1 'miscellaneous' vehicle. The latter was probably No. 58, a steel bodied van apparently used for conveying explosives. One of the timber trucks was later adapted for carrying oil by the fitting of a 'Royal Daylight' tank to its superstructure. Apart from the addition of a further open wagon in 1926 and the loss of one of the mineral wagons in 1936 these returns continued unchanged until 1947. In practice there was a steady reduction in railworthy vehicles as might be expected on any line making extensive use of gravity working. By 1949 it was observed that only 11 vehicles appeared to be in regular use.

For all the investment that had taken place there was no immediate transformation of the Snailbeach's fortunes. Instead there was a gentle increase in felspar traffic which was mined near Crowsnest and, together with fluctuating quantities of barytes, accounted for the bulk of the line's carrying until 1928. In that year stone traffic, only 199 tons in 1924 and 2589 tons in 1927, leapt to 4821 tons. The source of this new traffic was a quarry at Callow Hill about ¾ mile from Pontesbury. A loop siding was put in on the Snailbeach over which a crushing plant was erected. Crushed stone could therefore be loaded directly into Snailbeach wagons which would run in rakes of three or four down to Pontesbury by gravity. At Pontesbury the Shropshire County Council erected a tarring plant thus creating a most efficient unit for the supply and delivery of road making materials.

Apart from the continuing felspar traffic and small quantities of merchandise and coal, the roadstone operation became the mainstay of the Snailbeach's activities. Gravity trains ran from Callow Hill as required and two or three times a week a locomotive would be steamed at the far end of the line to run light to Pontesbury. It would haul the empty wagons gathered there the ¾ mile back to Callow Hill and then run light back to the locomotive shed at Crowsnest. According to the Snailbeach returns for 1930 this resulted in 1560 train miles being run of which only 780 were loaded. These figures smack of being a 'guesstimate' (1560 is twice 780) to save working out the real figures. Figures issued under the authority of W H Austen who took over after Stephens' death in 1931 indicate an effort to be more accurate: in 1935 2,144 train miles were run of which only 837 were loaded.

It has often been claimed that services on the Snailbeach at this time were entirely in the hands of one man, Driver Gatford, a veteran of the Bishops Castle Railway. It seems unlikely that just one man could have worked as brakesman on the gravity trains, driven and repaired the locomotives, kept the track in order and carried out the myriad other tasks necessary on even a small line such as the Snailbeach. Austen is quoted as giving the Snailbeach staff as four; one driver-fitter, one platelayer, one junctionman and one brakesman. It may be that in later years Gatford was the only full-time Snailbeach employee with labour being loaned as required by the Callow Hill Quarry and the nearby Shropshire & Montgomeryshire Railway, which is known to have carried out engineering work for the Snailbeach.

In one respect Gatford seems to have been extremely influential. Despite repeated exhortations from Stephens to get the 0-6-0T *Dennis* repaired, Gatford continued to find new delaying tactics to postpone this task. *Dennis* remained dismantled until officially withdrawn in 1936 and its components had all gone by 1938.

Stephens had devised a rota for the operation of the locomotives which was intended to extend their working life and reduce maintenance costs. Each locomotive would run for a spell of 2-3 weeks and then enjoy a period of rest and recuperation until its next turn came. The system worked well and was continued under Austen. Unfortunately when major overhaul did eventually become essential it was necessary for all three locomotives at the same time! All three locomotives were failed by the boiler inspector in 1946. Once again the Snailbeach was without motive power.

The solution this time was to hire a Fordson tractor, registration BUX174, to haul the empties back to Callow Hill. Fortunately the original Snailbeach District Railways Act had required sufficient land to be acquired and formation laid out for conversion of the line to standard gauge if so required in the future. This meant that there was sufficient level ground on either side of the Snailbeach track for a 'five foot gauge' tractor to run with one pair of wheels between the tracks and the other outside. The only significant differences in operation were that the tractor would run daily as it could manage fewer empties than the locomotives and that the tractor could be stabled at Pontesbury or Callow Hill, so the practice of running light to Crowsnest was abandoned.

On 14th April 1947 the Pontesbury to Callow Hill section of the Snailbeach was leased by Shropshire County Council who effectively became the sole operators of the line. In the following years the County Council acquired additional wagons to supplement the stock surviving at the time of their take over. The locomotives sat idle in the shed until cut up in 1950. The line between Callow Hill and Crowsnest was lifted shortly afterwards. By 1959 road access had been provided to Callow Hill Quarry and the remaining section of line fell out of use. The final lengths of rail were lifted in 1962, some being sold to the Talyllyn Railway, and the last wagons disposed of. The Snailbeach District Railways Company, however remains in existence to this day.

26.1   Photographed at the loco shed in the 1920s are 0-4-2T Kerr Stuart no. 2 (left), Baldwin 4-6-0T no. 4 and the remains of the Bagnall, Dennis.

26.2   The GWR siding at Pontesbury passed under the loading gantry.

26.3   This is Wharf Bridge at Snailbeach, looking north.

Chapter 27

A Railway on a Budget ND&CJLR

by Humphrey Brandram-Jones (1976)

In 1923, as a young civil engineer, I graduated from the Crystal Palace School of Engineering and began to look for a job where I could put to some advantage my newly acquired knowledge. I had emerged with the somewhat doubtful privilege of "student of the year", as jobs for young engineers were hard to come by at that time and the standard of mathematics taught by the college was not as high as that demanded by some employers.

I was, therefore, delighted when a Colonel Stephens applied to the college for someone to act as an "improver" on a light railway scheme with which Stephens was involved in North Devon and I was the recommended candidate. The severely practical curriculum of the college, with grounding in many aspects of engineering, was the ideal training for Stephens' requirements and following a brief interview at the RAC club in London, I was offered the job, which was accepted.

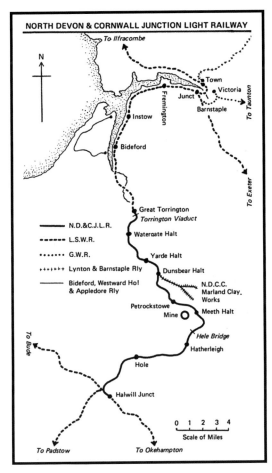

Stephens insisted that I should start work immediately and I was told to report to the headquarters of the Resident Engineer, Captain J H T Griffiths, at 9 Bridge Street, Hatherleigh, taking with me a bed and a bicycle. I arrived on or about 23rd December amidst appalling, snowy weather, only to find that Griffiths and his two junior engineers had just departed for the festive season, leaving me alone in the house, which was unfurnished and did not have even a semblance of mod cons, such as mains water or electricity. It was the most dismal Christmas that I could ever remember.

The North Devon & Cornwall Junction Light Railway was planned as a standard gauge line, running in a roughly North - South direction, from Great Torrington to Halwill Junction, a distance of some 20 miles. Although promoted as an independent concern, it was always intended that the railway would be worked by the London & South Western Company. The northern portion, some 5½ miles in length, followed the route of a 3 foot gauge china clay railway and, in fact, replaced it. The southern end was a completely new railway. The scheme was conceived partly to alleviate a chronic unemployment problem in the area and many of the labourers on the job were managers of commercial companies, chartered accountants and professional people of all types. As an "improver", my duties were to set out the centre lines and limits of earthworks, design and make drawings for small engineering structures such as cattle creeps and culverts and to measure up for the monthly certificates of payment to the contractor.

Captain Griffiths was an erudite and dedicated engineer, with a strong leaning towards the astronomical side of the work. He had been a lecturer in geodetic surveying at the University of Achimota in Ghana and I remembered that on all drawings calling for "north points" we had to make proper astronomical observations with the help of a nautical almanac. By the time that I left the job, I was fully competent to make these fixes and have often wished since, when working in various parts of Africa, where ordnance maps are few and far between, that I had kept up the knowledge that I had acquired at that time. Colonel Stephens visited the line several times whilst I was there. Stephens usually arrived by road at our Hatherleigh offices in a chauffeur-driven lorry, which possessed a spare set of flanged wheels which could be readily attached to the vehicle. By this means, he managed to visit all parts of the line where steel had been laid, in a very short time. Much of the railway was quite remote from even the most primitive lanes and the alternative was to walk or ride the route, which was continuously submerged in a sea of mud.

The line was constructed on "shoestring" finance and considerable use was made of local materials. For example, sleepers were cut from oak trees, bought standing and milled on site with portable, steam-driven sawbenches, although I remembered being sent to Newport to approve and stamp some 5000 creosoted fir sleepers that had been imported from the Baltic. Boundary fence posts were of larch, also obtained locally and I recalled two instances which show how tightly money, in particular payments to the contractor, were controlled. Part of my work was to inspect fence posts to see that they complied with the specification agreed with the contractor, which was 10 inches circumference at the top and 12 inches at ground level. I naturally assumed that this should be done when they were delivered on site and did so, until Colonel Stephens, on one of his periodic inspections, said that the posts should be inspected only after they had been driven into the ground and threaded with wire through the drilled holes. At this stage, the contractor was told that he might leave in (and forfeit payment) or replace any which did not hold up to the specification. Naturally, he chose the former course and in this way many serviceable posts were never paid for, until the timber contractor realised what was happening. A similar practice was applied in the case of sleepers.

Another of my responsibilities was the supervision of the steelwork for the construction of a viaduct over the River Torridge at the northern end of the line, to replace a flimsy, wooden viaduct which had carried the china clay railway. One of the piers of the new viaduct was undermined by winter flooding in 1924 and instead of demolishing and starting again, which should have been done, it was righted by winching and then underpinned to an annular foundation ring blasted out of the granite forming the river bed. This was not the only mishap experienced during the construction of the viaduct; some of the steelwork was bent whilst being unloaded from wagons at Halwill and rather than replacing what must have been a seriously weakened structure, an army of local blacksmiths was recruited to drill out the rivets and then straighten and reassemble it. The girders were transported from Halwill to Torrington by road, using a hired traction engine and many of the bends in the narrow lanes had to be specially excavated to get them round. Even so, a great deal of damage was caused to the highway and I often wondered why the girders were not delivered direct to the Torrington railhead, it would certainly have avoided many of the problems. Apart from myself, two other improvers were employed on the line. Transport from headquarters to the place where we happened to be working was quite a problem as it often involved distances of 12 miles or more. We had the use of a large horse to take us round the site, but it was a real penance to ride the beast, particularly after a long day's measuring up. A trap would have been a boon and it was, therefore, with some relief that we heard one was to be auctioned at the George Inn, Hatherleigh, and that the maximum sum the auctioneer anticipated it reaching was a modest £5. My colleague, Stanley Bunnell, duly wrote to Colonel Stephens at Tonbridge, requesting authority to bid for it. Stephens cannot have been devoid of a sense of humour, even if he was indifferent to our discomfort, for in a day or two he replied:

"My Dear Bunnell,

Transport facilities

With reference to your request, I regret the purchase of a trap is quite out of the question, as would be that of a sedan chair.

Yours faithfully"

Captain Griffiths enjoyed the use of the only other form of transport provided, a 680cc JAP engined Sunbeam motor cycle and sidecar and occasionally, during one of Griffiths' "Lost weekends", Bunnell and myself used to borrow this, after first casting off the sidecar, for a trip to London where I remembered we both had a powerful attraction.

The conditions under which those engaged on the line worked would be considered intolerable today. Many of the labourers slept out, under roughly constructed shelters in quarries near to where they were working, due to the difficult road access and there was undoubtedly a great deal of suffering. One particularly unpleasant task allotted to me was the fixing up of a "pulsometer" steam pump - just a hollow casting with two compartments and valves about 2 feet 6 inches long - to drain a quarry a few hundred yards from Halwill Junction to recover a body. The contractor's pay clerk had drowned himself when he found that he was some £100 short in his "float" and was unable to account for the discrepancy. At the inquest, it turned out that the missing sum was simply due to the practice of "subbing" a proportion of each man's weekly wages, something the head accounting office did not recognise and did not take into account when notifying the pay clerk of the cash that he should have had in hand.

I left Stephens' employment early in 1925, several months before the completion of the line, which was, I believe, on schedule. By then the London & South Western Railway had been merged into the Southern Railway and the latter concern automatically assumed responsibility for working the North Devon & Cornwall Junction line. Looking back on those days, now over half a century ago, many of the unorthodox methods and practices that were adopted in order to make the project a reality, within the constraints of a severely limited financial budget, would be entirely unacceptable today. Nevertheless, this small railway served the needs of the local community well for nearly 40 years, until in 1965 when it became just another "unremunerative branch line", ripe for deletion from the Western Region of British Railways.

27.1   W.H.Austen obtained this view of "work in progress on the southern half of the route".

Chapter 28

Memories of Salford Terrace

by Charles Clapper (1976)

I first encountered the stern, even fierce, face of Colonel Stephens in the pages of *The Railway Magazine*, where, in the May 1919 issue, it enlivened an article on the East Kent Light Railway. In the next decade I was able to see all the minor railways of England and Wales through the good offices of Ronald Shephard, founder of the Wimbledon Model Railway Club, who provided transport and was liable to fix rather arbitrary times of travel, having a penchant for night journeys.

There was plenty of talent on these expeditions - Fred Ashford, who became an industrial designer and was responsible for a range of diesel shunting locomotives at the designer stage; Andrew Earley, who after the Second World War left the London & North Eastern Railway, where he had been a traffic apprentice, to become ports director of East African Railways & Harbours, and Ronald Plummer, who even before the war had left the LMS service to become an industrial traffic manager. How little the railways thought of conserving their flow of brilliant young men. The two northern railways were particularly improvident in this respect.

On one of these trips, Fred Ashford and I set off towards Canterbury by coach and, arriving late at night, were overtaken by a cleric in a motorcar who was seeking a remote house to convey to the occupants a message about the death of a relative. As the cleric had no map and we were amply provided with the one-inch ordnance survey we offered him our services in return for a lift. This resulted in us being left somewhere along the East Kent line after 1 in the morning on a fine summer's night; we were far away from orthodox accommodation and so tired that we yielded to the temptation of sleeping rough on Ash station, where the shelter made some sort of protection from such wind as there was. The next day's easy walk landed us at Shepherdswell yard well in time for the afternoon train and we had a profitable conversation with the driver. He first invited us to wait outside Golgotha Hill tunnel and then to join him on the footplate. He then told us of Colonel Stephens's visit to Shepherdswell the previous week. Stephens had apparently taken exception to an engine photograph published by a railway enthusiast with the original lettering of "L.S.W.R." outlined in chalk and looking much more robust than the current lettering should have been. Actually the engine on our train when we boarded it had the insignia of the Kent & East Sussex Railway on its side tanks, for it was that company's 2-4-0 tank *"Tenterden"* which was on loan to the East Kent. It suffered pronounced big end knock only equalled by a Bulleid 4-6-2 on a 25% cut-off.

The description of the Stephens' wrath over the photograph (bowler hat one way, stick the other and withering words all round) made the two of us resolve to make a call at 23 Salford Terrace, Tonbridge, the next week when we were visiting hop-farming friends near by and this we duly did. Very happily we found the Colonel in jovial mood, not at all averse from having two railway enthusiasts turn up uninvited on a Friday afternoon and before long he was recounting the origins of the numerous miniature samples of sanitary ware that decorated the mantelpiece of the main office; showing off his collection of first-class passes of pre-grouping railways and apropos the Great Northern one telling them of the company's one-time ambition to revive the Llanymynech and Porthdinllaen project across the mountains of North Wales. He became very animated when he told how some members of the Great Northern board room had entertained the idea of acquiring the Potteries Shrewsbury & North Wales Railway and extending it to the port that is reputed to be nearest Ireland.

This gave me a lasting interest in the near misses of the railway world, from the Beckenham, Lewes and Brighton to the Mistley, Thorpe & Walton; railways that were planned to the last detail, but failed to secure Parliamentary approval; others like the Potteries Shrewsbury & North Wales, that received sanction from a Parliament that enforced no overall planning and particularly of planning the finances of the railway system. This let down more than one of Stephens's own ventures such as the Maidstone and Headcorn Junction, that would have given a logical outlet northward to the Kent & East Sussex, even though it would have involved surmounting four miles of a 1 in 47 bank to get over the Flagstone Hills by Sutton Valence. This, of course, was the reason the Kent & East Sussex had added a powerful 0-8-0 tank engine to its locomotive stock. A more intimate case for Stephens was the Southern Heights Light Railway, for which £400,000 was promised in American money and £140,000 in Southern Railway electrification capital when the launching of the London Passenger Transport Board scheme made the future of the 15½ miles of electrified single line round Biggin Hill too uncertain for contemplation and it was quietly dropped from Southern compartment maps.

Colonel Stephens was one of the best conversationalists; one had no time to be bored, for he produced such a variety of interesting topics and a thought back to that afternoon at Salford Terrace shows what a great range of subjects he not only touched upon, but in some cases went into in great depth. The pros and cons of passenger service on the Snailbeach District Railways was one of these; he showed us a plan of how a connection would be made to Pontesbury station if the capital expenditure for such a service (perhaps for a few summer weeks only) was thought to be justified. Another subject on which he was eloquent was that one of his East Kent men was an ex-Black-and-tan and during the "troubles" had had a shot-gun poked through his letter-box.

The friendship begun that afternoon lasted until Stephens's untimely death, enhanced by a number of meetings, usually at Euston, when he was on the way to North Wales; these were illuminated by pithy remarks on personalities at the Ministry of Transport and sometimes by rude remarks on Festiniog enginemen, such as the one who clouded a posed photograph with injector steam. In general, he had some admiration for the work done on the Festiniog in cramped conditions by the footplate crews. On these meetings at Euston, Stephens used to keep me posted with how the light railways connected with his organisation and the Southern Railway were progressing. It was evident that Sir Herbert Walker and Stephens, although operating in very different spheres, enjoyed more than a passing acquaintance and had a number of characteristics in common. Stephens, of course, was consultant to the Plymouth Devonport & South Western Junction Railway when they sought advice on the conversion of the less than standard gauge East Cornwall Minerals Railway into the standard-gauge Callington branch, connected with their main line at Bere Alston by the magnificent Calstock viaduct over the Tamar. The afternoon of the first meeting Stephens told me how the foundations of the viaduct are as far below the bed of the Tamar as the viaduct is high.

In this Stephens showed as not the man of little light railways, but as a man who could conceive and carry out majestic enterprises worthy to rank with the best of the Continental viaduct builders - ouvrages D'art. Admiration for this aspect of Stephens's character no doubt accounts for the considerable friendship that was generated between Walker and Stephens, even if it was of a somewhat intermittent type. One of the lines that was constructed as a result of this rather unlikely association eventually protected the northwest flank of the new Southern company, but, of course, was first thought of many years before 1923, in London & South Western days.

In the 1920s, motor transport was beginning to establish itself on a firm basis and the bus and the lorry was beginning to feel its feet; this was a fault in Stephens; he quoted statistics about buses dating from the 1907 vintage of vehicle, blissfully unaware of the great advance in commercial vehicle design that had come about with the London B-type bus in 1910 and had been accelerated by the 1914-18 war, although he made use of motor vehicle chassis on rails. At this period the light railway business, although fundamentally weak, still appeared comparatively flourishing.

The only thing wrong that we found with Headcorn station about 1926 was that some fish had taken it into their heads to thrive in the engine water tower. Most intriguing of the Kent & East Sussex rolling-stock was the Pickering railcar, which seemed to have had such great possibilities, but at that time was shown more or less perpetually "under repair". One wonders whether it would have had a better fate had it been equipped with a Sentinel boiler and power plant. For that matter I wondered what part Stephens himself took in its design, seeing how much out of the ordinary run of Pickering construction it was. As long before as 1895, Stephens had designed a compression-ignition railcar for the Rye & Camber Tramway which in the 1920s went modern with a Lister petrol tractor. He was so early in the diesel field that he continued to refer to the patentee as Ackroyd-Stuart, with no thought of the German claims to pioneering in this field.

Plans for the East Kent, which had been urged bombastically by its first chairman, who threatened the South Eastern & Chatham Company back in 1911 with building a new line from the coalfield to London if suitable "facilities" were not granted to the East Kent company, rather like the row that developed between the original East Kent company and the South Eastern that resulted in the formation of the London, Chatham & Dover company.

The directors of the light railway company had a number of plans for development - a triangular junction at Eastry and an outlet to port facilities at Richborough; a new port on the Thames; new facilities at Dover Harbour, including a 1½ mile tunnel from the neighbourhood of Kearsney to avoid the shipment coal traversing the streets below the cliffs, were explored by the Southern Railway on behalf of other collieries even after Tilmanstone Colliery had determined upon reaching Dover Harbour by aerial ropeway to rebuff the East Kent board; just after the 1914-18 war when the Channel Tunnel seemed quite a likely eventuality, an East Kent branch to Alkham, at that time a popular site for tunnel entrance and marshalling sidings, was planned.

In the upshot traffic from the coalfield proved far below the hopes entertained about 1910, when French syndicates were so interested in the possibilities of Kent. Optimism was a characteristic of Stephens; for example, until 1922 the Shropshire & Montgomeryshire Railway handled up to 20 wagons of freight daily into Shrewsbury from the Cambrian Railways. He saw no reason for such traffic to decline after the grouping of the railways, but decline it did, very sharply after 1 January 1923 because the Great Western Railway had its own route from Llanymynech and beyond into Shrewsbury and, again, beyond without recourse to routing traffic over the Shropshire & Montgomeryshire. As late as 1927 when I travelled the length of the S&M there still seemed to be a reasonable amount of freight presenting itself, although by then the popularity of road haulage was beginning to bite into railway traffics on railways great and small. Passenger traffic on the S&M was also beginning to diminish, discouraged by the comfortless railcars which Stephens had a year or two earlier deemed such an economical idea.

In these days of enthusiasts' railways, a line like the Weston Clevedon, & Portishead could have been exploited to the full, with the original locomotives and American-type passenger stock. It ended up with two Brighton Terriers which were overhauled at Swindon, but it had begun with a stock of 2-2-2 tank engines from the Furness Railway.

This imparted an archaic atmosphere to the railway which was not wholly deserved and not dispelled even by the passenger coaches, specially built for what was thought of at the opening as the Weston & Clevedon Steam Tramway. These vehicles had acetylene lighting (used also on the engine headlights) and tramcar-like longitudinal seating. In the spring of 1901 these Lancaster Railway Carriage & Wagon vehicles had the seats renewed, except in the leather-upholstered first-class compartment, after which they provided wooden transverse seats for 50 in the second and 10 firsts. Stephens was persuaded to take charge in 1911.

Another Stephens line that I knew in my youth from days when family holidays were usually at Bognor was the one built without specific powers which enjoyed the lengthy official title of Hundred of Manhood & Selsey Tramways. Shortened usually to the Selsey Tramway, it prospered before the days of cars and buses in linking Chichester to Selsey and it gained fame by Stephens wringing an Order from the Ministry of Transport to cover it under the Railway Construction Facilities Act of 1864; to the confusion of many, almost simultaneously he obtained the West Sussex Light Railway Order for the Wittering branch. A last tribute by Sir Herbert Walker to his late friend Stephens was that before plans for the Portsmouth No. 2 electrification were crystallised the possibilities of reopening and electrifying the Selsey line were investigated. It was a matter of some regret at Waterloo that not only were the physical limitations of the line against its development for sophisticated outer-suburban branch service with multiple-unit stock, but the operation of a useful service to Selsey in conjunction with Bognor and Portsmouth facilities presented insuperable problems.

28.1 *The former LSWR Beattie 0-6-0 was photographed on the EKLR on 14th May 1927, still with crude modified lettering. (H.C.Casserley)*

28.2 *The EKLR terminus at Shepherdswell was recorded in the 1920s. Centre is the curved connection to the main line. Much has been restored today.*

28.3   This is Calstock Viaduct on the PD&SWJR. According to Stephens, the foundations of the viaduct are as far below the bed of the Tamar as the viaduct is high.

28.4   The American style rolling stock of the WC&PR was recorded at Ebdon Lane.

Chapter 29

Colonel Stephens in the North Downs

by Tom Burnham (1980/81)

Part 1 - The Orpington Cudham and Tatsfield Light Railway

The dip slope of the North Downs, on the border of Kent and Surrey, has attracted railway promoters for many years, but their efforts have always been defeated by the difficult terrain and the speculative nature of the financial returns from this attractive but, relatively sparsely populated area. Before looking at the last two railways proposed for this area, both of which were engineered by H F Stephens, it will be helpful to review the earlier railway developments.

First in the field was the London to Brighton main line, passing through Coulsdon and Merstham and having a tunnel over a mile long under the Downs. This line was opened in 1841. In 1856, a branch from it was opened with the support of the South Eastern Railway from Purley along the Caterham Valley and shortly afterwards, between 1858 and 1860, the railways forming the London Chatham & Dover Railway main line were opened along the northern fringe of the area through Beckenham and Bromley. The main line pattern was completed with the SER Lewisham to Tonbridge cut-off line, opened to Chislehurst in 1865 and throughout in 1868. This had a ruling gradient of 1 in 100 to reach the summit at Polhill Tunnel.

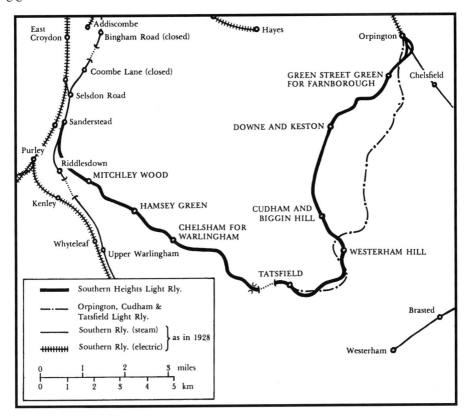

In 1863 the Beckenham, Lewes and Brighton Railway was promoted with the support of the LC&DR and the SER (co-operating for once) to give an alternative route to Brighton. Starting from junctions with both railways in the Beckenham area, it was to pass West Wickham and Hayes before taking a southerly course to Tatsfield, and on to Limpsfield, East Grinstead and Lewes. An Act of Parliament was obtained in 1866, but before construction could be started the financial crisis of that year resulted in the virtual bankruptcy of the LC&DR and a territorial agreement between the SER and LB&SCR and the project was abandoned. A scheme of more local interest, proposed in 1865, was the West Kent Railway, which was to have started with a junction with the LC&DR south of Penge and run through Eden Park and West Wickham to Keston. Here there was to be a branch to Farnborough, while the main line continued south to Titsey.

Another proposal for a competitive Brighton line, the Metropolitan and Brighton Railway of 1875, would have followed a similar course to the Beckenham, Lewes and Brighton between Beckenham and East Grinstead. In 1879, the Shortlands, Knockholt and Otford Railway was prompted by local landowners with active support from the LC&DR. This would have left the LC&DR main line near Shortlands and run through Hayes, Keston, Downe, Cudham and Knockholt to terminate in a cutting 74 feet deep at Knockholt Pound. Although ostensibly a local line, it is clear that the LC&DR hoped to extend it across the Darenth Valley to join their Otford to Maidstone and Ashford branch, giving an alternative route to Folkestone. This connection would have needed some heavy engineering works; it is interesting that the newly-formed SE&CR Managing Committee considered a rather similar link, from the south end of Polhill tunnel on the SER main line to a point between Otford and Kemsing on the LC&DR Maidstone branch, in 1899 but evidently did not consider the expense justified. The Shortlands, Knockholt and Otford Bill was rejected and the landowners turned to the SER for assistance, with the result that the Hayes branch from Elmers End on the Addiscombe Road extension of the SER Mid-Kent line was opened in 1882. Meanwhile, south of the North Downs scarp, the SER Westerham branch had been opened in 1881.

As a countermeasure to the SER threats to Brighton during the 1860s, the LB&SCR had obtained powers for the Surrey and Sussex Junction Railway from Croydon to Tunbridge Wells. Although some work was started on this, the 1867 agreement with the SER, and the Brighton's own financial difficulties led to its cessation. In 1878 the project was revived, this time jointly with the SER, and the Croydon, Oxted and East Grinstead Railway and this was opened in 1884. From a junction with the Brighton main line at South Croydon it climbed at about 1 in 100 for some six miles (including the half mile Riddlesdown Tunnel) to a summit north of Oxted Tunnel. The Woodside and South Croydon joint line was opened in 1885 from Woodside, on the SER Addiscombe Road branch, to a junction with the Croydon and Oxted at Selsdon Road (where a new station was opened). The object of this line was to provide the SER with an alternative access to the Oxted line and it completed the railway network in the area.

A Bill in the 1895 session for a Hayes and Farnborough Railway sought powers for a short branch from the LC&DR at Bromley to Hayes Common and Farnborough, competing with the SER. Although it was rejected at an early stage, it is clear that the old rivalry between the two companies was not dead and that there was still talk of invasions of other companies' territory and of blocking lines to protect one's own. It was against this background that a company entitled the Orpington Cudham and Tatsfield Light Railway Co Ltd. was incorporated in

November 1898. The nominal capital consisted of 1,000 £1 shares, of which only seven were issued, to William Pritchard, a Cheapside solicitor, and six of his clerks, but the objects were less modest, viz:

1. To construct, purchase, lease or otherwise acquire any light railway or tramway in the counties of Kent, Sussex, Surrey and the adjoining counties.
2. To equip, maintain and work all light railways and tramways belonging to the Company, or which this Company may possess a right to run over and work. And so on.

Two days after incorporation, this rather unlikely sounding company filed an application for a Light Railway Order for the construction of a standard gauge line some 7¾ miles long from the SER at Orpington; the engineer was H F Stephens, then corresponding from an office at 6 Old Jewry, London EC. Application for a Light Railway Order in the name of a limited company was a somewhat unusual procedure and was to create difficulty; it was usual for powers to be sought either by individual promoters or by an established railway company.

The line was to run south from Orpington along the Cudham valley and for the first 2½ miles was relatively level. A continuous 1 in 40 gradient for the next 2½ miles then took it on to high ground to which it kept for the last 2¾ miles of winding and undulating route to Tatsfield. In all, over the half the line was to be at a gradient of 1 in 50 or steeper, and the Board of Trade commented that this would make working difficult and some special regulations regarding the brake power on goods or mixed trains might be necessary. For this reason also, a proposal by Stephens that continuous brakes should be required only for trains with more than three passenger vehicles was rejected. (The same proposal was made and rejected in the case of the virtually flat Sheppey Light Railway.) No stations were shown on the plans submitted and their siting would have been difficult. Presumably a station for Cudham would have been provided at about 4 to 4½ miles, on the long 1 in 40 climb, and this is no doubt why Stephens requested powers to deviate from the line shown in the plans provided the gradient did not exceed 1 in 30. This request was also turned down by the Board, who considered that it should be possible to provide level sections for stations within the limits of deviation without increasing the ruling gradient beyond 1 to 40. The estimated cost of construction appeared high at £69,254 and the Board considered the proposed share capital of £80,000 with powers to borrow an additional £26,700 "quite outrageous".

A public enquiry was held by the Light Railway Commissioners at Orpington on Thursday 2 March 1899. There was a certain amount of opposition from some local landowners, such as Sir John Lubbock, although Lord Stanhope and others were in favour. Objections were also raised by the St. Joseph's Orphanage at Farnborough who were concerned at the loss of their playground to the railway and the possibility of wagons of manure being left in sidings adjacent to the premises; assurances were given by Stephens that appropriate deviations would be made. The most serious ground for objection was undoubtedly the fear that if the powers were granted the company would lack the financial resources needed to complete construction. William Rigby, the railway contractor, who was described as one of the promoters of the scheme (although the application was in the name of the limited company and he had no shares in that) said that he thought there would be no difficulty in raising the money required and that Mr. Willis of the SER had agreed that the company would work the line. In view of this, and the fact that several of the landowners approved and were prepared to sell land for the railway on favourable terms, the

Commissioners decided to grant an Order on condition that suitable persons were nominated as Directors of the company to be incorporated under the order. This condition caused considerable delay, but in January 1901 the promoters stated that Thomas H Fox and Richard Jones had consented to act as Directors. Mr. Fox was owner of a large brewery in Orpington and Chairman of Farnborough Parish Council and had supported the scheme from an early stage and Mr Jones, of East Wickham House, Welling, had been one of the promoters of the Bexley Heath Railway and so was presumably practised in the art of haggling with the SER!

The Orpington Cudham and Tatsfield Light Railway Order was confirmed on 10 June 1902. It provided for a line 7 miles 3 furlongs 5 chains in length, the last quarter of a mile at Tatsfield having been abandoned. Maximum axle load was 14 tons and a 25 mph speed limit was imposed, with lower limits of 20 mph on gradients steeper than 1 in 50 and 10 mph on curves of less than 9 chains radius. Rails were to be at least 60 lb per yd and check rails were required on all curves sharper than 9 chains. The three public road level crossings were to be gated. Clauses were included for the protection of the SER, the Earl of Derby (who had the right to have a siding built for him), A C Norman of Tubbenden and the St. Joseph's and St. Anne's Orphanages. The Board of Trade "intimated to the promotors that they must expect, owing to gradient &c. in this case, rather a more serious inspection of the line than usual and they were advised to ascertain the requirements of the inspecting officer beforehand".

It is interesting to consider how the SER might have operated this line had they ever been called upon to do so. Although a number of suburban trains terminated at Orpington, especially after 1905 when the main line was widened to four tracks as far as that point, axle load restrictions and short platforms would have favoured a self-contained service. The SER was poorly provided with small tank engines and worked most of its branch lines with elderly tender engines but the OC&TLR Order (like many others) stipulated a 15 mph speed limit for tender locomotives running tender first (many SER branch termini had turntables, but there is no indication of an intention to provide one at Tatsfield). Of the ex-Chatham types available to the SE&CR. the rebuilt "Sondes" class 2-4-0 tanks would have been acceptable (two worked the Sheppey line when it opened) and the "Scotchmen" class of Martley 0-4-2 well tanks would also have been just within the limit with reduced coal and water capacities (546 of this class was used on the Hawkhurst branch with its 1 in 60 gradients). The combination of gradient and axle loading would certainly have proved a severe test for steam traction in any form and the thought of this might well have inspired a forward-looking engineer such as H F Stephens to consider other types of motive power.

The period set in the LRO for the compulsory acquisition of land was two years with a further two years for construction. The powers lapsed with no attempt to make use of them and the promoters did not apply for an extension of time. It may, perhaps, be assumed that the line was originally promoted with the object of selling the powers to the SER as a blocking line against LC&DR attack. It was too late for this as the SER and LC&DR had formed a working union in 1899 and the Managing Committee had enough difficulty in coping with existing competitive lines of doubtful profitability without adding to their number. In the absence of such support, neither contractors nor landowners felt able to invest in the scheme. By 1905, letters from the Companies Registration Office to the Orpington Cudham and Tatsfield Light Railway Co Ltd's registered office were being returned marked "not known" and in November 1906 the company was dissolved. It only remains to add that although in this case Stephens was acting only as engineer and had no financial interest, the failure of the promoters to complete the line was remembered by the local people and was held against him when he put forward his next railway scheme for the district, the Southern Heights, nearly 25 years later.

* * * * * * * * * * * * * * * * * *

Part 2 – The Southern Heights Light Railway

This light railway was proposed in the same area by the same engineer - H F Stephens. The differences between the old and new railway schemes show the extent of the technical and social changes between the late Victorian and postwar eras.

Housing development had begun even without the stimulus of a railway. In the Biggin Hill area this was mainly in the form of shacks on large plots of land, which were especially popular after the war, while on the Surrey side larger and more expensive properties were the rule. Motor bus services had started just before the war and were provided mainly by the London General company and their East Surrey associates, although some independent operators also served the area in the 1920s. However, this development was slight compared with that in other areas around London, as in Middlesex where the Underground group's new and newly-electrified railways had turned country villages into suburbs within a few years. The recently formed Southern Railway was busily electrifying its extensive suburban network (reaching Orpington in July 1925) and it appeared that the faster, more frequent services made possible by electric traction would have the same effect south of the river. In short, it seemed that Sir Edmund Beckett's jibe (in connection with the Hayes & Farnborough Bill of 1895) that "whenever Mr. Forbes wants to make a railway, people will be born in London to go and use it" had become a reality.

No doubt this is what H M Bates, Sir Charles Igglesden, S R Jaggard. J MacVeagh and Lt Col. H F Stephens hoped when on 30 November 1925 they applied for a Light Railway Order for a 15½ mile line between Orpington and Sanderstead, a distance of less than 9½ miles in a straight line. This proposed line, the Southern Heights Light Railway, was very different from the rural backwaters we usually associate with Col Stephens. It would have had no level crossings with public roads and was designed to be worked by ordinary Southern Railway stock - electric trains for passengers and steam engines for goods. The ruling gradient of 1 in 50 was quite acceptable for electric traction - the Southern's Wimbledon-Sutton line built for electric trains in 1929-30 had a maximum gradient of 1 in 44.

Of the promoters, Sir Charles Igglesden (1861-1949); a resident of Ashford, Kent, was an author and for many years editor of the *Kentish Express*. Sargeant Robert Jaggard was a local landowner with an interest in some 750 acres at Leaves Green and Downe. Jeremiah MacVeagh (1870-1932), an Ulsterman, was MP for South Down and a director of various railways with which Stephens was connected, such as the North Devon & Cornwall Junction and the East Kent (he resigned from the East Kent board with Stephens in 1926 to make room for nominees of the SR).

The proposed line left the SR down slow line just south of Orpington station and dropped at 1 in 50 to pass under the main line on an 11 chain curve. A spur (Railway No. 2, 33 chains long) joined the up side of the SR line. The first station was a halt at Green Street Green for Farnborough (1m 7c); like all other non passing stations this would have had temporary buildings to facilitate subsequent widening.

The line undulated to the next halt, Downe and Keston (3m 5c) and then climbing started in earnest with over two miles continuous 1 in 50 to Cudham and Biggin Hill (5m 14c). A siding was to be provided for the Biggin Hill RAF station. Westerham Hill (6m 11c) was to be the first passing station and the line reached its summit of 740 feet (much higher than any point on the Southern Electric then or since) near the Kent-Surrey border just before Tatsfield (8m 9c), also a passing place. About a mile further on there would have been a 440 yard unlined tunnel through chalk, almost immediately followed by an 88 yard viaduct 60 feet high over a sand pit. From 10 miles the line was to fall at 1 in 50 to Chelsham for Warlingham (11m 44c, with a siding but no loop) and was then relatively level to Hamsey Green (12m 56c), the final passing station. From Hamsey Green there was again a 1 in 50 fall past Mitchley Wood (14m 12c) to the junction with the Oxted line of the SR (at 15m 32c) which was immediately south of the Purley Downs Road bridge, about half a mile south of Sanderstead station. 8¾ miles were at the ruling gradient of 1 in 50 and the sharpest curve, apart from the junction at Orpington, was of 15 chains. Fourteen bridges would have been built over roads and fourteen under, all of concrete; there were to be no level crossings with public roads. Apart from the tunnel and viaduct, major engineering works included an embankment 50 feet high at Limestone Bottom (7m 75c) and others 54 feet and 36 feet high at 9m 50c and 9m 70c.

The Ministry of Transport inspectors commented that "the works generally are of a much heavier character than one expects to find on a Light Railway. It is evidently to be regarded as a branch railway, intended for electrical operation by the Southern Railway. In the event of electrical operation the degree of equipment is likely to be higher than with steam in respect of fencing, platform accommodation, etc. The estimate of the cost of construction is under the mark, considering the works contemplated, especially bridging and, I think, tunnelling." There was in fact some variation in the estimated cost. This was originally given as £511,148 excluding electrification, but by March 1928 this figure had increased to £604,000.

The Southern were interested in the project from an early stage and the solicitor reported the application to the Board at their meeting on 17 December 1925. On 24 February 1926 the General Manager, Sir Herbert Walker, recommended that the SR should agree to work the SHLR when it was built and to guarantee the interest on debentures up to 5% on £300,000; this was agreed subject to powers for construction being granted and the SR being represented on the SHLR board. The following week it was agreed that if necessary the SR should pay for the fixed electrical equipment (about £140,000) and take payment in preference shares.

Objections to the application for a LRO were received from several local councils and landowners and from the London General and East Surrey bus companies - the latter, on the grounds of competition, being withdrawn later. A public enquiry was, therefore, held in the Village Hall at Orpington on 3 and 4 March 1926 before Mr. A D Erskine and Mr T L Peterson for the Ministry of Transport. Col H N Bidder, counsel for the promoters, opening the proceedings, "directed attention to the configuration of the country where the railway was proposed. It was high ground and the development of the railway system so far had been along the lower ground, so that the large piece of country of about 20 square miles, within 15 miles of London, remained untouched." He pointed out also that in consequence of the housing pressure in London it was difficult to find any suitable place to live and a piece of country such as that had vast possibilities of development from the residential point of view. As to the nature of the line, he thought it was very appropriate, in view of certain difficulties of construction, that it should be a light railway which allowed certain economics in construction, owing for instance to the fact that there would be a Parliamentary limitation of speed to 25 mph (the eventual LRO did not specify a maximum speed but empowered the Ministry of Transport to fix one). The lack of rail facilities was a distinct hindrance to the agricultural interests of the plateau, though a scheme of that sort, involving over half a million pounds, could not be started merely for improving the agricultural trade of the district. If the railway was made it would give direct access to London by a system of trains which would inevitably develop the district as a residential suburb - a development which, he maintained, it was very much in the public interest should take place. A district like that had got to grow and increase and he thought they would be satisfied that, if that railway were constructed and properly run, it would develop and grow rapidly as a suburb or dormitory for London. With regard to the opponents of the scheme, Col. Bidder said that the impression in his own mind was "that while there was a great deal of noise about them there was really not very much stuffing." He had never known a case where so much financial support had been forthcoming at the enquiry, as three quarters of the £600,000 required had been promised.

The first witness was Col. Stephens as engineer and promoter, who claimed that "it is difficult to talk about engineering matters on this line because there aren't any. It is a perfectly simple line. It is not an easy line to lay out because it is rather rough country, but as laid out there are no engineering matters worth talking about." The greatest problems were due to the fact that "Orpington is rather an awkward place to get out of" and the ruling gradient of 1 in 50 was "quite an ordinary gradient for a light railway". Mr. F G Thomas (counsel for Coulsdon & Purley UDC and Godstone RDC) in his examination raised the question of the Orpington Cudham and Tatsfield Light Railway:

Mr. Thomas: 'If this enquiry had been held yesterday it would have been a very interesting anniversary for you.'
Witness: 'I have not seen the papers for many years.'
Mr. Thomas: ' I have here a report taken from the "Bromley and District Times', of the 3rd March, 1899.'
Witness: 'The Order was not made until 1902.'
Mr. Thomas: 'The enquiry was held by the Light Railway Commissioners, I think in this very hall, 26 years ago yesterday.'
Mr. Erskine: 'I remember it.'
Mr. Thomas said that on that occasion evidence was called on behalf of the South Eastern Railway that they were prepared to make an agreement with the promoters, and it was on that assurance that the Commissioners recommended the railway.
Witness said he could not say; he was simply the engineer in connection with the original scheme, but he believed the agreement in question never was made. Mr. J Abady (counsel for Bromley RDC) also referred to the abortive attempt of 26 years before, the "dead hand" of which was still felt in the district.

Sir Herbert Walker, General Manager of the Southern Railway, was the next witness in favour of the line. He said that he was prepared to advise the SR to work the line and he thought they would be willing to guarantee the interest on the debentures. The SR would find the capital for electrification and take part of it in shares. He believed the district had "great possibilities for rapid development as a dormitory for London and otherwise" and said that "he did not consider it necessary to get out estimates of the probable traffic earnings of the line, but was satisfied, relying on his Company's experience as regards development on other new lines in the vicinity of London, that the railway would in a very few years be self-supporting." The SR would electrify the first part of their Oxted line to Sanderstead and would provide a circular service from Charing Cross.

Other witnesses called by the promoters were the Assistant General Manager of the SR, Mr. G S Szlumper, the Electrical Engineer, Mr H Jones - who confirmed that their standard system of electrification with a third rail at 600V dc would be used - and Mr. Carl Lockheed of the contractors Sir Robert McAlpine & Sons, who said his firm would be willing to undertake the construction of the line for the amount of the estimate and to take some of this in shares (Stephens expected them to take £20,000). A number of landowners and farmers also spoke in favour. A representative of the Ministry of Labour gave figures for unemployment in the district and Squadron Leader Buckeridge from the Biggin Hill RAF station said that "the Air Minister's view is that the proximity of a railway to the air station would be considered very valuable." The only promoter other than Col. Stephens to appear was Mr. Jaggard. He said in his opinion the line was absolutely essential if the district was to be developed. He was prepared to support the undertaking financially, but would not say to what extent.
Mr. Thomas: Are you prepared to find £100?
Witness: I would prefer not to go into that.

Sir Henry Lennard, the Chairman of Bromley RDC, opened the case against the line by saying that they felt the project was of such magnitude that it ought to be submitted to Parliament instead of coming before the Light Railway Commissioners. The Council felt very strongly that no Order should be made until the money was absolutely secured and there remained no fear of the line coming derelict. His knowledge of the district did not lead him to share the optimism of the promoters as to the revenue that would be forthcoming. He could not hold out any prospect for the ordinary shareholders and would think it would be at least 20 years before a dividend on the ordinary capital would be paid.

Col. Bidder pressed the witness very closely as to whether his Council would not welcome a satisfactory railway across the district. Sir Henry said they would not oppose it. Counsel pressed the point and said he was asking whether the Council would not welcome it, which was a different thing from not opposing.
Witness: That I am not prepared to say.

The other objection raised by the Councils was that the LRO might interfere with their town planning proposals, although the railway promoters argued that these were only schemes on paper and it was unfair to burden them with making provision for bridges over roads that might never be built. Mr. Thomas, for the Surrey councils, observed that on the most favourable working agreement the SHLR would have to earn £8,000 per mile to produce the necessary revenue (this would in fact have left the ordinary shareholders with a 3.6% dividend) and that this was unlikely. If the SR were prepared to go so far in support of the line why were they not prepared to find the capital? He submitted that no evidence had been called that the line was really needed. Objections were also made by the owners of the Aperfield Court estate and by Lord Avebury, whose private burial ground was within 100 yards of the planned line.

Reviewing the enquiry, the Ministry of Transport were generally in favour of the application, provided there was a reasonable chance of the money being raised and the line built. One comment was that "the line will, in fact form an integral part of the Southern Railway, and it might have been better if the Southern Railway Company had themselves accepted full responsibility for its promotion and for financing it." The promoters continued their discussions with the Ministry, with the local authorities and landowners and over the working agreement with the SR, Stephens was under pressure to make the line more like a SR suburban line, finally (on 21 December 1927) writing "the Promoters applied for a Light Railway Order, and they are unable to accept the burden, which might be put upon them, of constructing the railway as a Heavy Railway, with the means at their disposal." Nevertheless, an agreement was eventually drafted and was approved by the SR shareholders at their meeting on 21 February 28. The main points were:

The SHLR were to acquire land and construct the line and the SR would work and maintain it for 75% of the gross receipts. The SR would equip the line for electric working and be paid by the SHLR in cash or shares.

The SR would guarantee interest of 5% on £330,000 of SHLR debentures.

If the SR had to pay £10,000 a year or more under the guarantee they would have the right to appoint two (later increased to three) directors to the SHLR board.

If the SR wished to take over the SHLR, the SHLR would support it.

In April 1928, Sir Herbert Walker, Col. Stephens and a number of SR senior officers inspected the route and approved the sites chosen for stations. Later that year, on 29 December, the LRO was granted and soon afterwards an article describing the line appeared in *The Times*. 'Our Correspondent' in Tonbridge (could this have been the Colonel himself?) said "the line will touch the highest points in Kent and Surrey ... Various estates in this district are being rapidly developed and at present are entirely unserved by the railway... The opposition entered at the Ministry of Transport inquiry by the local authorities and landowners has been withdrawn or settled on agreed terms... No less than 631,000 cubic yards of chalk will have to be excavated; 20,000 cubic yards of concrete will be used for the foundations of bridges, &c.; 1,000 tons of steelwork will be utilized... The length of the contract will be from 18 months to 21 months... The engineer and promoter of the scheme is Col. H F Stephens, who has been associated with light railways all over the country. He has constructed 146 miles at a cost of £842,000."

The LRO allowed a share capital of £400,000 with powers to borrow a further £400,000. As we have seen, the SR had agreed to guarantee the interest of £330,000 of debentures and this would have made it relatively easy to find takers; Stephens had counted on issuing them at 95%. The ordinary shares of what would at best be a long-term investment were a different matter, however. The promoters would have been able to take only a modest proportion of them themselves and proposed to issue them at 60% of their nominal value.

Against this gloomy financial background planning continued. A A Jackson describes a meeting in May 1929 between Col. Stephens and senior officers of the SR at which the layout of the connection at Orpington, including a berthing siding on the down side, was agreed. The SR Assistant Engineer (New Works) was to begin tipping spoil to widen the embankment and it was agreed to build the SHLR bridge under the main line to double track width, perhaps as an alternative to the spur to the up fast line. Col. Stephens refused a suggestion by the SR that the formation of the whole line should be built to double track width (at an additional cost of

£50,000) but agreed to consider this from Orpington to Green Street Green and possibly also from Sanderstead to Chelsham. The SR also required the realignment of certain curves and ballasting and fencing to their usual standards for electric lines.

It seems that no construction on the SHLR was ever carried out. Although there is a persistent local rumour that some work was done on a cutting near Farnborough, as the embankment of the main line south of Orpington is thickly wooded, evidence of any tipping is not easily seen.

It was reported in October 1930 that the SHLR was about to apply for an extension of time. Order and plans were submitted in 1931 for a deviation for about 1½ miles just west of Tatsfield. This would have avoided the tunnel at the expense of a rather higher viaduct - 75 feet instead of 60 feet. The promoters were evidently still finding it difficult to raise unsecured ordinary capital - according to C F Klapper, the railway historian, Col. Stephens hoped to raise £400,000 in the United States and intended to go there to complete the deal. A further severe blow to the project came in July 1931 when the SR board decided that as the SHLR powers had lapsed "and having regard to the altered position in view of the new Board to be set up under the London Passenger Transport Bill to control all transport within the London Traffic Area, the promoters should be informed that the Company was not prepared to support any application for a revival of those powers." By then the chief driving force behind the project was removed as Col Stephens became seriously ill at the beginning of 1931 and died in October of that year. Indeed the worry associated with the scheme had been a contributory factor to his death. However, an attempt was made to continue without him and in June 1932 Sir Herbert Walker informed his board that the SHLR board "having been reconstituted (with Mr M M Parkes as Chairman), he had again been approached as to whether, in the event of the line being constructed, the Southern would support the Light Railway Co by the provision of rolling stock, the supply of reasonable passenger and goods services, and the furnishing of staff for the stations, on the understanding that the Light Railway Co will not ask for any guarantee of interest on the Debenture stock. If so, the promoters state that they have every reason to believe that the necessary capital for the purchase of the land and the construction of the line will be forthcoming." The proposals were generally approved but nothing further was heard from the new promoters, who were faced not only with the usual lack of finance, but also with opposition from the Ministry of Transport on the grounds that the SHLR would complicate the Passenger Pooling Scheme introduced by the London Passenger Transport Act of 1933. It is ironic that one of the last references to the SHLR was by the Bromley RDC who, after strongly opposing it in 1926, used the fact of its expected construction as an argument in support of an (unsuccessful) application for Urban District status in 1933.

Electric trains did eventually reach Sanderstead, on 30 September 1935. Although the SHLR was by this time effectively dead, the SR decided to tidy up a loose end in their suburban network by reopening the Woodside to Selsdon line (closed to local traffic since 1915) and running an electric service from the Mid Kent line to Sanderstead.

Fifty years on, it is easy to dismiss the SHLR as a speculative venture which never had a real chance of success - the *Folie de Grandeur* of a dedicated entrepreneur who refused to accept the inevitable demise of the light railway era. Nevertheless, if the line had been built, would the sight of electric trains grinding through the hilly suburbia between Farnborough and Hamsey Green have been any more remarkable than other projects of the thirties, for instance the

Northern Line to Edgware or the Southern Railway to Tolworth and Chessington? One might have regretted so many beautiful downland valleys given over to the speculative builder; as it is, some have been left in peace - except when a late traveller hears a ghostly 3-SUB rattling back to Charing Cross and thinks on what might have been.

29.1   This view south from the up fast platform is of the area that would have accommodated the junction at Orpington.

29.2   Here is an example of the type of station that would have been built on the SHLR. This is the 1929 Merton South station, on the Wimbledon-Sutton route of the SR.

Chapter 30

Passenger Stock of the East Kent Light Railways

By Stephen Garrett (1980)

The East Kent Light Railways Company was not primarily a passenger undertaking. Its main aim was to open up the Kent coalfield and in particular to develop links with new port facilities at Richborough and, later, Birchington. The intervention of the First World War, the failure of either Richborough or Birchington to develop as expected and, even more disastrously, the failure of the Kent coalfield to prove as extensive as had been hoped all led to the situation in which the East Kent was left as a collection of straggling branches serving nowhere in particular with a life-giving nucleus of coal traffic between Tilmanstone Colliery and Shepherdswell on the South Eastern & Chatham main line. Until 1929 the East Kent ran a relatively intensive service in workmen's trains, but when these were deserted in favour of more reliable bus services only a vestigial passenger service remained to make use of the immensely varied collection of antique carriages that the Company had acquired.

Even in the period up to the cessation of workmen's trains in 1929 the East Kent rarely carried more than 500 passengers a week but from 1930 onwards the figures fell from an average of 65 a week in that year to a record low of 11 a week in 1947! Adequate bus services compared with slow and infrequent trains amply explain this, but perhaps the sorry story of passenger services on the East Kent can be best understood from this letter to the Editor of the *Dover Express* in October 1925:

Dear Sir,

I think the sooner the managers of the East Kent Railway discard their old engine, the 'Walton Park', and put on the line an engine that can do the journey and up to time, the better it will be for all concerned. A month ago it missed the connection with the main line at Shepherdswell and passengers to Dover had to wait an hour for the next train; on the return journey, with a struggle, it crawled to Wingham an hour and a quarter late, and above all, passengers to Wingham were invited to walk from Staple as he could not keep up his steam. The climax came last Saturday night when the 'Walton Park' could not do the journey at all and the passengers home were conveyed by motor car. No blame is attached to the officials who do all they can to run to time and are very courteous.

"A SUPPORTER OF THE LOCAL LINE"

Unfortunately the early history of the East Kent passenger stock will probably never be known for certain as the Company appears to have acquired and disposed of some stock in its early years of which no official records nor photographs survived. These carriages were probably acquired in anticipation of an earlier commencement of passenger services than actually occurred, a result of unforeseen difficulties in developing the various pits and the shortage of labour resulting from the outbreak of war in 1914. It is not really until 1920 that a confident account of the line's carriages can begin. Even then, although it is possible to identify the line's carriages it is not always possible to ascribe running numbers to all of them as the paintwork on some vehicles had already deteriorated sufficiently to obscure such numbers as they may

179

have carried. I have seen photographs in which the numbers of carriages 2, 7, 8, 10, 11 and the second 5 and 6 can be made out and I believe that numbers 1 and 4 have also been identified but the ascription of numbers 3, 5, 6, and 9 to the particular vehicles which follow must remain conjectural until further evidence comes to light. It must be admitted that on a small concern like the East Kent the numbering of carriages, no two of which until 1946 were alike, can hardly have been a major preoccupation.

In the descriptions that follow I have given the class of each carriage as that for which it was built. Although carriages on the East Kent were labelled first and third and were distinguished as such in the Company's official returns the self same returns divide actual passengers solely into third class and workmen. It would be very interesting to know whether first class tickets were ever issued by the East Kent.

The first carriage known to be owned by the East Kent was a light bogie saloon brake composite acquired from the Kent & East Sussex in 1912. This had formed part of a rake of three 41' 0" carriages, delivered to the Kent & East Sussex by R.Y. Pickering in 1905, possibly in anticipation of the extension to Maidstone. Two of these carriages had been sold to the War Department in 1909 for use on the Woolmer Instructional Railway, but the third was still available when the East Kent sought a suitable vehicle to convey its guests and dignitaries at the official opening ceremony on 27th November 1912. What use was found for the carriage in the years between 1912 and the introduction of passenger services in 1916 is not known though it may have seen its fair share of inspection trips for anxious directors and shareholders. It seems to have been used regularly on the line once passenger services had begun and its saloon would have given it great advantages for fare collection over the compartment stock otherwise in use. By the late 1930s it appeared worn out but this hardly distinguished it from the rest of the line's stock and it survived until nationalization. Not surprisingly British Railways promptly condemned the carriage and it was scrapped in 1948.

Carriage No.2 was a four-wheeled North London Railway full brake probably acquired from the Kent & East Sussex which had inherited two from the Rother Valley Railway, only one of which, No. 15, seems to have been in evidence after 1912 or so. Quite what use the East Kent made of this vehicle is not clear but it may have proved useful for fruit traffic and parcels. Officially it was withdrawn in 1946, but does not seem to have been scrapped until 1948.

No.3 was a Cheshire Lines Committee five compartment third class four-wheeler which may also have come from the Kent & East Sussex. A peculiar characteristic, presumably not original, was the presence of a pair of windows in each end. This carriage seems to have been used intensively on workmen's trains, but does not seem to have seen much use once these had ceased. It was withdrawn around 1940, but its body was retained and used as lineside accommodation.

No.4 was a six-wheeled Midland Railway four compartment first and second brake composite built in 1882. This often ran with No.5 which was a six-wheeled London & Southern Western three compartment brake third. Both carriages survived until 1948 though latterly in a very dilapidated condition.

No.6 was a Great Eastern four-wheeled four compartment first. This closely resembled a carriage inherited from the Rother Valley by the Kent & East Sussex and subsequently unaccounted for so there is some probability that this is the same vehicle. It appears to have been withdrawn in 1937 according to the official returns.

Carriages 7 and 8 were London Chatham & Dover four compartment four-wheeled stock. Respectively they were first class and third class and it is believed that they may have been South Eastern & Chatham Nos 2771 and 2773. They were acquired in 1920 and usually kept company with a further London Chatham & Dover vehicle acquired at the same time. This was a four-wheeled three compartment brake third with an antiquated 'birdcage' roof lookout. All three survived until 1948 though in poor condition from the mid 1930s.

Carriages 10 and 11 were also of LCDR origin, but were six-wheeled stock. Both were built as first/second brake composites, but on the East Kent, No. 10 ran with its compartments labelled as two firsts and a third originally whilst No. 11's were all labelled as thirds. They were probably SECR and 2691. They were acquired in 1926 and seem to have borne the brunt of passenger services until the acquisition of the line's first corridor stock in 1946. These were two London & South Western five compartment bogie brake seconds, Southern Railway Nos 3126 and 3128, and became Nos 5 and 6 on the East Kent. They must have been a great improvement over the rest of the line's stock, but they seem to have attracted few passengers back to the line in the short period until passenger services ceased in October 1948.

30.1   An ex-LCDR 1st class coach leads and a brake third from the same company follows. The locomotive is O class no. 8.

30.2   A line up from about 1931 begins with a Cheshire Lines 3rd class, followed by a North London Railway full brake, a LC&DR 3rd class and a GER 1st class.

30.3   Ex-LCDR composite no. 10 was photographed in fair condition in June 1934. (H.C.Casserley)

Chapter 31

Colonel Stephens -The Twilight Years

by Philip Shaw (1983)

Colonel Stephens died at the Lord Warden Hotel, Dover, on Friday 23 October 1931, in his 63rd year. A tragic figure in his declining years, Stephens had suffered a debilitating illness which paralysed the right side of his body and deprived him of the power of speech. The Lord Warden, a grand, Mid-Victorian establishment situated adjacent to the Marine Station and catering mainly for boat train traffic, had been his principal residence throughout the 1920s and he travelled each day by train to Tonbridge, from which it was but a stone's throw to his offices at Salford Terrace.

Stephens was well known to the train crews, as he would frequently tip the driver half a crown particularly if he had to pass directly by the engine cab for the station exit. Certainly, he would have had no lack of opportunity for implementing these little gestures of generosity. According to Bradshaw, an early-morning journey from Dover to Tonbridge in 1926 would have involved catching the 7.01 am train from the Marine Station, changing at Ashford with a wait of 41 minutes, arriving at 9.15am.

Ernie Rodgers, now living in retirement at Dover, was employed at the Lord Warden between 1927 and 1934, initially as a page boy and latterly as hall porter. He remembers Stephens quite clearly as the occupant of room 11 on the first floor and one of only two permanent residents at the hotel: "The Colonel was a distinctive figure, punctilious in dress and usually attired in dark clothes, including an overcoat or Burberry and he always carried an umbrella. He was quiet and courteous with the staff, but mingled little with the other guests and usually dined alone, returning to the hotel lounge afterwards for whisky, which he drank in large quantities without any noticeable effect, and a cigar."

Stephens may have first become acquainted with the Lord Warden at the time of the construction of the East Kent Railway at Shepherdswell nearby, but it was not until some years later that he took up permanent residence there. In the early years of the century he had rented rooms at a house in Station Road, Robertsbridge, and also lived part of the time at Ashby House, Priory Road, Tonbridge, premises which he owned and kept going even when he was at the Lord Warden, presided over by his housekeeper, Miss Flo Standen. The move to Dover may have taken place in 1923 (surviving correspondence shows him to have been there in 1926) possibly for the reason that he could be close at hand to his Territorial Army activities.

The heyday of Stephens' light railway empire was immediately after the Great War and by the end of the 1920s the creative days were over. The last two lines that he engineered were the North Devon & Cornwall Junction Light Railway and the Ashover, both of which were opened in 1925. Several others were planned at around this time but not built, including the Newport & Four Ashes, Worcester & Broom, Southern Heights and various extensions to the East Kent. Apart from this, it was merely a case of administering the existing railways, including the tiresome Festiniog and its truculent Traffic Manager, Robert Evans, with whom there was a voluminous exchange of correspondence (but more one way) between 1925 and 1930. Indeed, it is following a perusal of the Festiniog archives, which have miraculously survived virtually intact, that one can pinpoint almost exactly the onset of Stephens' illness. The Great Man always insisted on signing all letters emanating from the office personally, but after 24 January 1930 this became at first spasmodic and then stopped altogether. Nevertheless, all correspondence continued to go out under his name, although written by his clerks, right up until the end. Inevitably, the style of the writing changed and by the early Spring of 1930 the urgency and the humour of the prose, so characteristic of the man, had gone forever. Stephens is believed to have suffered his first stroke at the end of January 1930, following a visit to London to attend a function. Nevertheless, he still managed to make his way regularly to Salford Terrace, despite a pronounced limp, some paralysis and impairment of speech. By the late Spring he suffered a second and more serious stroke, which further incapacitated him. In June, he was reported as "not being well enough to be consulted" and about this time, at the suggestion of his physician, Sir Percival Horton-Smith Hartley, entered a London nursing home, where from all accounts he proved to be a difficult patient. A nurse confided to a member of the Salford Terrace staff that on at least one occasion he had to be restrained from throwing banknotes out of the window, during a period of frustration with his condition. After 6 weeks he discharged himself and went to convalesce at Hastings. Unable to communicate either physically or verbally, Stephens grew tired of his isolation and arrangements were made for him to return to the Lord Warden, where at least everybody knew him.

From then on he was nursed, virtually night and day by the hotel staff, communicating by means of a nod or a shake of the head and unable to feed or dress himself; clear in the mind, but totally inarticulate, except for a pathetic utterance "Wo, Wo, Wo", which he used to draw attention. Several times a week, Arthur Iggulden, his secretary, went down to see him, often being kept so late that he would arrive back at Tonbridge at midnight, having just caught the mail train. Iggulden had been granted Power of Attorney to deal with Stephens' personal affairs on 17 January 1931. Despite his grave disabilities, Stephens continued to visit his lines when he felt able, going even as far as the Festiniog at Portmadoc, where it is recorded he went in April 1931. On these occasions he was accompanied and physically supported by a member of the staff (usually Alfred Willard) or in the case of the nearby East Kent, frequently by Ernie Rodgers, who would hire a taxi to take him to Shepherdswell for the afternoon. The end came quite suddenly, when the hotel night porter, Rigden, went up with the morning papers, drew the curtains and found him dead in bed - he had suffered a fatal heart attack.

The funeral was held at St Peter's church, Hammersmith, the mourners consisting mainly of staff members and business acquaintances, there being no surviving relatives. Amongst several representatives of the Southern Railway were C F Barfoot, on behalf of the Chairman, Sir Herbert Walker and in person R E L Maunsell, Chief Mechanical Engineer. Interment was in the family grave at the Brompton Cemetery, Fulham Road. Four staff members shared equally in his estate of some £30,000, under a will dated 19 January 1931, initialled "H F S" in a shaky hand and included W H Austen, J A Iggulden, A Willard and G H Willard. The family collection of mainly Pre-Raphaelite paintings was bequeathed to the Tate Gallery. Stephens' close friend, Gilbert Szlumper, General Manager of the Southern Railway, wrote after the funeral to Austen, "My little mother sent the poor old Colonel a photo of herself as he always had a soft spot in his heart for her and she is wondering if you can send it back now he is gone? I am glad he looked after you and some of his other 'boys' in his will - you were certainly very good friends to him and it is a just reward. I suppose you have not had time yet to consider what you are going to do about carrying on the office and some of the jobs".

In the event, Austen assumed overall responsibility for the office after Stephens' death - a role that he had been obliged to fill anyway since the beginning of 1930, but with the depression years ahead and the growth in road competition, its days were clearly numbered. The War provided a temporary respite for the East Kent, Kent & East Sussex and Shropshire & Montgomeryshire lines, but with nationalisation in 1948, the doors of number 23 Salford Terrace, Tonbridge were finally closed to light railway administration forever.

The Colonel's death certificate shows the primary causes of death as Coronary Thrombosis and Polycythaemia Rubra Vera. The latter condition is interesting in that it was undoubtedly the real cause of the deterioration in his health in the last year. The disease is one of middle age and is more common in men. It is characterised by the over production of red cells in the blood and may give rise to a rather ruddy appearance in the sufferer. The patient may complain of headache, dizziness and tiredness and indeed it is possibly not surprising that the Colonel, feeling far from well, may have seemed rude and lacking in patience in his latter days. Among the complications of polycythaemia is the possibility of blood clot formation and this may be particularly devastating if a clot (thrombosis) occurs in the brain.

Stephens had probably suffered from the complaint for some time and the earlier episodes of cerebral thrombosis (or "strokes"), may well have been attributable to this. Because the nerve pathways cross over at the base of the brain, the left side of the brain controls the right hand side of the body and vice versa. Stephens seems to have had, firstly a "mild" thrombosis in the left side of the brain which resulted in a partial paralysis on his right side, hence the limp and difficulty with writing. Unfortunately for the Colonel, the left side of the brain also controls our powers of speech, so that when he was struck down with a more "severe" thrombosis, he lost not only his power of writing but verbal communication as well. If only he had been left-handed!

Although the emotions may be disturbed following a "stroke", the victim of such a catastrophe may be intellectually unimpaired. The frustration of a man such as Stephens, unable to communicate his ideas and wishes either in writing or speech may be imagined. The fatal coronary thrombosis in the early hours of the 23 October 1931 at least spared him from further suffering.

31.1   The Lord Warden Hotel was convenient to Dover Marine station. Steps in the structure behind the second coach gave access to the walkway (left), this leading to the platforms. A train from Folkestone is arriving in 1921 behind class E1 4-4-0 no. 179.

31.2   Stephens' room was on the west aspect and is seen in 1983, by which time it was in use as an office by Calvanbridge, a forwarding company. Note that the view includes many sidings at the foot of Shakespeare Cliff.

Chapter 32

The Colonel Stephens Railway Museum

by Philip Shaw (2005)

The Colonel Stephens Railway Museum was officially opened to the public by Sir Neil Cossons OBE, Director of the Science Museum on 22nd May 1998. The nucleus of the collection of artefacts had been accumulated over a period of some 25 years and consisted initially of the very considerable amount of material accumulated by W.H.Austen, Colonel Stephens' right hand man and successor, which passed to his son and ultimately to the Kent & East Sussex Railway. Subsequently, additional items have been added including those in the possession of Salford Terrace accountant, J A Iggulden, and a significant number of purchases have been made at auction, as and when items have become available. The museum premises are at Tenterden Town Station in Kent and the organisation is part of the Kent & East Sussex Railway Company, the registered charity which runs the line between Tenterden and Bodiam. It was built by Colonel Stephens and opened between 1900 and 1903.

The displays were constructed under the supervision of John Miller, the Company's Curator and Archivist and are arranged chronologically to tell the story of Stephens and each of the lines with which he was closely associated. The first room contains personal and family items, including reproduction of some of the paintings of Stephens' father, F G Stephens, one of the original members of the Pre-Raphaelite Brotherhood. There are then displays with literature and hardware items for all of his 16 lines. There is a military display containing his camping gear and also his commission certificates. There is also a re-creation of his office at 23, Salford Terrace, Tonbridge which contains his original roll-top desk and chair and many other authentic items. Pride of place is gven to *Gazelle*, the little 0-4-2 locomotive of 1893, which was purchased by Stephens to run on the Shropshire & Montgomeryshire Railway and is on loan to the museum from the National Collection.

The museum is open to the public on most days that the Kent & East Sussex Railway is running train services.

32.1 The interior of Colonel Stephens' office includes many relevant pictures. Most of the artefacts are authentic, including the filing basket, books and pictures. Members of staff were summoned to his presence by means of the bell push seen to the right of the fireplace. It was operated with a series of codes. (B.Stephenson)

32.2 The contents of Colonel Stephens' desk were always in pandemonium! (B.Stephenson)

32.3 Colonel Stephens' camping gear includes a canvas wash basin, table and chair, plus a bag in which to carry it all. (B.Stephenson)

32.4 The East Kent Railway's display includes models and a diorama featuring the station at Wingham, Canterbury Road. (B.Stephenson)

32.5 The Bere Alston & Callington Light Railway display includes a nameplate from one of the locomotives. (B.Stephenson)

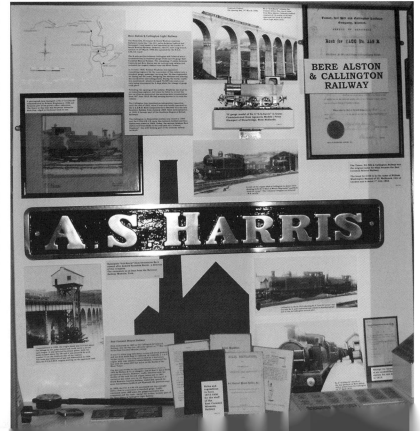

Index to Railways

(Most main line companies not included)

**Middleton Press albums featuring lines
with which Colonel Stephens was involved:**

Branch Lines to Clevedon and Portishead
Branch Lines around Portmadoc 1923-46
Branch Line to Selsey
Branch Lines around Sheerness
Branch Line to Shrewsbury
Branch Line to Tenterden
Branch Lines to Torrington
East Kent Light Railway
Sussex Narrow Gauge

MP Middleton Press

EVOLVING THE ULTIMATE RAIL ENCYCLOPEDIA

Easebourne Lane, Midhurst, West Sussex.
GU29 9AZ   Tel:01730 813169

www.middletonpress.co.uk   email:info@middletonpress.co.uk
A-0 906520 B-1 873793 C-1 901706 D-1 904474

OOP Out of Print at time of printing - Please check current availability   **BROCHURE AVAILABLE SHOWING NEW TITLES**